Practical Artificial Intelligence and Blockchain

A guide to converging blockchain and AI to build smart applications for new economies

Ganesh Prasad Kumble

BIRMINGHAM - MUMBAI

Practical Artificial Intelligence and Blockchain

Commissioning Editor: Sunith Shetty
Acquisition Editor: Devika Battike
Content Development Editor: Nathanya Dias
Senior Editor: David Sugarman
Technical Editor: Utkarsha S. Kadam
Copy Editor: Safis Editing
Project Coordinator: Aishwarya Mohan
Proofreader: Safis Editing
Indexer: Priyanka Dhadke
Production Designer: Nathanya Dias

First published: July 2020

Production reference: 1300720

Published by Packt Publishing Ltd.
Livery Place
35 Livery Street
Birmingham
B3 2PB, UK.

ISBN 978-1-83882-229-3

www.packt.com

Packt.com

Subscribe to our online digital library for full access to over 7,000 books and videos, as well as industry leading tools to help you plan your personal development and advance your career. For more information, please visit our website.

Why subscribe?

- Spend less time learning and more time coding with practical eBooks and Videos from over 4,000 industry professionals

- Improve your learning with Skill Plans built especially for you

- Get a free eBook or video every month

- Fully searchable for easy access to vital information

- Copy and paste, print, and bookmark content

Did you know that Packt offers eBook versions of every book published, with PDF and ePub files available? You can upgrade to the eBook version at www.packt.com and as a print book customer, you are entitled to a discount on the eBook copy. Get in touch with us at customercare@packtpub.com for more details.

At www.packt.com, you can also read a collection of free technical articles, sign up for a range of free newsletters, and receive exclusive discounts and offers on Packt books and eBooks.

Foreword

We are at a pivotal point in the journey of human civilization. From hunting to agrarian to industrial revolutions, most of human advancement was functional. We primarily used our physical faculties and focused on developing, coping, and survival methods. But with the advent of the knowledge era, this is about to change exponentially. We are embarking on the grandest of discoveries. We're using our mind to understand its own working, to discover the commonness in all of us and the world, and to create a co-operative equilibrium in all our societal interactions. A journey where we move from episodic functional growth to constantly evolving networked learning. A model that maximizes the **happiness quotient** of society at large.

It is against this backdrop, we have technologies such as blockchain, artificial intelligence, and peer-to-peer networks taking shape. As the knowledge era progresses, technology is rapidly moving from a supporting cast to become the main actor in our lives. Lines between real and virtual are blurring at exponential rates. Human networks are rapidly being replaced by their digital look alike. Interactions are becoming the new value driver, opening up transformational opportunities for the society and enabling a new **way of living**. This is a paradigm shift. But, societal changes of this magnitude inherently increase the entropy and require a new framework for harnessing value from the change. A framework where the building blocks of new technology, their interplay, and the context of their connectedness is well understood and implemented. In this book, the author has connected the basics of the new technology, its usefulness, and the business context in an effective way to wean away from the **noise** of change and has clearly articulated the practical business benefits of the new model.

Chapter 1, *Getting Started with Blockchain*, Chapter 2, *Introduction to the AI Landscape* and Chapter 3, *Domain-Specific Applications of AI and Blockchain*, provide a good foundational understanding of AI and blockchain, focused more on practical usability of the technology and the context of its usage. This approach allows readers, especially the beginners, to gently **get into** the topic without getting overwhelmed by the algorithmic and mathematical complexity of some components.

Chapter 4, *AI- and Blockchain-Driven Databases*, focuses on the different data storage models of the new world. The author has covered all the major new models here. I particularly liked the comparison between centralized, distributed, and decentralized database models. Chapter 5, *Empowering Blockchain Using AI*, is where all the **dots** are connected. The author brings in specific and practical use cases where blockchain, AI, and digital interactions are seamlessly connected and shows how they deliver clear business benefits. Readers will be excited to learn about how the novel **digital reimagination** process harnesses value from the new technologies and the thoughts behind the KIP protocol to humanize the networks. Chapter 6, *Cryptocurrency and Artificial Intelligence*, talks about cryptocurrencies, their role, and uses. It was interesting to read about how AI can de-risk some of the inherent challenges of cryptocurrencies and bring it closer to common use.

Chapter 7, *Development Life Cycle of a DIApp*, gives a very detailed and practical guide to building a DIApp. This is a great resource for programmers who are starting to build decentralized applications. The sample DIApp **DICTAO** presented in Chapter 8, *Implementing DIApps*, is an excellent example of how to connect IOT, blockchain, and AI to solve today's real-world problems. This application clearly demonstrates the power of these new technologies and how to combine them for effective value creation.

The author closes the book with Chapter 9, *The Future of AI with Blockchain*, on the future of blockchain and AI with specific opportunities in different industries. The chapter has multiple greenfield ideas for building practical solutions using blockchain and AI.

Whenever I met Ganesh, I have always enjoyed his insight, passion, and commitment to the craft. He has brought all of that to bear in this book with the goal of passing on his learnings to the new warriors entering this field. *Practical Artificial Intelligence and Blockchain* is an excellent book for students and working professionals who are planning to kickstart their career in Blockchain and AI and provides the right balance between theory and practice with clear guidance on how to build decentralized applications.

It is often said **Knowledge is power**. But it is most powerful when **wielded** correctly. In this book, Ganesh has shown how to wield the power of blockchain and AI to create maximum benefit for all.

I wish Ganesh Kumble all the best.

Anantha Krishnan

Founder & CEO

Aicumen Technologies Inc

Contributors

About the author

Ganesh Prasad Kumble is an expert in emerging technologies and business strategy. He has co-founded, bootstrapped, and mentored several start-ups and initiatives across SaaS, e-commerce, IoT, Blockchain, and AI. He is a contributor to several open source projects, including Ethereum and IPFS. He authored **TEXA** in 2017 - an ethical AI initiative based on the Turing test that is used to safely assess multi-context robots and AI models in a quantifiable manner.

He is currently leading platform innovation efforts at Aicumen Technologies, Inc. and KIP Foundation, building a general-purpose business protocol featuring identity management, third-party services, distributed compute, and immutable storage. Ganesh is also a moderator at the Ethereum Research forum.

There are several people whose encouragement and support made this book possible. I would like to begin by thanking the Packt Publishing and its entire team. My foremost thanks goes to Sanket Thodge and Devika Battike who persuaded me to take up this opportunity. As a first-time author, I am eternally thankful to Kirti Pisat, Nathanya Dias, and Gebin George who guided me in every step of this book. I'd also like to extend my thanks to Vaibhav Saini who gladly accepted my request to review the technical aspects of the book. I also thank my dear brother Madhusudhan Kumble for helping me in building the tutorials.

This acknowledgment is not complete without showcasing my gratitude to my employer Aicumen Technologies Inc., my co-workers, and the Co-founders Mr. Anantha Krishnan and Mr. Karthik Balasubramanian. Under Anantha's and Karthik's visionary leadership and constant mentorship over the past three years, I have been privileged to articulate some of the next-gen thoughts and design patterns in this book. I'd also like to thank all industry colleagues for supporting me in this endeavor.

Finally, my humble pranams go to my parents, family members, and teachers for all the support and well-wishes.

About the reviewers

Vaibhav Saini is an entrepreneur and advocate of an open and decentralized world. He is an IIT Delhi student, co-founder of Signy Advanced Technologies, and founder of open source projects including Dappkit, AvionDB, and SimpleAsWater. He is an open source contributor to projects such as IPFS and Ethereum and an active contributing writer at freeCodeCamp and Hacker Noon. He is also an author of *Data Analytics and Data Mining: Strategy to Improve Quality, Performance, and Decision Making*, from Springer Nature.

Ankur Daharwal is a technology expert in enterprise blockchain. He has been designing, architecting, and developing blockchain solutions for over 4 years. Embarking on his journey with IBM Blockchain Garage, he has brought numerous projects to fruition. He builds real-life solutions for asset management, value exchange, and traceability in many industries worldwide. Currently, he leads blockchain practice at NTT Data and serves an auxiliary role as a client solutions manager at SettleMint. He is a member of ISO TC307 DLT Standards Technical Committee as well as a member of IIB Council Blockchain Advisory Board. He has also reviewed other Packt titles, including *Oracle Blockchain Services Quick Start Guide* and *Security Tokens and Stablecoin Quick Start Guide*. He believes in fulfilling social responsibilities and supporting humanitarian causes with entrepreneurial skills in technology.

Packt is searching for authors like you

If you're interested in becoming an author for Packt, please visit `authors.packtpub.com` and apply today. We have worked with thousands of developers and tech professionals, just like you, to help them share their insight with the global tech community. You can make a general application, apply for a specific hot topic that we are recruiting an author for, or submit your own idea.

Table of Contents

Section 3: Developing Blockchain Products

Preface

Over the past 10 years, blockchain and its affiliated technologies have been used to add transparency and dis-intermediate unnecessary parties involved in critical processes. Along similar lines, AI has been adopted to optimize processes and predict outcomes in an accurate and cheap way. Together, AI and blockchain are catalyzing the pace of enterprise innovation. The convergence of these two technologies is expected to revolutionize some aspects of the digital landscape as we know it today. This book is a guide to help you understand the basic concepts of blockchain and AI, analyze their use cases, and implement these technologies across various industries such as healthcare, finance, trade, and supply chain management. The book also guides you to build applications using Ethereum, machine learning, and MóiBit.

Who this book is for

This book is for blockchain and AI architects, developers, data scientists, data engineers, and evangelists who want to bring the power of AI to blockchain applications. If you want a perfect blend of theoretical and practical use cases to understand how to implement smart cognitive insights in blockchain solutions, this book is what you need! Having some familiarity with the concepts involved in machine learning and blockchain is required.

What this book covers

Chapter 1, *Getting Started with Blockchain*, helps you understand the basics of blockchain and the contrasts between various forms and implementations. If you are already comfortable with the basics of blockchain and its applications, you may skip this chapter and start with Chapter 2, *Introduction to the AI Landscape*.

Chapter 2, *Introduction to the AI Landscape*, as the name suggests, introduces you to the basics of AI and its history, and draws contrasts between some of its basic forms and implementations. If you are already comfortable with the basics of AI and its applications, you can directly head to Chapter 4, *AI- and Blockchain-Driven Databases*.

Chapter 3, *Domain-Specific Applications of AI and Blockchain,* covers some of the well-known applications of blockchain and AI.

Chapter 4, *AI- and Blockchain-Driven Databases,* is crucial for learning how to connect blockchain with AI. We will be introducing and contrasting traditional data management tools and decentralized databases, as well as filesystems.

Chapter 5, *Empowering Blockchain Using AI,* covers some of the exclusive applications that use both AI and blockchain to address some real-world challenges.

Chapter 6, *Cryptocurrency and Artificial Intelligence,* examines some of the applications of AI in cryptocurrency trading.

Chapter 7, *Development Life Cycle of a DIApp,* introduces you to the DIApp design pattern and outlines the **Software Development Life Cycle** (**SDLC**) processes involved.

Chapter 8, *Implementing DIApps,* demonstrates how to build a live application that utilizes blockchain, AI, and decentralized databases to solve a real-world challenge.

Chapter 9, *The Future of AI with Blockchain,* ends the book by suggesting new use cases to analyze and ways to apply the learnings from the book to build your own DIApp.

To get the most out of this book

Although we don't expect you to be thoroughly acquainted with the basics of blockchain and AI, it would be helpful to be familiar with these technologies. Also, one of the learning outcomes for the book is to see how to build a DIApp, which combines the best of blockchain and AI. If you are interested in learning how to build a DIApp, you should be familiar with the basics of Solidity smart contracts, machine learning, and Python.

Software/hardware covered in the book	OS requirements
Developing a DIApp that can help track COVID-19 infections in animals and objects requires the following: • Python 3.7 • Node.js 12 • Firefox or a Chromium-based browser with access to the internet	• macOS Mojave or higher • Ubuntu 18.04 LTS or higher

If you are using the digital version of this book, we advise you to type the code yourself or access the code via the GitHub repository (link available in the next section). Doing so will help you avoid any potential errors related to the copying and pasting of code.

Download the example code files

You can download the example code files for this book from your account at www.packt.com. If you purchased this book elsewhere, you can visit www.packtpub.com/support and register to have the files emailed directly to you.

You can download the code files by following these steps:

1. Log in or register at www.packt.com.
2. Select the **Support** tab.
3. Click on **Code Downloads**.
4. Enter the name of the book in the **Search** box and follow the onscreen instructions.

Once the file is downloaded, please make sure that you unzip or extract the folder using the latest version of:

- WinRAR/7-Zip for Windows
- Zipeg/iZip/UnRarX for Mac
- 7-Zip/PeaZip for Linux

The code bundle for the book is also hosted on GitHub at https://github.com/PacktPublishing/Hands-On-Artificial-Intelligence-for-Blockchain. In case there's an update to the code, it will be updated on the existing GitHub repository.

We also have other code bundles from our rich catalog of books and videos available at https://github.com/PacktPublishing/. Check them out!

Download the color images

We also provide a PDF file that has color images of the screenshots/diagrams used in this book. You can download it here: https://static.packt-cdn.com/downloads/9781838822293_ColorImages.pdf.

Conventions used

There are a number of text conventions used throughout this book.

`CodeInText`: Indicates code words in text, database table names, folder names, filenames, file extensions, pathnames, dummy URLs, user input, and Twitter handles. Here is an example: "Mount the downloaded `WebStorm-10*.dmg` disk image file as another disk in your system."

A block of code is set as follows:

```
modifier onlyBy(address _account) {
      require(
          msg.sender == _account,
          "Sender not authorized to update this mapping!"
      );
      _; // The "_;"! will be replaced by the actual function body when
the modifier is used.
   }
```

Any command-line input or output is written as follows:

```
just run-server
```

Bold: Indicates a new term, an important word, or words that you see onscreen. For example, words in menus or dialog boxes appear in the text like this. Here is an example: "The rules of creating blocks and the acceptance of blocks are specified by consensus algorithms called PoW or **Proof of Stake (PoS)**."

Warnings or important notes appear like this.

Tips and tricks appear like this.

Get in touch

Feedback from our readers is always welcome.

General feedback: If you have questions about any aspect of this book, mention the book title in the subject of your message and email us at customercare@packtpub.com.

Errata: Although we have taken every care to ensure the accuracy of our content, mistakes do happen. If you have found a mistake in this book, we would be grateful if you would report this to us. Please visit www.packtpub.com/support/errata, selecting your book, clicking on the Errata Submission Form link, and entering the details.

Piracy: If you come across any illegal copies of our works in any form on the Internet, we would be grateful if you would provide us with the location address or website name. Please contact us at copyright@packt.com with a link to the material.

If you are interested in becoming an author: If there is a topic that you have expertise in and you are interested in either writing or contributing to a book, please visit authors.packtpub.com.

Reviews

Please leave a review. Once you have read and used this book, why not leave a review on the site that you purchased it from? Potential readers can then see and use your unbiased opinion to make purchase decisions, we at Packt can understand what you think about our products, and our authors can see your feedback on their book. Thank you!

For more information about Packt, please visit packt.com.

1
Section 1: Overview of Blockchain Technology

In this section, we will cover the basic concepts of Blockchain and AI, and compare their various forms and implementations.

This section comprises the following chapters:

- Chapter 1, *Getting Started with Blockchain*
- Chapter 2, *Introduction to the AI Landscape*

Getting Started with Blockchain

1

"A blockchain a day keeps centralization away!"

Emerging technologies such as blockchain and AI have reached the pinnacle of visibility, acceptance, and also some speculation from various academics and industry experts. With a common aim to reduce operational inefficiency and add transparency, these two emerging technologies are now in great demand. From disruptive start-ups to large-scale enterprises, everyone is racing toward the opportunity to become a leader in blockchain- and AI-based solutions. This book aims to prepare you for the next leap of convergence of these two technologies and guide you to become technically capable of building these solutions.

This chapter provides a brief overview of the current blockchain landscape. The key topics covered in this chapter are as follows:

- Blockchain versus distributed ledger technology versus distributed databases
- Public versus private versus permissioned blockchain
- Privacy in blockchains
- Understanding Bitcoin
- Introduction to Ethereum
- Introduction to Hyperledger
- Other blockchain platforms – Hashgraph, Corda, and IOTA
- Consensus algorithms
- Building DApps with blockchain tools

Technical requirements

This chapter assumes you have a basic awareness of blockchain and its impact on traditional systems for transactions.

Blockchain versus distributed ledger technology versus distributed databases

There have been several debates on how to differentiate blockchains from **Distributed Ledger Technology** (**DLT**) and distributed databases. Based on some of the user- and application-level features and heuristics, we can observe the following differences:

Feature	Blockchain	DLT	Distributed Database
Immutability	The information persisted in blockchains cannot be removed or updated without a new identifier to the target data.	Although most DLTs are pro-immutability, there are a few exceptions where immutability is not a design constraint.	Most distributed databases are not immutable due to design limitations.
Logical execution	Smart contracts can be used to enforce business logic on data from a blockchain.	DLTs offer the execution of logic on the data within them, as well as on user inputs.	User-defined functions and stored procedures are normal approaches that are used here.
Accessibility	Data in a public blockchain is stored in the form of a transaction or account states in a block and is visible and accessible with middleware.	Data is private in a DLT and may, in some cases, be encrypted in the DLT entry. Data can only be accessed by participating stakeholders.	Data is persisted within the distributed data clusters spread across the globe for faster access, using traditional client-server techniques.
Verifiability	All the transactions are verified before a change is made to the state of an account.	Most DLTs do not offer verification algorithms or modules as a design restriction to applications.	The verifiability of data is not offered as the state of accounts is not persisted in a specific structure.
Incentivization	Most blockchains use several economic models to incentivize their stakeholders.	Stakeholders in a DLT group host the nodes and are self-incentivized to run their business more confidently.	The company manages the data for sustainability and so no extra incentivization can be observed.

Let's now compare these technologies with an example use case discussed in the following section.

Comparing the technologies with examples

The following scenario is provided to aid your understanding of the core differences between the preceding three implementations.

Imagine that you plan to create a new digital platform for stock photography. If you want to invite photographers all over the world to use the platform and allow them to upload their work and be incentivized with their royalties automatically paid off by the consumers, you'd want to use blockchain to offer public access and incentivization and to transfer the royalties directly from the consumer to the photographer, thereby eliminating the need for a third party performing the duty payment collection, guaranteeing the return of royalties but with a service fee.

However, if you want your platform to form a private consortium of photographers, with their art exclusively available to a limited audience, and to handle royalties in conjunction with other means, you would use a DLT.

Finally, if you intend to use your platform to exhibit art by an eligible set of photographers that are accessible across the globe, with or without royalties (which is handled offline), you'd form a cluster of nodes that host this data and logic to handle access and payments. So, you would use distributed databases.

Let's now further discuss the types of blockchains available for different use cases.

Public versus private versus permissioned blockchains

Public blockchains were designed and developed with a focus on ensuring that any number of interested parties can execute the business logic and access transactional information. Similarly, any interested party can also verify and validate the transactions incoming to the network, as well as be rewarded for the process.

Private blockchains are implemented to ensure that access to business information is limited and only accessible to a limited set of participating stakeholders.

Permissioned blockchains are a hybrid implementation of what both public and private blockchains have to offer. Permissioned blockchains are implemented if data is to be accessed by a specific stakeholder. This is achieved by leveraging private networking, as well as the encryption of transactional user data, which is also stored in blocks that may consist of transactions relating to other stakeholders in the consortium.

Comparing usage scenarios

The following table shows how the three types of blockchain can be used in various scenarios. They are:

Attribute versus variant	Public blockchains	Private blockchains	Permissioned blockchains
Network barrier	Access to the network is not restricted. The details inside public blockchains are widely accessible to all users.	Access to the network is limited by an IP or a DNS. Only a few people with suitable credentials can join the network.	Access to the network is limited to verified participants. Only selected people can join the network with limited permissions to read, write, or both.
Restrictions	There are many different actions that the user can perform, such as develop a smart contract and use it, host a node as a validator, and so on.	Virtually, there are only two common roles for members in a private blockchain—facilitated nodes as validators and DApps users.	Based on the role of the members, the users may be able to deploy DApps, use DApps, validate transactions, or all three.
Encryption	Almost all of the user data in blocks is not encrypted as the general goal is to serve the information to a public audience.	Encryption may not be used if there is a trust quotient between the participating stakeholders.	Encryption is widely used as it involves various stakeholders in the networks with potential conflicts of interest.

In the next section, we will further understand the privacy options in blockchains.

Privacy in blockchains

Blockchains add new values, such as transparency and provenance of information. However, many people mistakenly believe that all transactions are publicly viewable in a blockchain. However, in reality, not all the blockchains necessarily facilitate transactions with public viewability:

- **Motivations:** Several applications on blockchains are not just built for enterprise use cases. Many blockchain applications are now targeting mass consumer audiences. The internet, in recent years, has become a testbed for various approaches in preserving the privacy of users. Unlike any other trend or improvement on the current state of the internet, most blockchain projects aim to deliver a privacy-first mode of operation to users by leveraging pseudonymous cryptographic wallets without revealing the identity of the senders and receivers. Some examples of privacy-first blockchains include Monero, Quorum, and Zcash.

- **Approaches:** As we already know, public blockchains have design limitations with respect to privacy. As global access to user data is one of the prominent objectives of a public blockchain, we see very few applications of cryptography in them. However, the emerging blockchains such as Zcash, Monero aim to offer untraceable, secure, and analysis-resistant transactional environments for users with their own cryptocurrencies. This is made possible by leveraging a Zero-Knowledge proof mechanism that prevents double spend of the same cryptocurrencies, but at the same time preserves the fundamental values of blockchain.

On the other hand, private and permissioned blockchains consider protecting the privacy of the participating stakeholders as high priority. One well-known private implementation is the Quorum blockchain, which was developed by JP Morgan Chase & Co. Quorum offers transaction-level privacy, yet at the same time offers network-level transparency on the actions by all the stakeholders in the network by using a privacy engine called **Constellation**. Constellation encrypts the transaction payload with a special key generated from the public/private key pair of the users involved in the transaction. It also facilitates the deployment and operation of private smart contracts within an existing network.

Let's now explore Bitcoin, the earliest cryptocurrency with the largest market capitalization of them all.

Understanding Bitcoin

Bitcoin is a virtual currency on a peer-to-peer network with users and validators distributed across the network. With the help of the Bitcoin blockchain network, users can transfer cryptocurrency in a truly decentralized manner, without a need for either a central bank, a clearing house, or an intermediary. The transfer of Bitcoin between users is recorded in the form of a transaction, which is later verified, mined, and added to a canonical link of blocks.

Bitcoin is believed to have been created by a group work working under the pseudonym Satoshi Nakamoto, with most of its features and functionalities derived based on existing techniques in cryptographic hashes, peer-to-peer network communication, and immutable data structures.

In the following diagram, we have illustrated how Bitcoin mining works in a single node, as well as in pool environments:

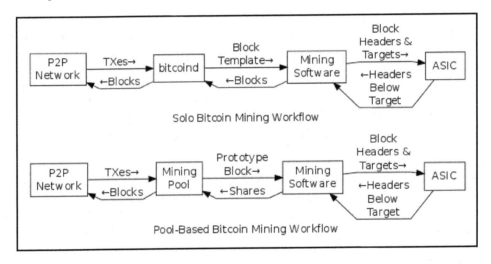

Fig 1.1: Two types of mining in the Bitcoin blockchain network

You can check it out in detail by going to, https://git.io/JJZzN and https://git.io/JJZzx.

A brief overview of Bitcoin

This section offers historical background on the Bitcoin cryptocurrency, along with factual information on its current state as well as the technical and architectural limitations perceived by experts in the market.

We will now quickly dive into some of the necessary details required for further chapters:

- **Motivation**: One of the core motivations behind this cryptocurrency was that the currencies rolled out by central banks could not be trusted as they may not be backed by real collateral. This led to the adoption of a free-market approach to the production, distribution, and management of the money, with proof of work for every Bitcoin minted, thereby eliminating the need for central banks and other intermediaries.
- **Facts**: The virtual currency was open sourced in 2009 with a maximum supply of 21 million Bitcoin that can be minted. Around 18.3 million Bitcoin has been mined to date, with at least three forks.

The following are the prominent Bitcoin forks:

- Bitcoin Cash (with larger block sizes)
- Bitcoin Gold (preserving GPU-based **Proof of Work** (**PoW**) mining instead of ASICs) and Bitcoin **Adjustable Block-Size Cap** (**ABC**) with 32 MB of blocksize)
- Bitcoin **Satoshi's Vision** (**SV**) with an increased block size of 128 MB
  At the time of writing this book, each **Bitcoin** was valued at around USD 6,806.00. The Bitcoin blockchain network incentivizes validating miners by charging users who transfer Bitcoin with a small fee, which is awarded to the winning block maker as per the PoW algorithm.
- **Criticism**: The cryptocurrency is alleged to be one of the prime choices of medium for illicit transactions. One of the major crackdowns of this sort of use came from a renowned online black market on the darknet, **Silk Road**. The FBI shut down the website in late 2013.

With basic knowledge of blockchains, let's now move on and learn about Ethereum.

Introduction to Ethereum

Ethereum is a public blockchain that was designed by Vitalik Buterin in 2013 as an enhancement to the incumbent Bitcoin blockchain, by including transaction-based state management with business logic scripting using a special-purpose programming language and a virtual machine called the **Ethereum Virtual Machine** (**EVM**).

The following diagram outlines the basics of block creation in Ethereum:

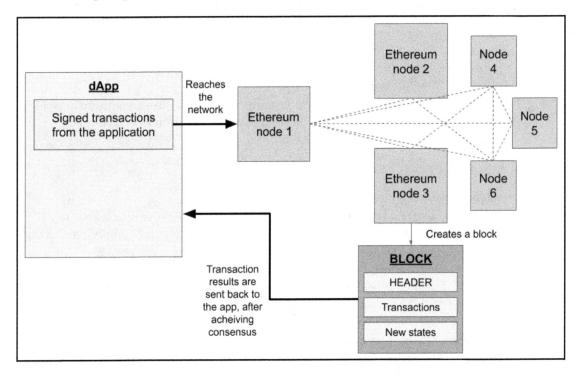

Fig 1.2: Block creation in Ethereum

In the next section, we will look at a brief description of Ethereum.

A brief overview of Ethereum

This section offers historical background on the Ethereum cryptocurrency, along with factual information on its current state as well as the technical and architectural limitations perceived by experts in the market:

- **Motivation**: The main motivation behind Ethereum was to support building decentralized applications on the powerful medium of blockchain. Unable to convince the Bitcoin community of the need for a scripting language, Vitalik and a like-minded group of people created Ethereum.

- **Facts**: The project was open sourced with an initial release date of July 30, 2015. The research and development upgrades to the Ethereum network is managed under the Ethereum Foundation, financially supported by the initial crowd sale of the **Ether (ETH)** token from July to August 2014. Around 105 million ETH has been minted so far. Ethereum has one major fork called Ethereum Classic (the original Ethereum blockchain that denied the DAO hard fork and retained the original unaltered state of the Ethereum network). At the time of writing this book, each ETH is valued at around USD 156.00. The Ethereum blockchain network also incentivizes the validating nodes by charging users who make transactions on DApps or transfer ETH with a small fee, which is awarded to the winning block maker. The rules of creating blocks and the acceptance of blocks are specified by consensus algorithms called PoW or **Proof of Stake (PoS)**. We will explore PoW and PoS in more detail in the upcoming sections of this chapter.

- **Criticism**: The Ethereum community has had to face some of the earliest criticism due to the hard-fork decision taken by the team, thereby contradicting some of the ideology and values of blockchain, such as immutability and immunity from human political dynamics. The network was later criticized and heavily scrutinized by the regulatory authorities due to the alleged Ponzi schemes offered by the **Initial Coin Offerings (ICOs)** without a stable product or service.

 A hard fork is defined as a radical change made to the protocol, thereby rendering some of the previous blocks and its transactions invalid.

With this basic understanding of Ethereum, let's move on to look at the Hyperledger platform.

Introduction to Hyperledger

Hyperledger is an open source project hosted by the Linux Foundation in collaboration with various industry leaders in finance, banking, supply chain, manufacturing, and other domains to create standard blockchain technologies. We will now dive deeper into Hyperledger and some of the projects under the Hyperledger umbrella.

Overview of the project

Linux Foundation announced the Hyperledger project on February 9, 2016, with an initial 30 founding corporate members, including Accenture, IBM, DTCC, Intel, and R3, among others. At the time of writing, the Hyperledger governing board consists of 21 board members and around 200 corporate members around the globe. The project hosts a dozen code repositories of blockchain frameworks and tools. A few significant examples are mentioned in the following section.

Hyperledger Fabric

Hyperledger Fabric is a blockchain framework initially developed by the IBM and Digital Assets members. Fabric is a DLT that aims to provide a modular architecture for developers to use only what is needed. The framework supports the execution of logic abstracted into containers called **chaincode**. Using Fabric is easily enabled by the plethora of documentation, tutorials, and tools available for deploying business networks without much hassle.

Hyperledger Sawtooth

Hyperledger Sawtooth is a blockchain framework that offers enterprises a secure leadership election of nodes in the network, with special modes for executing instructions. Sawtooth offers a powerful, developer-friendly **Software Development Kit (SDK)** for a majority of languages to write and deploy smart contracts. Notably, Sawtooth is one of the early live projects to experiment with **WebAssembly (WASM)** as a virtual medium for the execution of smart contracts.

Other Hyperledger frameworks and tools

Some of the other notable projects incubated under the Hyperledger umbrella are as follows:

- **Hyperledger Indy**: A blockchain platform to specially handle decentralized identities from inside or external systems
- **Hyperledger Grid**: A WASM-based project for building supply chain solutions
- **Hyperledger Quilt**: A blockchain tool to connect blockchain realms of different protocols using the **Interledger Protocol (ILP)** specifications
- **Hyperledger Caliper**: A blockchain benchmarking tool to assess the performance of a specific blockchain with specific parameters such as **Transactions Per Second (TPS)**, transaction latency, resource utilization, and so on

With this basic understanding of Hyperledger, let's now explore other blockchain platforms available to developers.

Other blockchain platforms – Hashgraph, Corda, and IOTA

Hashgraph is a DLT with a superior consensus mechanism leveraging **Directed Acyclic Graphs (DAGs)**. Notably, the implementation of this project is not fully open source. The algorithm was designed and published by Leemon Baird and was initially released in 2017.

Corda is an open source DLT maintained by the financial services consortium R3. Corda offers a smart contracts platform to allow businesses to execute complex agreements, associating multiple variants of asset classes across various business domains, including supply chain, healthcare, and finance.

IOTA is an open source DLT that offers payment automation and secure communication between IoT devices. This project is maintained by the non-profit IOTA Foundation. Quoted as one of the promising ICOs, the project has delivered impressive wallets, a data marketplace for sensor data, and payment channels for quicker transaction settlements using a new special data structure called **Tangle**, eliminating the need for miners and traditional canonical representations of transactional data in blocks.

With this basic knowledge of blockchain platforms, let's now move on to look at the internal components of a typical blockchain network.

Consensus algorithms

The laws that human society relies on to function are much more difficult to enforce when it comes to computers. **Consensus algorithms** are the specific instructions programmed on computers in a network so that they have a common definition of objects and instructions to agree on changes. Crashes, failures, and Byzantine faults in computers led to a better approach in forming an agreement in a digital network and so consensus algorithms rose to great heights, well before the dawn of the internet. This concept has been revisited thanks to the new leap in innovation to blockchains.

The following sections look at some of the important consensus algorithms used by blockchains.

Proof of work

Proof of work (PoW) is a consensus algorithm introduced by the anonymous founder of Bitcoin—Satoshi Nakamoto. The PoW consensus algorithm is one of the earliest consensus algorithms used in a blockchain environment. It leverages a combination of cryptography, P2P network communications, and a Merkle data structure to offer a distributed, immutable, and cumulative state of accounts in the Bitcoin blockchain. The solution computed by the first node is verified by the remaining nodes and the block producer is broadcast in the network:

- **Merit**: The PoW algorithm has been time tested in the Bitcoin blockchain network and there is not a single hack/compromise of the account states in the network leading to double spend.
- **Demerit**: As the PoW algorithm needs to find a solution to a mathematical problem, significant CPU cycles are required to generate hashes and so it is an energy-intensive technique.

Proof of stake

Proof of stake (PoS) is a new consensus algorithm designed and developed to address some of the trade-offs of the PoW algorithm. The block-producing node is determined by an application of mathematical function involving a few determining factors, such as the stake (for example, ETH), the age of the node, and the randomization of eligible node candidates:

- **Merit**: The PoS algorithm is energy-efficient as there are fewer computational requirements and it does not select a block-producing node based on a solution-verification model.
- **Demerit**: Although the PoS algorithm is efficient in its block times and is environment-friendly, there have been criticisms relating to the algorithm's vulnerability to capitalist attacks on the network of the node owner and tries to compete with other candidates with a stupendous amount of cryptocurrency at stake, higher than all the other candidates.

Proof of burn

Proof of Burn (PoB) is a consensus algorithm with an interesting approach to solving transition problems from one version of cryptocurrency to another in the blockchains. Through the PoB algorithm, the old cryptocurrency (or its preceding version) is burnt in order to reduce its supply and gradually increase the supply of the new cryptocurrency (or its succeeding version). This consensus algorithm is practiced in various forms, including a method wherein users can transfer the old cryptocurrency to an unspendable wallet address in exchange for new ones:

- **Merit**: The PoB algorithm is convenient during the transition of cryptocurrencies and network upgrades if the system trusts the participating entities.
- **Demerit**: The PoB algorithm is usually applicable in PoW-based blockchains and so has a limitation of applicability. This is due to the requirement of verifiable proofs and the ability to decay the burnt coins over time, which is naturally capable through PoW algorithms.

Delegated Proof of Stake

Delegated Proof of Stake (**dPOS**) is a consensus algorithm developed and used by the Block.one EOS platform. Under dPOS, the token holders reserve the right to nominate the validators (also called block producers). The selection of block producers is a continuous process and performs the duties of packaging user transactions into blocks with Byzantine fault-tolerant safety:

- **Merit**: dPOS is **Byzantine Fault Tolerance** (**BFT**) -ready and scales easily in a public network environment.
- **Demerit**: Although dPOS is efficient, it is prone to capitalistic efforts to supersede other minor token stakeholders.

Proof of authority

As the name suggests, the **Proof of Authority** (**PoA**) algorithm facilitates a distributed consensus with a few eligible verifiable nodes preserving the right to add transactions to blocks, if some criteria is met. There are many variants of the PoA algorithm, with or without the reputations of the validating nodes used in the public, private, and permissioned blockchains:

- **Merit**: The PoA algorithm is energy-efficient and not prone to capitalistic pitfalls as the validator nodes are authorized to add transactions to blocks based on their reputation. If the node is observed to malfunction, its reputation is severely affected and cannot proceed as a validator.
- **Demerit**: The PoA algorithm is partially centralized as the authority of adding or rejecting transactions lies in the purview of very few nodes in the network.

Practical Byzantine fault tolerance

Practical Byzantine Fault Tolerance (**PBFT**) is one of the replication algorithms brought to light by academic research. Authored by Miguel Castro and Barbara Liskov in 1999 (http:/ /pmg.csail.mit.edu/papers/osdi99.pdf), this algorithm was primarily aimed at solving the Byzantine faults caused by the arbitrary point of failures in the nodes of a network.

Notably, the PBFT algorithm is used by the Hyperledger Fabric blockchain framework:

- **Merit**: The PBFT algorithm is efficient, with fast transaction processing and scalable to hundreds of nodes in a private network.
- **Demerit**: The algorithm is based on a gatekeeper technique and is hence criticized for its centralized approaches. PBFT is not suitable for public blockchains.

Proof of elapsed time

Proof of Elapsed Time (PoET) is a consensus algorithm developed and used by the Hyperledger Sawtooth blockchain framework. The PoET algorithm ensures security and randomness involved in the leadership of validator nodes with special CPU instructions available in most of the advanced processors featuring secure virtual environments:

- **Merit**: PoET allows anyone with eligible hardware to participate as a validator node, allowing legitimate ways of verifying the leader election.
- **Demerit**: Although PoET does not involve staking cryptocurrencies to form a validatory node, the cost of affording specialized hardware does not come cheap. So, there have been criticisms highlighting this as an unfair bar to enter the network.

RAFT

RAFT is a consensus algorithm designed and developed by Diego Ongaro and John Ousterhout with the main motivation to bring about a distributed consensus algorithm that is much easier to understand than Paxos. Notably, RAFT ensures safe leader election, appending log entries in a distributed manner, and state machine consistency. The RAFT consensus is implemented in the Quorum blockchain to inherit the preceding described safety features:

- **Merit**: RAFT is one of the fastest algorithms in processing complex transaction payloads with the security of leadership and state machine consistency.
- **Demerit**: RAFT is suitable for permissioned or private blockchains only.

Ternary augmented RAFT architecture

Ternary Augmented RAFT Architecture (TARA) is a consensus algorithm designed for large-scale Byzantine-distributed networks. It is an enhanced version of the RAFT consensus algorithm to address heterogeneous transactions identifiable by their asset classes by leveraging PBFT hardening and cryptographic message exchanges. TARA introduces dynamic hierarchy to networks to ensure that their authority is not concentrated among a few nodes:

- **Merits**: TARA offers service clusters to ensure high availability, throughput, and scale. It has the hardware of all form factors with the ability to compute and store transactions can participate. TARA can be applied in all three environments—public, private, and permissioned blockchain networks.
- **Demerit**: Leadership election is not inherently dependent on the node's reputation, thereby allowing a potential attack on systems. These constraints must be implemented explicitly.

Avalanche

The **Avalanche** consensus is a protocol for distributed systems, introducing leaderless Byzantine fault tolerance, using a metastable mechanism achieving the same level of security and consistency among the nodes. Avalanche depends on the Snowball family to form a DAG, which stores the user transactional data, instead of blocks:

- **Merit**: Avalanche guarantees liveness and is immune to race conditions in the network.
- **Demerit**: Leadership consensus may not be applicable to all blockchain environments as there is not a carefully analyzed set of heuristics to ensure consistency.

With this detailed analysis of consensus algorithms, let's now go through the development tools available to blockchain developers.

Building DApps with blockchain tools

One of the main causes of the mainstream adoption of blockchain is the developer-led wave of evangelism for the technology. This has been observed in the form of frameworks and tools at developer's disposal. In the following section, we will go through the various tools and platforms that are available for public consumption to build blockchain-based software solutions.

Blockchain toolchains and frameworks

The following list introduces several blockchain toolchains and frameworks that are popular with both developers and the associated solution community:

- **Truffle**: The Truffle framework was developed by ConsenSys as an open source project, offering a pipeline for the development, testing, and deployment of smart contracts targeted on the EVM.
- **Embark**: The Embark framework was developed by Status as an open source project, offering a debugging and integration environment for Ethereum smart contract developers. Notably, Embark offers tighter integration with IPFS for the decentralized storage of contract data.
- **Hyperledger Composer**: This is an open source effort from the Linux Foundation, which offers tools to assist developers with converting requirements into **proof of concept** for the DevOps process, for spinning a new network as required.
- **MetaMask**: This is a middleware that bridges an application running in the browser with the Ethereum blockchain. It is an open source initiative supported and consumed widely by all Ethereum developers. Users can perform transactions in a web application through MetaMask.
- **Ethers.js**: This is a JavaScript-based library with full implementation of the Ethereum wallet as per the specification. Developers use this open source library to create user wallets, perform transactions, and much more. This library is also well known for its recent support for **Ethereum Name Service** (**ENS**).
- **Nethereum**: This is an open source library used to build Ethereum-based blockchain solutions in .NET environments. Nethereum offers .NET developers an SDK called NuGet, which is integrated into the Visual Studio **Integrated Development Environment** (**IDE**) for using web3 functionalities across web and mobile applications.

Next, let us look into developing smart with IDEs and plugins.

Developing smart contracts using IDEs and plugins

Traditional software developers are more familiar and comfortable with working in IDEs, and the vibrant developer communities of blockchain have considered this. In the following section, we will observe a few famous web-based IDEs and plugins available for standalone IDEs.

The Remix IDE

Remix has been the de facto IDE for smart contract development and deployment. This open source IDE is used by developers who are interested in developing, debugging, and deploying solidity smart contracts for Ethereum network. Notably, this IDE works well with private networks and offers regular updates.

The EthFiddle IDE

EthFiddle is an open source initiative by Loom Network to facilitate code experimentation online and provides the ability to share experimental code snippets of solidity smart contracts among developers for easier collaboration.

The YAKINDU plugin for Eclipse

Several enterprise developers have yearned for plugins for current IDEs, and this plugin offers just that. YAKINDU offers basic syntax highlighting and other common language package features for solidity smart contract development in the Eclipse IDE.

The Solidity plugin for Visual Studio Code

This plugin can be installed on **Visual Studio Code**, one of the most used IDEs. It boasts to be one of the leading plugins used for solidity smart contract development.

The Etheratom plugin for Visual Studio Code

Etheratom is a plugin available for GitHub's Atom editor, offering IDE features such as syntax highlighting, including a deployment interface to a local Ethereum node. It uses web3.js to interact with a local Ethereum node.

Summary

Blockchain has enjoyed a lot of hype, and we are now observing some of the excitement that came out of this hype coming to fruition in the form of well-established practices, frameworks, tools, and live use cases. Understanding the current landscape of blockchain and its current offerings helps us to assess the ability to convert the emerging requirements into products, with less friction to the market.

In this chapter, we explored what blockchain is, and we are now confidently able to identify the similarities and differences between DLT and distributed databases. We also observed different types of design patterns within open and private blockchain with practical examples. We enumerated multiple blockchain projects, cryptocurrency implementations, frameworks, and tools.

In the next chapter, we will introduce you to the contemporary basics of AI, and we will observe different types and forms of AI, as well as more applications of AI.

Introduction to the AI Landscape

2

"AI sees the invisible and reaches the unreachable."

Artificial Intelligence (AI) is one of the fundamental concepts that evolved well before computers existed on every desk in homes and offices across the world. Today, AI is applied across various domains to optimize processes and address issues where human abilities and outreach do not provide a feasible solution. In this chapter, we will briefly examine the history of AI, its classifications, and the applications of AI in enterprises.

This chapter provides a detailed overview of the AI landscape, covering the following key topics:

- AI – key concepts
- Types of AI
- Forms of AI and approaches
- AI in digital transformation
- AI platforms and tools

Technical requirements

This chapter assumes that you are aware of a few basic concepts of AI in various forms, with some knowledge of how AI is impacting daily life. This chapter explains the fundamental concepts for beginners, so technical know-how is not a mandatory requirement.

AI – key concepts

AI has many definitions based on the nature of its techniques, its usage, and also the timeline of its research. However, the most common definition is as follows—AI is the intelligence and capability exhibited by a computer to perceive, learn, and solve problems, with minimal probability of failure.

The ability of AI to compute and achieve results within a shorter period of time than humans has made computers the cornerstone of automation across various industries. The computational work of humans is often prone to errors, is time-consuming, and exhibits diminishing accuracy as the problem gets harder to solve. However, computers have been able to fill this role for a long time, from the early beginnings of automation that can be observed in many passive forms in our daily life. One of the best examples of such automation is the introduction of **Optical Character Recognition** (**OCR**), which converts embedded text in an image or document into a text source ready for computation. Computers enabled with OCR devices are more accurate and consume less time in reproducing the content than humans. Similarly, barcode scanners have led the way to faster checkout times at retail shops. Although the early systems were not completely *intelligent* per se, they are still recognized for their efficiency.

Although there was a lack of general criteria for AI in the early days, we will consider the major efforts made by researchers over the past eight decades in the following section.

History of AI

Numerous depictions of AI in the form of robots, artificial humans, or androids can be observed in art, literature, and computer science dating back to as early as the 4th century BC in Greek mythology. AI research and development gained mainstream progress in the early 20th century. The phrase **artificial intelligence** was coined during a summer workshop held at Dartmouth College in 1956 in New Hampshire. The workshop was called the **Dartmouth Summer Research Project on Artificial Intelligence** and was organized by Prof. John McCarthy, one of the mathematics professors at **Massachusetts Institute of Technology** (**MIT**). This workshop led to the development of AI as a special field within the overlapping disciplines of mathematics and computer science.

However, it is also notable that two decades before the Dartmouth workshop, the British mathematician Alan Turing had proposed the concept of the **Turing machine**, a computational model that can process algorithms, in 1936. He later published the paper *Computing Machinery and Intelligence* (https://www.csee.umbc.edu/courses/471/papers/turing.pdf) in which he proposed the concept of differentiating the response of machine intelligence from a human. This concept is widely known as the **Turing test** today.

In the following diagram, we can see how the Turing test is performed to test whether the response from an AI can be distinguished from a human response by another human:

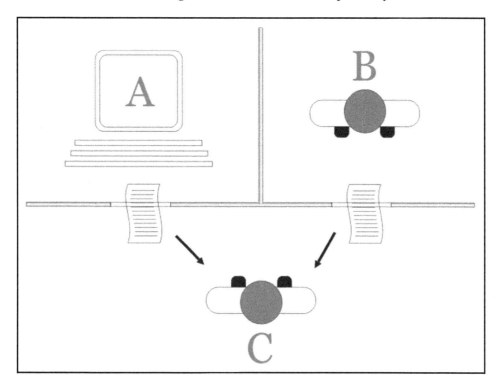

Fig 2.1: The Turing test performed by an interrogator (**C**) between an AI (**A**) and a human (**B**).

You can check out the preceding diagram by Juan Alberto Sánchez Margallo in more detail at `https://en.wikipedia.org/wiki/Turing_test#/media/File:Turing_test_diagram.png`. Here is the license to the diagram, `https://creativecommons.org/licenses/by/2.5/`.

Almost a decade after the summer workshop at Dartmouth College, the first chatbot, named ELIZA, was showcased by AI researcher Joseph Weizenbaum at MIT in 1966. It was one of the first few chatbots to attempt the Turing test. After the invention of ELIZA, a new range of expert systems and learning patterns evolved over the next two decades until the 1980s.

With the preceding basic understanding of AI and its history under our belts, let's consider some of the impediments faced by researchers in the early days of AI in the following section.

AI winter

AI winter is a term used by many in the IT industry to define a period of time when AI researchers faced many challenges, leading to severe cuts in funding and the slowdown of AI as a specialized field.

During the early 1970s, academic research and development in the field of AI were suddenly halted by the US and British governments, due to some unreasonable speculations about AI and the criticisms that followed. The complex international situations at the time also contributed to the complete halt of many AI research projects.

It is commonly observed that AI winter started in the early 1970s, but ended nearly two decades later due to research failures, setbacks in motivation, and consensus among government bodies, as well as the collapse of some of the original foundational goals set prior to the commencement of a few research programs.

Now that we have learned a bit about the history of AI, in the following section, we will explore the different types of AI and the different forms in which AI is manifested.

Types of AI

There are several forms of AI, each conceived to solve different problems. AI can be categorized and classified by various different criteria, including the theoretical approach used to design it and the application domain for which it is intended to be used.

Efforts at categorization were directly influenced by some parameters such as the ability to learn a particular task without supervision, obtaining cognitive abilities, and the ability to perform reasoning similar to humans. Based on these and a complex set of expectations, we will look into the three basic types of AI.

Weak AI

Also generally known as **narrow AI**, **weak AI** can be used to execute narrow and repetitive tasks. Weak AI functions are based on a preexisting combination of logic and data. User inputs are processed based on the same logic, and hence, weak AI lacks self-consciousness and aggressive learning abilities. Some prominent examples of weak AI implementations are voice assistants, chatbots, and linguistic expert systems. Due to the narrow implementation of logic, weak AI is suitable for scenarios where the user's inputs and expected outputs are well defined.

Chatbots receive textual inputs from a user and process the input data to identify the information required to convert the textual input into some form of action. Chatbots are generally applied in the areas of e-commerce and support where human intervention may not be necessary all the time. In the case of online shopping, the presence of a chatbot provides a personal touch to the user and provides the user with a traditional way of communicating with the system instead of conventional searching. Similarly, in the case of support, the application of chatbots can reduce the per capita cost of maintaining a support team for a product. It is also important to realize that newer generations of users are more prone to communicating via messaging over conventional phone calls. Chatbots can leverage this cultural shift and also reduce the potential friction involved in the support process.

Strong AI

Also generally known as **Artificial General Intelligence (AGI)**, strong AI can be used to apply aggressive learning abilities to solve problems with multivariate range. Strong AIs are capable of perception, being conscious of the given problems and aided by its cognitive abilities. Strong AI has been one of the more prominent fields of research due to its potential ability in cutting down operational costs in existing processes, as well as exploring applications in uncharted territories.

Due to the capabilities of strong AI to reason and make optimal judgments, applications of strong AI can be observed in the business landscape. Expert systems, machine learning, and deep learning techniques are some of the most renowned manifestations of strong AI. These manifestations are commonly used by businesses due to their ability to predict and reason based on given data points.

Some other examples of strong AI applied across various industries include **Computer Vision (CV)**, **Natural Language Processing (NLP)**, **Natural Language Understanding (NLU)**, and **Reinforcement Learning (RL)**.

For example, NLP can be used to adapt a system according to the user's mood and help the system to communicate with the user more effectively compared to weak AI implementations. Similarly, strong AI can also be applied for efficient language translation with greater accuracy in the conversion between languages.

Super AI

Super AI, or **Artificial Super Intelligence** (**ASI**), is the hypothetical ability of a computer to surpass the consciousness of the human mind. It is speculated by many experts that an AI may achieve this stage after reaching the singularity. It is also widely believed that super AI would ultimately lead to the technological dominance of computers over human thinking. Although super AIs are nonexistent, there are a handful of institutions and organizations preparing for the leap from AGI to super AI, with extraordinary focus on genetic engineering, artificial digital neurons, and quantum computing. The application of super AI is surprisingly unclear at the moment, as few can comprehend what could be achieved after the singularity. However, a few primitive variants of super AI are expected to help in exploring space, creating new languages, and predicting unintended consequences in war.

Singularity is a hypothetical situation proposed by John von Neumann wherein the AI's cognitive capabilities surpass that of a human mind. As a result, it is believed that singularity could lead to a varied range of outcomes in which the extinction of the human race is considered a probable outcome.

With the preceding understanding of weak AI, strong AI, and super AI on a theoretical basis, let's now examine how AI is manifested practically in various forms.

Forms of AI and approaches

Implementations of AI have come in various forms due to the varying nature of the intended application and the technology available for the solution. Hence, AI has been manifested in code in various forms, utilized by a wide range of developers in different domains for respective problems.

In the following Venn diagram, we can see various forms of AI:

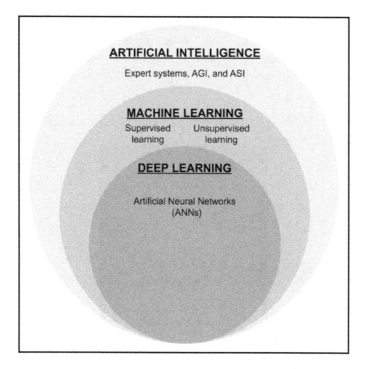

Fig 2.2: Relationships between forms of AI

In the preceding diagram, I have mentioned all the major forms of AI categorized into three major manifestations. Each form is explained in detail in the following section, broken down into expert systems, machine learning, and neural networks.

We will now explore these primary approaches and forms of AI with brief introductions to their backgrounds and applications.

Statistical and expert systems

Statistical systems were one of the most primitive forms of AI, dating back to the late 1960s. As the name suggests, statistical approaches used a huge amount of data to arrive at the most desirable result. However, it was soon recognized that the results were virtually unrelated to real-world scenarios and produced output only based on the AI's rational decision-making ability. These limitations led to the decline of statistical AI, paving the way for expert systems in the early 1980s.

Expert systems were a mature form of strong AI with the ability to mine datasets and derive answers that were more related to the context of the problem. This leap was aided by information theory, combined with new abilities in hardware. Although expert systems were developed in the early 1960s, they only became affordable during the 1980s thanks to the PC revolution. Unlike the scientific approaches used by statistical AIs, expert systems leveraged semantic and linguistic programming to arrive at the expected outputs with high probability.

An example of an expert system in use can be seen in the following photo:

Fig 2.3: Photo of an expert system in use

You can check out the preceding photograph by Michael L. Umbricht and Carl R. Friend at https://en.wikipedia.org/wiki/Expert_system#/media/File:Symbolics3640_ Modified.JPG. Here is the license to the photo, https://creativecommons.org/licenses/ by-sa/3.0/.

Although expert systems opened the doors for early AI adoption, it is machine learning that really met the demands of industry. In the following section, we will learn about machine learning.

Machine learning

Machine learning is a form of AI that depends on a preexisting dataset as input, with or without a variation in the expected output to produce human-like thinking based on applying a mathematical model on the given data. The term was coined in 1959 by Arthur Samuel, one of the pioneers of AI research at IBM. If a particular machine learning algorithmic system aims to extrapolate a result based on the given forecast data, it is called **predictive analytics**, which is used in various emerging fields of computer applications.

Although similar forms of AI existed before machine learning, it is believed that most of the research has now been consolidated under this label since the early 1990s, also known as the golden age of machine learning. Some of the earliest applications of the concepts of machine learning were CV, email spam filtering, and operation optimizations.

There are three approaches to machine learning algorithms that have been observed in use very consistently in the recent past. We will look at them in the following sections.

Supervised learning

Models in this approach directly depend on the datasets that serve as the input for training data, and also on the expected outputs. The model uses the input data in the training phase by itself, learning outcomes associated with a few ranges of inputs in the form of labeled samples. Such samples are fed into the algorithm model to be able to successfully achieve the expected result. Usually, the expected outcomes are either in the form of classification, regression, or prediction.

Unsupervised learning

Under this approach, the models are provided with the training data as the input, but lack any expected output to be specified by the end user. This approach is justified as the intended outcome of this practice is to gain visibility on the unexplored rational commonalities present within the data.

Reinforcement learning

This is a reward-based learning approach used to achieve all-round optimization by enforcing a wide range of techniques in rewarding successful agents in a cumulative manner.

Now that we have a basic understanding of machine learning, let's proceed to examine neural networks.

Neural networks

An **Artificial Neural Network (ANN)**, also called **deep learning**, is a group of synthetic neurons forming a circuit to solve difficult problems. This is a specialized form of AI with aggressive strategies designed to achieve the desired goal. However, unlike machine learning algorithms, the heuristics and execution patterns in ANNs are not linear, and hence this kind of AI can be found in a wide range of applications such as autonomous driving, textual and facial pattern recognition, decision-making software for trading, digital art, and drug formulation.

The following diagram is a general representation of a neural network, along with the basic relationship between the three layers—**Input**, **Hidden**, and **Output**:

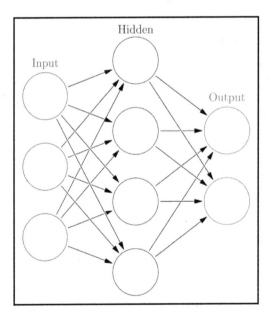

Fig 2.4: Pictorial representation of a typical neural network

You can check out the preceding diagram by Glosser.ca at `https://commons.wikimedia.org/wiki/File:Colored_neural_network.svg`. Here is the license to the diagram, `https://creativecommons.org/licenses/by-sa/3.0/`.

Evolutionary computation

AI has long been identified as a key enabler for the future of biotechnology. Evolutionary AI in forms such as genetic algorithms have also been one of the early fields of research in this domain. AI has been helpful in analyzing, simulating, and predicting the behavior of mutations in our bodies. It is also notable that some AI practices in genome research have been actively criticized, fearing severe repercussions for the future of mankind in the process of experimentation.

Swarm computation

Apart from behaving in a centralized manner, AI is also significantly known to have disrupted the functioning of distributed and collaborative computer systems. **Swarm intelligence** is the capability of a group of systems to achieve a common goal by cooperating in an ordered manner. Swarm intelligence is leveraged to understand group behaviors and optimize processes wherever possible.

Multiple agents work together based on a set of heuristics to consume vast amounts of data and produce meaningful results based on the coordination between one or more computing devices. Applications of swarm AI can be observed in robotics, logistical automation such as truck platooning, and so on.

The following photograph is a real-world example of a coordinated application using swarm computation techniques:

Fig 2.5: A group of coordinating robots in a swarm for recharging

You can check out the preceding photo by Serge Kernbach at `https://commons.wikimedia.org/wiki/File:RechargingSwarm.jpg`. Here is the license to photo, `https://creativecommons.org/licenses/by-sa/3.0/`.

With this basic understanding of AI and its types, forms, and approaches, we will now explore the procedure of applying AI in the next section.

AI in digital transformation

Many organizations have already prepared for the next wave of digital transformation. While a few digital solutions have adopted AI techniques successfully and are reaping the benefits, a significant portion of the digital solution space is busy preparing for the upcoming leaps in AI. We will briefly observe some of the key milestones where AI can enable future digital transformation programs and address major challenges.

We'll begin by observing some of the key milestones involved in a digital transformation project enabled by AI in the following diagram:

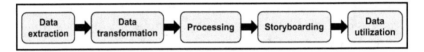

Fig 2.6: Important milestones in digital transformation using AI

The preceding diagram represents all the important milestones of an AI-led digital transformation project. The diagram also represents the flow connecting one milestone to another. Each milestone is elaborated in the following sections.

Data extraction

Before AI can be used to fuel a digital transformation project, essential information related to processes and practices must be collected and archived into suitable bundles for further structuring.

The data extraction step involves rigorous sourcing of raw data and information from various modules of the existing system. The extracted data not only helps us in understanding existing processes but also helps us quantify and establish boundaries and checkpoints for further analysis.

The method used for extracting the data is the most fundamental step for AI to empower a digital transformation project. Hence, it is essential to make sure that the quality of data is reviewed and measured by the team along with key stakeholders.

Assume that a dairy company is planning for a digital transformation of its business and is interested in leveraging AI for better insights. We'll begin by understanding the topline information of the dairy business by identifying the products and revenue, followed by specific information on raw materials sourced from many areas. The data extraction process also includes the identification of business processes with key checkpoints.

Consider the following graph of the performance of AI models:

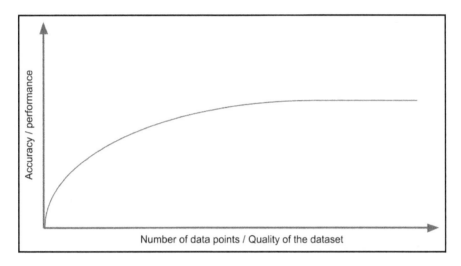

Fig 2.7: Generic illustration of the increase in AI model's performance

The preceding line graph is a generic illustration of how AI models can perform better and gain accuracy, represented by the *y* axis, with the increase in the quality of datasets using new data points represented by the *x* axis. This means that over time, AI models can get better with a careful review of the quality of the growing datasets.

Data transformation

The data collected from the previous phase could be unstructured or semi-structured. This means there is a higher chance that the data points are inconsistent when put together, which could become an impediment to the analysis of the collected data.

To help AI understand the given scenario, the collected data must be structured based on agreed standard formats by the key stakeholders. However, if the data is extracted from a data warehouse, the effort required might be minimal.

If the data is a stream of unstructured data, several **Extract**, **Transform**, **Load** (**ETL**) tools are available in the market to structure the humongous amounts of data with minimal effort, including Apache NiFi and Apache StreamSets (`https://dzone.com/articles/top-5-enterprise-etl-tools`).

Apart from standalone and on-premises software, there are cloud-hosted ETL services available in the market, such as AWS Data Pipeline and AWS Glue.

Once the data is transformed according to the specified scheme, we can forward it to data processing.

Assume that we have obtained the necessary information from the dairy company. Now, we can separate the data from the noise by identifying the key information in the dataset. In the data transformation process, we remove the unnecessary columns. We also consolidate some of the columns depending on the type of data, such as latitude and longitude. If the latitude and longitude data of the local dairy is maintained in separate columns, we can aim to consolidate them into one column. Similarly, we can consider skipping the rows that may not have values for critical columns.

Processing

The structured data from various business units, along with training data, is now used as the input data to mine, simulate, and extrapolate the expected results to better understand any efforts planned under a digital transformation program.

Based on the nature, source, and complexity of the data point, you may opt for various sets of AI models and techniques. For example, if the data is a conversation between a seller and a buyer, you may use **NLP**.

Assuming that the data from the dairy business is cleaned up, we can now supply the data into a prediction model for training. Once the data is fed in, we can check the results of the model with the business team to confirm that the results are favorable to the given business goal. For example, the model could be predicting the likely stocks of surplus milk from local cattle farms. Based on the surplus milk data generated, we may also be able to identify the dairy products we could produce with it. As such, these results from processing the data can help us get better insights.

Storyboarding

Once the expected results are computed, the information should be communicated and shared for feedback. This helps identify the relevance of the results.

In the dairy product example, we can use the predictions to make business decisions to allocate surplus milk on time for manufacturing the chosen dairy products. The costs saved and the revenue increased by the sale of dairy products can be communicated in the storyboard using visualization libraries and dashboard software available on the market.

Data utilization

Once a common agreement has been achieved on the obtained results, the gathered insights are converted into renewed practices and put to work across multiple agents in the ecosystem through web, mobile, and **Internet of Things (IoT)** devices. This engagement cycle repeats until the desired results of optimizations are achieved through continuous innovation in the refinement of data sourcing, data processing, and the efficient design of algorithms.

In the dairy product example, the insights and profit predictions generated with the help of AI are not only communicated to key personnel through storyboards. The insights can also be put into further action by making suitable changes to existing business processes.

Now that we have understood the key milestones in an AI-based digital transformation project, let's also explore the possible failure scenarios by enumerating the reasons behind a potential failure.

Failure scenarios

An AI-based digital transformation project may fail due to various reasons, including market requirements, adaptability, skill gaps, and unexpected changes in the business processes. Let's learn more about these reasons in the following sections.

Business requirements

We must ensure that the business requirements are unanimously agreed upon before assessing any applications of AI in the digital transformation project. A list of all the stakeholders whose processes will see improvements must be created to assess any potential risk among other stakeholders involved in the process.

Adaptability

Although technologies have become accessible to the majority of organizations in the enterprise landscape, it does not necessarily mean that the business benefits from the application of AI in transformation. Applications of AI may actually increase the complexity and complications in the process established. Hence, we must be sensitive to the morale of the industry and take a firm decision only if the majority of the stakeholders are open to adopting emerging solutions.

Skill gaps

There are a few industry verticals wherein not all the stakeholders involved are educated about or aware of emerging technologies. There might be a serious impediment in introducing AI-enabled digital transformation to a group of stakeholders who do not feel comfortable operating under the conditions required by standard AI practices, which often involve analytical capabilities from the user group.

Process overhaul

As we know, humans tend to react negatively to change in their lives. Just as in life, it is very important to assess the risk of introducing these emerging solutions to stakeholders who are very sensitive to the changes introduced to the business. Also, a major breakthrough in digital transformation may affect the current business models and affect the privacy policy of the stakeholders involved in the business. It must be reviewed carefully to ensure that data is governed in line with the local data regulations and laws.

With a basic overview of the processes involved in an AI-based digital transformation project, let's now explore some of the tools available to support such digital transformations.

AI platforms and tools

One of the major signs of maturity in an AI ecosystem is identified by the application of new tools and frameworks. Other indicators such as innovation, interoperability, and accuracy also play a major role in identifying the maturity of an AI ecosystem and its tools. In the following sections, we can see a short list of a few AI platforms and tools that are leveraged by many engineers around the world.

TensorFlow

TensorFlow is an open source project anchored by internet giant Google. It is a sophisticated framework used for machine learning projects. It offers a wide ecosystem with comprehensive toolkits, libraries, and documentation that enable researchers and developers to easily design, build, and deploy machine learning-powered applications. Find out more about the tools at `https://www.tensorflow.org`.

Microsoft Cognitive Toolkit

The **Microsoft Cognitive Toolkit (CNTK)** is an open source toolkit for commercial-grade distributed deep learning. It describes neural networks as a series of computational steps by using a directed graph. Find out more about the toolkit on GitHub, at `https://github.com/Microsoft/CNTK`.

IBM Watson

IBM Watson is an open source, multi-cloud platform that lets you build powerful models and deploy them with a smoother, more streamlined experience. This IBM suite offers enterprise-ready AI services, applications, and tooling with rich support. Find out more about IBM Watson at `https://www.ibm.com/watson/about/`.

Summary

AI has been at the cutting edge of innovation, with the majority of business applications adopting it across all domains. In this chapter, we were able to observe the key concepts, brief history, and progress of AI so far. We also covered different approaches used in the AI landscape and understood multiple implementations and categories within AI with the help of a diagram. We then observed the steps required to apply AI in a digital transformation program to achieve the best results. Finally, we concluded the chapter with an introduction to some of the latest tools and platforms used proactively by the AI community globally.

In the next chapter, we will explore some interesting applications of AI and blockchain, along with some detailed case studies of real-world scenarios.

Section 2: Blockchain and Artificial Intelligence

In this section, we will cover the applications of Blockchain and AI. We will observe some of the live applications that use both blockchain and AI combined. We will also learn about decentralized databases and filesystems. Finally, we will observe how AI is applied in cryptocurrency trading.

This section comprises the following chapters:

- Chapter 3, *Domain-Specific Applications of AI and Blockchain*
- Chapter 4, *AI- and Blockchain-Driven Databases*
- Chapter 5, *Empowering Blockchain Using AI*
- Chapter 6, *Cryptocurrency and Artificial Intelligence*

Domain-Specific Applications of AI and Blockchain

3

"Blockchain and AI: The hands of the future."

Blockchain and AI have been leveraged to build many solutions. In this chapter, we will showcase some of the applications of blockchain technology. We will also showcase some of the applications that use AI techniques. We will analyze the problems faced and the solutions offered, and also provide you with a perspective of the current solutions.

We will be covering solutions across several domain verticals, such as the following:

- Applying AI and blockchain to healthcare
- Applying AI and blockchain to supply chains
- Applying AI and blockchain to financial services
- Applying AI and blockchain to other domains

Let's get started!

Technical requirements

This chapter requires you to be able to analyze the applications of AI and blockchain, based on its crucial abilities in application domains.

Applying AI and blockchain to healthcare

AI was used experimentally in the healthcare domain back in the early 1970s. One of the earliest AIs that was applied to this domain was an expert system called **Dendral**. However, Dendral did not become a mainstream application in healthcare; one of its successors called **MYCIN** took over some of the challenging problems in the domain of medicine for therapeutic treatments. Today, the applications of AI and blockchain in the domain of healthcare are crowded by top brass companies such as IBM, Microsoft, Google, and other start-ups.

In the following screenshot, you can see an **Electronic Health Record** (**EHR**) of a patient:

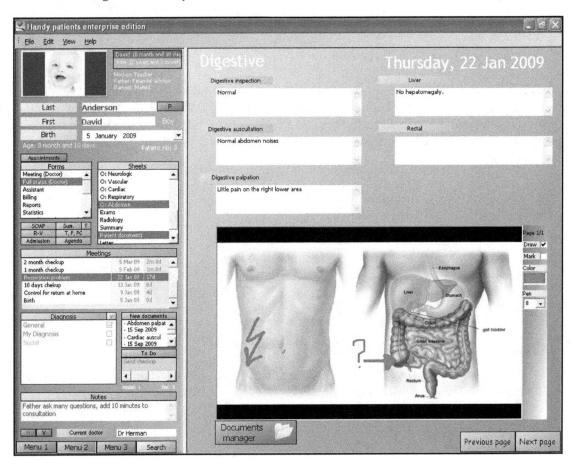

Fig 3.1: Sample view of an EHR

You can check out the diagram at, `https://en.wikipedia.org/wiki/Electronic_health_record#/media/File:Electronic_medical_record.jpg`.

Now, let's understand some of the issues faced by the healthcare industry.

Issues in the domain

Although applications of AI has made significant advancements in healthcare, they have failed to address some of the governance issues and a few unlawful practices plaguing the space. Blockchain serves as a powerful combination here in that it aids the AI as a store of lawful data supported by transparent and discoverable actions. Let's take a look:

- **EMR privacy and security**: Electronic Medical Records (also called Electronic Health Records) are digital copies of the patient's health information and are populated by doctors over the course of treatment. Generally, EHRs are composed of a patient's medical history, symptoms, diagnosis information, and lab results. EHRs enable organizations to provide more connected, efficient, and convenient care. Applications of EHRs have been heavily regulated by developed countries in the previous decades, predominantly the European Union and the United States of America, who passed the Cross Border Health Directive and **Health Insurance Portability and Accountability Act (HIPAA)** of 1996 Privacy and Security Rule, respectively. Despite the strong enforcement of these rules, there have been multiple EMR data breaches that have affected millions of users. This can be partially traced back to the centralized information architecture, which led to portal-level hacks being discovered by hackers.

- **Drug formulation**: Drug formulation (also called pharmaceutical formulation) is the process of researching a combination of chemical substances to form a new drug or medicinal product to treat a particular ailment. Finding an ethical way of sharing clinical trial records to perfect the analytical process of drug formulation is a challenge. Most of the new techniques used in drug formulation leverage various analytical processes based on the data obtained from drug delivery, as well as clinical testing records. Similar to EMR, the underlying data is very sensitive.

- **Predictive healthcare**: The common goal of predictive healthcare is to provide treatments or notifications prior to the patients presenting symptoms. This is made possible by performing predictive analytics on the patient's personal data in a near real-time manner. Access to unprecedented data regarding the body could be very useful but must also be treated sensitively. AI practices based on blockchain data can aid in providing preventive treatments during diagnosis using verifiable data discovery.

Now, let's learn how to use either blockchain or AI to solve the problems in the healthcare industry.

Emerging solutions in healthcare

The following list includes some of the blockchain-based initiatives being started by active enterprises and startups alike in the healthcare domain:

- **IOTA eHealth**: IOTA eHealth is a solution-based initiative spearheaded by the IOTA Foundation that offers features such as Remote Patient Monitoring, Patient's Health Data Exchange, and ensuring clinical research data integrity is supported by the IOTA ledger. You can learn more about IOTA eHealth at `https://www.iota.org/verticals/ehealth`.
- **IBM blockchain**: IBM blockchain research groups are reportedly researching a solution to prevent counterfeit drugs by using a permissioned blockchain, along with a special mobile interface. The solution reportedly hosts a blockchain network, wherein participants on the network are certified and authorized to perform transactions, as well as track and verify them. You can learn more and catch the latest actions being made on the current efforts at `http://www.research.ibm.com/haifa//dept/services/bc-iot.shtml`.

Now that we've looked at the key solutions, let's take a retrospective look at the current scenario in the healthcare industry.

Retrospective

The usage of AI and blockchain can help revolutionize healthcare, and regulators and international bodies such as the **World Health Organization (WHO)** and **Food and Drug Administration (FDA)** are reportedly keen on taking advantage of this technology. They are actively collaborating with enterprises making efforts in this direction. Wellness and healthcare are expected to grow substantially in this coming decade, and I urge you to keep an open tab on this domain for more innovation through both blockchain and AI.

Now that we have had a look at the current solutions for the healthcare industry, let's explore the products and solutions used in supply chains, powered either by blockchain or AI.

Applying AI and blockchain to supply chains

Supply chain management is crucial to the success of many industries and growing economies around the world; some consider supply chains to be the nervous system of trade. Managing a supply chain is an operation-oriented practice that requires efficiency and effectiveness, from the early phases of planning, procurement, and warehousing, to the logistics of shipping goods from producers to consumers.

The following sample diagram identifies the stakeholders involved in the supply chain management of a laptop:

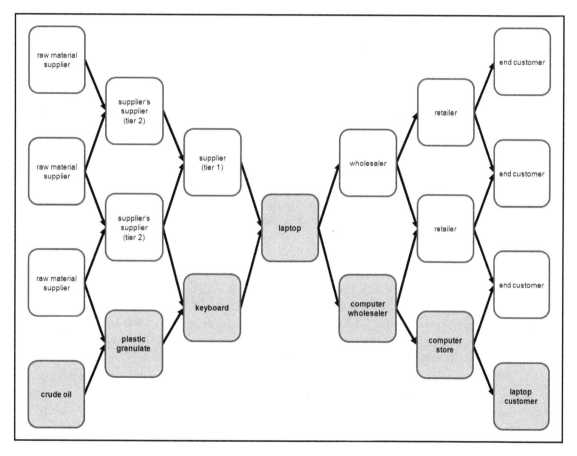

Fig 3.2: Stakeholders in the supply chain of a laptop

You can check out this diagram by Andreas Wieland at, `https://en.wikipedia.org/wiki/Supply_chain_management#/media/File:Supply_and_demand_network_(en).png`. Here is the license to the diagram, `https://creativecommons.org/licenses/by-sa/3.0/`.

Now, let's understand some of the issues faced by the supply chain industry.

Issues in the domain

The following are three of the top issues faced by the supply chain industry:

- **Operational costs and risks**: A high proportion of the supply chain is still in paperwork mode. This means that data across the system is highly vulnerable to being tampered with. The data in supply chains is crucial for identifying the value of the products, including its basic attributes such as validity and shelf life. If the paperwork of the shipment has been tampered with, there could be a large gap across the value chain. Manual paperwork-based supply chains can also attract financial glitches due to potential scenarios such as double billing, thereby creating more audit problems and confusion among the stakeholders. Although relatively newer supply chain solutions have been effective in digitally transforming the paperwork nature of a few supply chain transactions, there are fewer systems technically capable of handling potential data loss or forgery in the process. Blockchain can alleviate these problems with the help of smart contracts and can automate several critical processes.

- **Security and authenticity**: Although the end-to-end processes of the supply chain are digitally connected using traditional enterprise software, they are loosely defined and coupled among themselves. This means that data integrity is not treated as a first-class feature. This can be resolved with blockchain technologies based on the immutability concepts and ensure that no records can be stolen, withdrawn, or replaced with inaccurate data. Since transactional data on the blockchain is open, relevant stakeholders can access information and verify the single source of truth.

- **Real-time visibility**: Transactions on native digital platforms that are closely coupled to traditional finance can also invite other business challenges, such as delays in settlements. Businesses in the supply chain heavily rely on working capital, and the major source for capital is either through loans or the revenue for their services. Enabling real-time payments across the value chain can enable faster payment processing at relatively lower costs compared to traditional finance. This is a game-changer for the industry.

Let's go through some of the solutions using either blockchain or AI to solve the problems in the supply chain industry.

Emerging solutions in the supply chain industry

Here are some of the applications that either use blockchain or AI in order to address some of the issues mentioned earlier:

- **IBM Sterling Supply Chain Suite**: Powered by IBM Watson, this cloud-based digital business network provides real-time intelligence and actionable recommendations. This suite offers a wide range of features across supplier management, inventory management, and order management. It is also notable that the suite offers an open platform and a developer hub for building tailored solutions in the supply chain using blockchain and AI. You can learn more about their product and offerings here: `https://www.ibm.com/in-en/supply-chain`.
- **OpenText**: With the aim of making supply chains more connected, collaborative, intelligent, and secure, OpenText is working on an autonomous and intelligent supply chain that can be used to apply AI, IoT, and blockchain. You can learn more about their product and offerings here: `https://www.opentext.com/info/ai-iot/connected-supply-chain#form`.

Next, we'll take a look at the current scenario in the supply chain industry.

Retrospective

Although AI and blockchain are being used to track orders and manage inventory more effectively, there are many business gaps that need to be filled. It is important to lower the bar of entry to bring in a diverse set of stakeholders across the globe so that they can participate in a globally verifiable supply chain network with a vision to increase quality and efficiency and promote transparency. This can happen by exposing APIs so that not all vendors have to be running on the same blockchain or network; instead, they could simply exchange trustworthy data and record them as cross-transactions across the networks for better compatibility. Effort must be made to make these products interoperable so that it becomes easier for the global supply chain economy to thrive on the diversity offered by the blockchain.

Now, let's explore the products and solutions used in the **Banking and Financial Services Industry** (**BFSI**) that are powered either by blockchain or AI.

Applying AI and blockchain to financial services

The BFSI is the backbone of the economic operations of the whole world as we know it. With trillions of dollars of assets under management, managing money effectively at a digital scale has become a lucrative opportunity and hence needs to be revisited due to some inefficiencies in the current systems that generally rely on traditional methods.

The following diagram depicts the relationship between stakeholders in the BFSI industry:

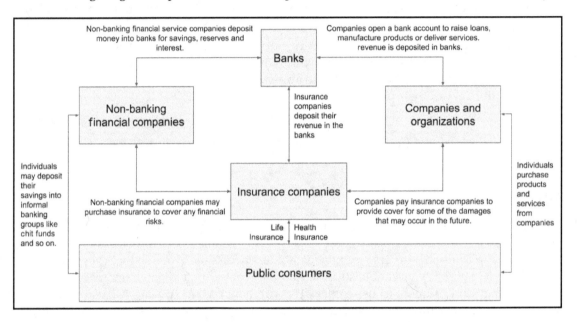

Fig 3.3: Stakeholders in BFSI

As shown in the preceding diagram, public consumers like you and me access capital and services through banks, insurance companies, and **Non-Banking Financial Companies (NBFC)**. Also, note that companies and organizations that provide services to us also rely on these financial institutions.

Now, let's explore some of the issues faced by the BFSI industry.

Issues in the domain

The following are the top three issues faced by the BFSI industry:

- **Access to capital**: The unbanked and the underbanked are severely affected by the problem of eligibility criteria, thereby creating a gaping hole in the market, thus leading to informal economies. If accessing the capital is made easier, we can streamline the informal economy and maximize its potential.
- **Fraud and delinquency**: It's estimated that financial fraud and delinquency are affecting the global economy through a loss of 600 billion USD. This is a serious problem plaguing the BFSI industry, especially in India due to the recent revelations about bad loans. At the time of writing, India ranks second in bad loans, piling up to 160 billion US dollars according to a Bloomberg article. You can read more at this link: `https://www.bloomberg.com/news/articles/2019-09-27/asia-s-640-billion-bad-loan-pile-lures-investors-deloitte-says`.
- **Lack of proper process automation**: Although numerous attempts have been made to secure and automate the BFSI sector, we need a better model that can bring about a striking balance between transparency in the industry but also preserves order among institutions. Hence, using blockchain to bring about transparency and using AI techniques to enable optimized workflows for automation could be the key to revolutionizing this industry.

Now, let's go through some of the solutions that can be used to solve the problems in the BFSI industry.

Emerging solutions in BFSI

Here are some of the applications that either use blockchain or AI in order to address some of the issues in BFSI mentioned earlier:

- **Teradata**: Teradata is a California-based corporation well-known for its data analytics products for the financial services industry. There is an interesting case study where deep learning and AI were used to detect sophisticated fraud and reduce the false positives at a reputed bank. Compared to the traditional rules engine, which reportedly detects about 40 percent of total fraud, Teradata's analytic solution increased the rate to as high as 80 percent. The solution also drastically reduced the false positives by 60 percent and increased true positives by 50 percent. The champion/challenger method is used to ensure that the best deep learning model is used in real time for detecting fraud.

You can find out more about the solution by reading Teradata's case study document at, `https://www.teradata.co.uk/Resources/Case-Studies/Danske-Bank-Fight-Fraud-With-Deep-Learning-and-AI`.

- **Nuo Network**: Nuo is a peer-to-peer network of lenders and borrowers that enable crypto-backed loans. Lenders can provide their cryptocurrencies for an interest rate, while borrowers can raise loans against collateral at a discounted price of the pledged asset, followed by a payment of a premium at the end of the loan's term. At the time of writing, the Nuo network has been used by many users to raise loans of up to 30 million USD. Also, it is important to note that Nuo Network is non-custodial, meaning that the wallets with funds in them are not in direct or indirect control of the company. This is enabled by using the Ethereum blockchain, where smart contracts are used to trade **Ethers** (**ETH**) and ERC20 tokens. You can find out more about their products and offerings here: `https://nuo.network/index.html`.

Next, we'll take a retrospective look at the current scenario in the BFSI industry.

Retrospective

A few emerging solutions have addressed the key issues in the BFSI industry. However, it is possible to achieve leaps in the solution space if we are able to connect the dots. AI solves optimization issues and blockchain enables transparency, but mostly, these technologies are deployed in individual silos that may not be able to carry value across the chain. Hence, it is imperative to connect these silos in a way that allows users and institutions alike to discover value beyond their own systems so that they can discover new potential and revenue streams.

Now that we've looked at retrospective offered on the current solutions for the BFSI industry, let's explore the products and solutions used across other domains, powered either by blockchain or AI.

Applying AI and blockchain to other domains

Although the majority of the solutions today are commercially deployed across supply chains and financial services, many more emerging solutions are being applied across various domains. We will observe such solutions using AI and blockchain to solve the current problems in businesses and unlock their true potential.

Now, let's explore the products and solutions used in the knowledge management domain, powered either by blockchain or AI.

Applying AI and blockchain to knowledge management

Most of you, including myself, gained exposure to the internet through open source knowledge bases such as Wikipedia. Things are moving fast in this generation and some content in this book could also possibly become outdated by the time it reaches your hands or devices. In this rapid world of changes, agility is very important in maintaining the accuracy of any documented knowledge base on the internet. This is a huge problem if the knowledge base consists of multiple topics and each topic is maintaining several sub-topics and articles.

Now, let's explore some of the issues faced by the knowledge management domain.

Issues in the domain

There is one top issue that's faced in knowledge management, known as accuracy of information.

Maintaining the accuracy and relevance of any outdated information across articles in Wikipedia requires a huge amount of time and several rounds of manual effort by human editors. With millions of articles stored and served by one of the largest encyclopedias on the planet, Wikipedia also has to maintain factual correctness. Also, this open information should not become susceptible to fake news or propaganda over time.

Now, let's take a look at a solution to the problems in the knowledge management domain.

Emerging solutions in knowledge management

Let's look at an example of an application that either uses blockchain or AI in order to address some of the issues mentioned earlier.

A group of researchers at the **Computer Science and Artificial Intelligence Laboratory** (**CSAIL**) of **Massachusetts Institute of Technology** (**MIT**) have created an automated text-generating system that can pinpoint and replace specific information in Wikipedia sentences, wherever required, while preserving human grammar and styles.

While many rule-based bots exist today that can make certain predefined or programmatic changes, bots may generally lack reasoning and hence be unable to put two facts together coherently in a human-readable format. This could not only create a disruption in the flow of the document but also lead to doubling efforts to fix such issues. Moreover, fact-checking becomes essential while updating any document to ensure that fake news or propaganda does not pivot the perception of a concept, leading to bias. Using an augmented dataset, the researchers were reportedly able to reduce the false positives by 13 percent, by making the model look at both the evidence and the sample in agree-disagree pairs. You can find out more about this research at, `https://news.mit.edu/2020/automated-rewrite-wikipedia-articles-0212`.

Now, let's look at a retrospective regarding the current scenario in the knowledge management domain.

Retrospective

The practice of knowledge management systems is being rethought, with constant innovation being made on the cloud. I think that now is a prime period to also inculcate the effectiveness of blockchain technologies and AI techniques to enrich the user experience, reduce overall costs, and to keep the data safe.

Now, let's explore the products and solutions used in the real estate domain, powered either by blockchain or AI.

Applying AI and blockchain to real estate

Over the past few decades, India's growing economy has resulted in the rise of many metropolitan cities and an active market for new purchases. However, there have been cases of aggressive land-grabbing, among other serious issues, due to bad record-keeping practices and/or corruption. Verifying titles is a cumbersome process before transacting on any piece of real estate. We can also observe some historic cases where ethnic clashes persist to this day regarding claiming land in some places in India.

Although I have explained the contemporary issues in the Indian real estate, these are common issues plaguing many developing economies.

Now, let's explore some of the issues faced by the real estate domain.

Issues in the domain

The following are two of the top issues faced by the real estate industry:

- **Inconsistency in land records**: A sale or transfer of rights pertaining to property involves several departments. Unfortunately, these departments work as silos, thereby making way for discrepancies if the same data is not available to all the authorities. This can lead to complicated legal positions for landowners.
- **Lack of instant traceability**: If a buyer wishes to buy a specific property, there must be a method to trace the transfer of ownership through the title deeds or any other complying documents within seconds. Today, the services offered by local authorities usually take some time and may come at a considerable cost.

Now, let's take a look at a solution to solving the problems in the real estate domain.

Emerging solutions in real estate

In this section, we'll take a look at an application, **emBlock**, that uses blockchain in order to address some of the issues mentioned earlier:

Based on Hyperledger Fabric, emBlock is a solution that was built out of eMudhra's emLabs. emBlock was built for enterprises and governments to benefit from immediate consensus, real-time information sharing, and smart contracts. eMudhra was established in 2008 and is a Certifying Authority in India and Mauritius for issuing digital signature certificates. They are a market leader in India that have worked with large banks, financial services companies, and several Government agencies in India to implement digital signature-based solutions.

This solution proposes recording sale deeds so that they're stored on a blockchain, thus allowing various government bodies to access it, such as registration and stamp revenue departments, survey and settlement departments, revenue departments, and courts, along with business entities such as banks. You can learn more about emBlock's case study for land records at, https://www.emudhra.com/us/case-studies/blockchain/emBlock_land_records_case_study.pdf.

Now, let's take a retrospective look at the current scenario in the real estate domain.

Retrospective

Although there are a few blockchain-based solutions that may be conforming to the existing requirements, AI should also be used to recognize potential frauds or sense any corruption of data. Also, government agencies and concerned regulatory authorities must be encouraged to use these new technologies in the form of pilot projects.

Some Indian states have embraced this change in technology but required broader thinking to establish a proper digital strategy to move toward a 100% digital record-keeping practice. Personally, I am confident that this will be achieved in the next 5 to 10 years.

Now, let's explore the products and solutions used in the media domain, powered either by blockchain or AI.

Applying AI and blockchain to media

Fake news has become a serious issue over the past few years, leading to political unrest among many countries. The recent outbreak of coronavirus also garnered some abnormal reactions from several communities outside China, spreading fear and stigma.

Now, let's look at some of the issues faced by the media domain.

Issues in the domain

Let's take a look at the top issue that's faced in this domain.

Suppose you are reading the news daily from an established newspaper. You may trust that newspaper for its information, but also because of its history and the reputations of the journalists, all of which can be socially identified. Now, consider you are reading a bit from an online magazine – the tables have totally turned against you. Although you might be an avid reader of that website, there is no guarantee that the article has been published by a credible author. Sometimes, there is a good chance that an imposter is posting an article while using the name of a journalist who has a good reputation and trust from readers. In these situations, it becomes very difficult to evaluate the validity of the information, either by the reader or the website publishing the news, since the volume of such articles is so high. Blockchain can be used not only to help verify that the story is originating from your favorite journalist, but also verify the claims through the help of fact-checkers that can learn on their own in real-time.

Now, let's take a look at a solution that can be used to solve the problems in the media domain.

Emerging solutions in media

In this section, we'll look at a solution that can tackle some of the issues mentioned earlier:

Civil is a blockchain-based network that propagates community-owned journalism, enabling trust and transparency. Civil allows both readers and journalists to set a level of trust. Journalists earn reputation and approval, making their content trustworthy. Readers can decide on which newsrooms they want to trust as their source of news. This enables the users to customize their news feeds based on their own preference and level of trust; this isn't decided by the vendors who traditionally mine the user's behavior data. This also means that newsrooms have discovered a new means of raising funds or generating revenue since the traditional subscription models have declined. At the time of writing, Civil allows users to directly pay the journalists, without a cut. Also, Civil proudly boasts of having more than 1,000 journalists across 28 countries and 6 continents. Unfortunately, at the time of publishing this book, Civil has shut down their operations. However, you can still find the code behind Civil at, `https://github.com/joincivil`.

Now, let's take a retrospective look at the current scenario in the media domain.

Retrospective

Many more companies like Civil are able to help readers differentiate between noise and signals. This is fundamental progress in the quality of content thanks to blockchain. However, it becomes difficult to personalize stories if the design is stringent and extremely pro-privacy. We should encourage DApps to ethically use AI only for customizing the feed, provided the user opts in.

Now, let's explore the products and solutions used in the identity management domain, powered either by blockchain or AI.

Applying AI and blockchain to identity management

Prior to the advent of the internet, the only proof of identity we probably had was a government-issued photo ID, which was used to avail a few services such as rationing and so on. In the second generation of the internet, most of the digital services we use are linked to our email ID. This alleviated the need for photo IDs but did not become independent of it. Since traditional IDs and digital versions of our IDs are being abused in one way or the other, it becomes extremely difficult today for users to manage this. This issue of managing identities and tying it to a **Decentralized Identifier (DID)** has been one of the cutting-edge research areas in the past few years.

DID is a new type of identifier that offers verifiable digital identity. These identifiers are of **self-sovereign** nature, meaning that the digital identity is not dependent on a centralized identity provider. Hence, users control their own DIDs.

The following diagram depicts the stakeholders in the identity management domain of enterprise users:

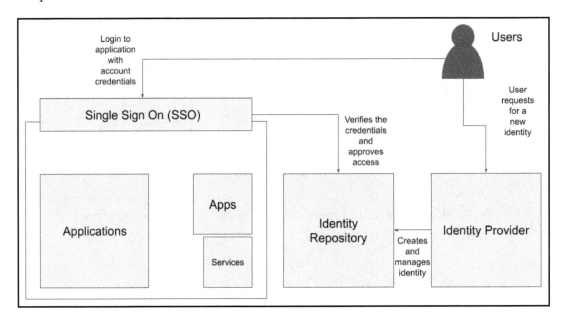

Fig 3.4: Stakeholders in the enterprise identity management domain

As shown in the preceding diagram, enterprise users such as employees, customers, and vendors generally access the application through an SSO authentication mechanism. This SSO requires an enterprise ID that originated from a set of whitelisted domains or providers. The will be managed by all the companies collaborating in the industry.

Now, let's explore some of the issues faced in the identity management domain.

Issues in the domain

Let's take a look at the top issue faced in identity management.

Most of us use cellphones and thus have used our photo IDs at some point to verify ourselves before we could get access to cellular services. Although this is required to maintain accountability and keep our society secure, some bad actors can misuse your identity proofs and act as imposters – without your knowledge.

Now, let's take a look at the solution that can help solve the problems in the identity management domain.

Emerging solutions in identity management

Let's take a look at one of the decentralized identity applications that uses blockchain in order to address some of the issues mentioned earlier.

Using DIDs, the Sovrin Network allows users to securely verify and issue their own digital credentials, control them, and manage them using a security standard called **zero-knowledge proofs** (**ZKPs**). Let's assume that you were required to have more than 1,000 USD in your bank balance to enter a casino. Today, if there were such a rule, the only way to verify your balance to the casino is by showing your account's statement, which has also been attested by a bank manager. You probably do not want to do that because you are exposing your bank balance, which could lead to certain social and personal risks. ZKPs are used to solve the same problem, in an innovative way – you do not have to show your current balance, as long as you have more than 50,000 USD. You do not have to disclose your bank balance, but service providers, such as casinos in the preceding example, would still be able to verify the fact that you have more than 1,000 USD. This is a huge win for user privacy because sensitive data such as your current bank balance has not been shared. The same may apply to verifying residential addresses, birth dates, and so on. You can find out more about ZKP concepts at, `https://sovrin.org/the-sovrin-network-and-zero-knowledge-proofs/`. To learn more about Sovrin, you can read their whitepaper at, `https://sovrin.org/wp-content/uploads/2018/03/Sovrin-Protocol-and-Token-White-Paper.pdf`.

Now, let's take a retrospective look at the current scenario in the identity management domain.

Retrospective

Adoption is the key issue for DIDs and ZKPs. Issuers need to use ZKPs before users can try them at service providers who wish to verify them. Today, there are bottlenecks in all three levels of participation:

- **Issuer**: Government agencies and authorities need to understand the benefits of using ZKP-based DIDs to reduce their own managed costs and potential data breaches.
- **User**: User needs to be aware of privacy and start using some of the socially verifiable proofs that are available today.
- **Verifiers**: Service providers should also be motivated to use these technologies and avert from data leaks on their end.

Now, let's explore the products and solutions used in the royalty management domain, powered either by Blockchain or AI.

Applying AI and blockchain to royalty management

Content creators and publishers spend a vast amount of time creating various forms of novel art such as music, videos, and games, among others. Users access this content through applications but often do not pay the content creators directly. Although this is not expected, companies pay on behalf of all the users for their consumption on a periodic basis. As you may be able to tell, the middleman here is the app facilitating the content over a platform. However, there is no surety that these platforms are paying royalties to the content creators in a justifiable manner.

The following diagram highlights the key stakeholders involved in royalty management:

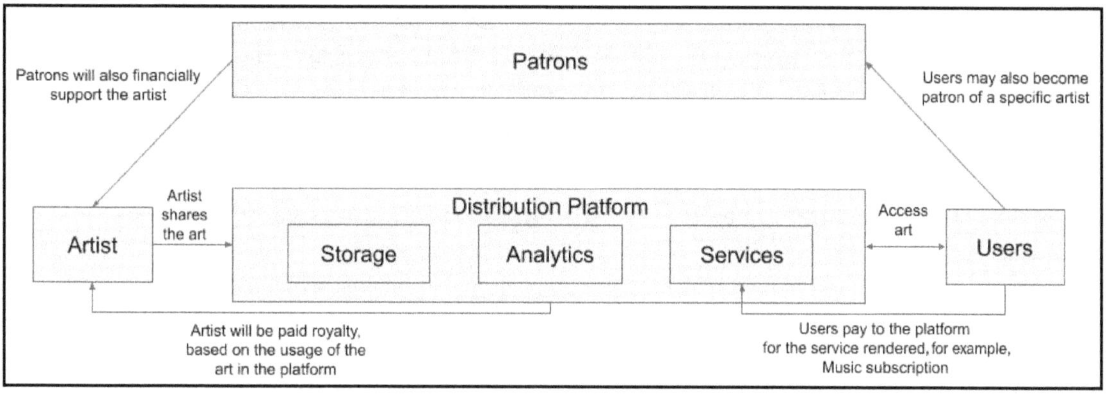

Fig 3.5: Stakeholders in the royalty sector

As shown in the preceding diagram, artists get paid in royalty when users access their artwork through a distribution platform. It is evident that users and patrons are sources of income for artists.

Now, let's examine some of the issues faced in the royalty management domain.

Issues in the domain

In this section, we'll look at one top issue faced in royalty management.

Content creators do not get full visibility of the sales statistics if the organization is not public. Products may not provide a complete reconciliation or justify the amount all the time, keeping contributors or content creators in the dark.

Now, let's take a look at the solution that can help solve the problems in the royalty management domain.

Emerging solutions in royalty management

Let's take a look at an application that uses blockchain to address the issue mentioned earlier.

The Microsoft corporation, partnered with **Ernst and Young** (**EY**), has developed a blockchain-based solution that allows Xbox game publishers to access their royalty statements in near real-time, without having to wait for days of reconciliation. This solution uses Microsoft Azure, Azure Blockchain Service, Azure Cosmos DB, and Microsoft Power BI. You can learn more about this solution by taking a look at the case study document on Microsoft's site: https://customers.microsoft.com/en-us/story/microsoft-financial-operations-professional-services-azure.

Now, let's take a retrospective look at the current scenario in the royalty management domain.

Retrospective

Over the past few years, we have seen an uptick in people subscribing to on-demand content services such as Hulu, Netflix, and Amazon Prime. Some estimate the total market size of on-demand content services will grow up to 100 billion USD in the next 5 years. This significant shift means the end user's perception of content, such as music and video, has drastically moved from **free** to **paid**. Although users are ready to pay for these services, we are yet to see major reform in how the content creators and artists will be paid on the platform.

Now, let's explore the products and solutions used in the information security domain, powered either by Blockchain or AI.

Applying AI and blockchain to information security

We may have heard the saying **Information is the new oil**. Information is pervasive. As a reader, most of your digital identity and your interactions are persisted online today compared to your offline relationship with the world. Calling this a seismic shift in humanity is not an over-exaggeration. Hence, we must pay attention to keeping our information safe and secure. Over the course of a few decades, we have observed many inefficient architectures that have failed to protect our identities and our interactions online. This can be rectified today with the application of AI as it can be used to closely monitor any backdoor vulnerabilities in systems. But fundamentally, the ownership of data mostly remains with the vendors. This has to change and, thanks to blockchain, we can easily establish some of the ground rules regarding the privacy of information and its ownership.

Now, let's look at some of the issues faced by the information security domain.

Issues in the domain

Let's take a look at one top issue that's faced by the information security industry.

Storing, reading, changing, and persisting information comes at a cost. Most blockchains and decentralized file storage services today use volatile cryptocurrencies to charge fees for the data you manage. This means several users have a high barrier to entry, either because the volatility affects their budget to persist information or the usage of cryptocurrency is severely limited or strictly prohibited in a few countries. Hence, we must find a way to offer a decentralized file storage service that can charge users in a traditional manner with fiat currencies, but also provide full control of the data they own.

Now, let's take a look at a solution that can be used to solve the problems in the information security domain.

Emerging solutions in information security

Let's take a look at a special application of IPFS that addresses the issue we mentioned earlier.

MóiBit provides a personalized and decentralized secure storage network, powered by the immutability and provenance of blockchain systems. **Moi** in French means **me**. **Bit** is an amalgamation of two words – **binary digit**, which refers to a unit of data. MóiBit offers enterprises and DApp developers the ability to use all the benefits of a blockchain and a decentralized filesystem in a predicted cost environment. To learn more about MóiBit, go to, `https://www.moibit.io`. If you are interested in developing applications on top of MóiBit, refer to this link: `https://github.com/moibit/Moibit-Sample-DApp/tree/matic-dapp`.

Now, let's take a retrospective look at the current scenario in the information security domain.

Retrospective

Enterprises are yet to show a keen interest in secure file storage systems because most of them are decentralized. We must understand that it is a very important but uphill battle to convince enterprises to adopt such systems. Although MóiBit and other solutions have addressed this problem, the barrier is the cheap cost of centralization versus the duplication or replication of data in decentralization. Efforts are being made to customize the control of data replication both at the application level and also at the network level by making these operations more atomic to walled systems.

However, this may result in the creation of silos again. Hence, attention must be paid to creating balance in the ecosystem between walled systems guaranteeing cost and decentralization guaranteeing accountability, as well as security.

Now, let's explore the products and solutions that are used in the document management domain, powered either by blockchain or AI.

Applying AI and blockchain to document management

Documents and paper trails have become necessary in recent times for establishing authenticity, provenance, and legal precedence. Although the majority of business operations are now carried out online, we need to identify ways to achieve immutable and verifiable mechanisms that can protect us from hacks or leakages of sensitive business data.

The following diagram depicts the stakeholders in a document and knowledge management system:

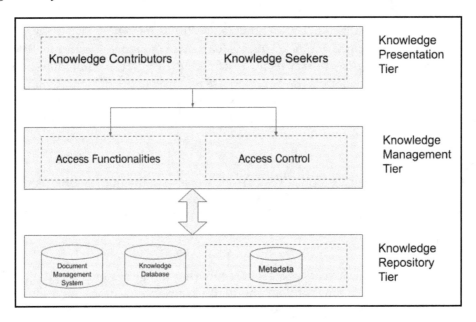

Fig 3.6: Stakeholders in document and knowledge management systems

As shown in the preceding diagram, document management mostly consists of users who contribute content, and another set of users who seek this content. These functionalities are managed by access control and are then stored in a database.

Now, let us look at some of the issues faced by the document management domain.

Issues in the domain

The following are the top two issues that are faced in document management:

- **Permission management**: Although there are several applications that can provide **proof of existence** for a document, very few can customize access to the document. This is largely due to the nature of blockchain, wherein the data is accessible to everyone.
- **Reporting**: Access to sensitive business data must be reported accurately after it's been shared. Monitoring this access and looking for anomalies is still an open problem in companies who may suffer from data leaks from their own employees as part of corporate espionage.

Now, let's take a look at a solution that can be used to solve the problems in the document management domain.

Emerging solutions in document management

In this section, we'll look at an application that uses blockchain and AI in order to address the issue mentioned earlier.

Signy is a blockchain and AI-based application suite that allows users to submit any type of application form, digitally sign and cosign certificates, create and customize their own smart-certificates, and share digital certificates with complete security and an audit trail. It leverages blockchain for the transparency, safety, and security of documents, certificates, and assets. It also uses AI and ML technologies to create innovative products and services and augment its blockchain solutions to make them more adaptive and intelligent. You can learn more about Signy's use cases for customer on-boarding, certificate, and document management here, `https://signy.io/certificates`.

Now, let's take a retrospective look at the current scenario in the document management domain.

Retrospective

Although the pace of adoption for decentralized document management is picking up, there is a need to provide fine-grained control to business owners. The design paradigm of blockchain alone does not provide enough capabilities to build such systems. Marrying these technologies with existing **Identity and Access Management (IAM)** systems is the key to integration and growth going forward.

Summary

In this chapter, we identified some of the best use cases in large-scale industries, identified the issues faced by these industries, and articulated the real-world applications of AI and blockchain across several domains. We covered these aspects across several domains such as knowledge management, real estate, media, identity management, and royalty management. We have also covered some special issues that are faced by the information security domain and how IPFS can be used to address them. I hope that what you've learned in this chapter enables you to develop your hands-on skill in terms of observing, analyzing, and developing relevant case studies, as well as help you come up with extensive ideas so that you can craft better solutions and develop an eye for critical thinking.

In the next chapter, we will understand the basics of decentralized database concepts and learn more about the decentralized data service providers and their offerings.

4

AI- and Blockchain-Driven Databases

"From store of value ... toward value of storage"

Databases have been a critical component in the development of applications, across all generations of the web. While the advent of databases started from a centralized design pattern, there have been several iterations of innovations over the past three decades. These new patterns address key pain points of centralized databases.

In this chapter, we will dive deep into a new generation of decentralized databases and filesystems based on innovative design patterns. Some of these design patterns inspire traditional applications to blend **Artificial Intelligence** (**AI**) and blockchain technologies. We will observe different types of decentralized databases and understand how they help to perform better AI analysis alongside blockchains.

In this chapter, we will cover the following topics:

- Centralized versus distributed data
- Blockchain data—big data for AI analysis
- Global databases
- Data management in a DAO
- Emerging patterns for database solutions

Technical requirements

This chapter assumes your acquaintance with the basics of database design and the application of AI techniques in related scenarios.

Centralized versus distributed data

Databases have been primarily consumed in a centralized manner since their earliest applications, dawning in the mid-1960s. Databases were meant to provide **direct access** to the information requested by either users or client applications. This centralized approach was influenced majorly by the client-server architecture introduced in the early days. This design paradigm was popularly followed by the market with successful products in commercial- and consumer-level databases such as DB2 and dBASE, respectively. **Relational Database Management System** (RDBMS)-based databases followed the client-server model. These centralized databases managed data redundancy by making regular copies of the data on disks and magnetic tapes.

However, the dawn of NoSQL in the 2000s is credited with distributed databases that scale horizontally, with higher tolerance to failures and less chance of data corruption. NoSQL databases are able to manage data without schemas and facilitate swift operations between clients, along with reasonable data consistency maintained across multiple nodes. In contrast, RDBMSes needed schemas and maintained a point-to-point relationship between the client and the server. Backups were not visible to the clients, and rollbacks had to be initiated by database administrators to read any potentially lost data. Newer NoSQL-based databases such as MongoDB addressed some of these issues.

NoSQL-based databases could also power pseudo-decentralized projects by persisting business data on a network of computers hosted by all the stakeholders of an initiative, but the main limitation of such a setup is that such databases lack transparent record keeping. In addition, these databases do not allow the voting and execution of business logic with cryptographic security inherent to the network. These capabilities must be built externally in order to compete with blockchains.

With key background information regarding centralized and distributed databases, let's now understand the motivations for using decentralized databases in the following section.

Motivations for using decentralized databases

Over the past three decades, most user data on the internet has been stored in either a centralized or a distributed fashion. The common issue with both approaches is that very few stakeholders administer, manage, and sometimes *own* all the data. Recent events of breaches and data abuse at some of the reputed social networking sites and online aggregator services highlight the fact that we are no longer in control of our own data. Careless administration of data can lead to such detrimental events and create panic among users and business stakeholders.

In the past few years, multiple accounts of data breaches and abuse have called for fundamental innovation in how data can be defined, stored, accessed, and managed. This has motivated many individuals and organizations across the world to build decentralized databases in the past decade.

Some of the common properties of decentralized databases are detailed as follows:

- Allow anybody to store and access information across boundaries
- Allow anybody to participate in persisting the data
- Persist the updated data and record the changes made to the data in a traceable manner
- Allow all users to control and manage their data by facilitating the persistence of encrypted data

These values are well represented and contrast with traditional databases, as shown in the following diagram:

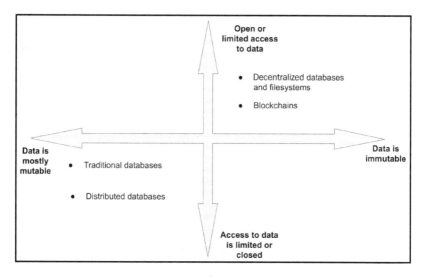

Fig 4.1: Comparing the values of traditional database patterns with decentralized database patterns

In the preceding diagram, we can observe the *y* axis representing the modes of accessing the business data or user data. Along the *x* axis, the mutable properties of the data are represented. The first quadrant defines whether the data is immutable and accessible to the general public. The third quadrant defines whether the data is mutable and inaccessible to the masses. As we can see from the preceding diagram, decentralized databases and filesystems fall under the first quadrant. We can also observe that most traditional and distributed databases fall under the third quadrant.

Immutability does not mean permanence—decentralized databases offering immutability may not store all the versions of changes forever. The data might get garbage collected and recent changes may be persisted.

With this basic information on the motivations for decentralized databases and their values, let's now contrast data management techniques and analyze consumption patterns.

Contrast and analysis

Decentralized databases organize information in a new manner that offers control back to the users, by allowing users to specify where data can be stored, along with effective governance.

Before we move forward with the analysis of using databases in Web 2.0 and Web 3.0, let's round up the key differences between all three types of databases (centralized, distributed, and decentralized databases) in the following table:

	Centralized database	**Distributed database**	**Decentralized database**
Ownership	Owned and hosted by one company.	One or more than one company can host the database.	Anyone with sufficient system resources can join and host the database.
Data definition	Most of the centralized databases are RDBMS-based, hence data definition is mandatory. Schemas are required to store data.	Most distributed databases are NoSQL-based, hence data definition is not mandatory. Schemas are optionally used.	Most decentralized databases use content addressing, hence there is no need for schemas to store data.
Failure	Single point of failure. The point-to-point connection between the app and the database will not work, and the app cannot function until the database is fixed.	There is no single point of failure. Apps can read from another node if the database fails to provide information from one node.	There is no single point of failure. Apps can read from another node if the database fails to provide information from one node.

Redundancy management	Backups of the data are stored on disks and magnetic tapes, securely stored in a physical location.	Replication of data is fixed, and all the nodes may comply with the replication policy set by the database admin.	There is no replication policy in public networks. There is a guarantee of replication upon incentivization only. However, policies can be built for permissioned decentralized databases used in consortiums.
Access and transparency	The connection to the database is closed. Only dedicated applications can access the database with credentials.	The connection to the database is neither closed nor open, but it is permissioned. Only permitted apps can access the database.	Users can access the data openly, with just a hash of the file or data. Users who care about privacy need to encrypt their data before storing it.

With the contrasts made in the preceding table, the analysis continues as follows.

In the second generation of Web (Web 2.0), applications have predominantly depended on centralized and distributed databases to leverage the new fuel in the market, which is **user information**. After multiple breaches, scandals, and reports of data abuse, the internet citizen is warier about where data should reside, and what degree of control should go back to applications.

As we are entering Web 3.0, most decentralized applications may not consider using traditional databases, as they do not support the properties of decentralized databases. Also, it is important to realize that some of the legacy applications in various domains running on Web 2.0 are considering using decentralized databases, to ensure that new demands from conscious users are met.

Having understood the basic contrasts between Web 2.0 and Web 3.0, let's now understand how data persisted on decentralized databases can be consumed to perform analytics.

Blockchain data – big data for AI analysis

As you may be aware, blockchains generate enormous amounts of data due to their transactional nature. At the time of writing, the size of some of the prominent blockchain networks is as follows:

Blockchain	Total size of the blockchain (approx. in GB)
Bitcoin	323
Ethereum	4,233

Some experts in the industry have speculated that the size of blockchains will soar 10 times more, due to an increase in the number of users and the adoption of public networks in the **business-to-business** (**B2B**) landscape.

The growing size of blockchain data enables new avenues of growth for data science. The application of AI and analytical practices on this giant heap of transactional data in the blockchain can create a large impact on most of the current blockchain products. Analytics derived from qualified data sources such as blockchain can also lead to new digital transformation projects. In order to facilitate this, we need a secondary source of information that can persist user data, business data, and the transactional data generated by the blockchain. Decentralized databases can persist this data in a cryptographically secure and verifiable manner.

The following diagram depicts how AI models can leverage decentralized databases:

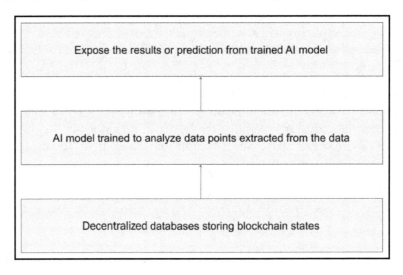

Fig 4.2: Generic illustration of AI modeling using decentralized databases

As shown in the preceding diagram, data residing on the decentralized databases is qualified to be used for training suitable AI models. Most of the transactional data stored on the decentralized databases is inherently valid to be considered a data point, meaning that the transactions are signed by the user wallet with an intent. Hence, such transactions are not trivial in their nature. When suitable AI models are trained using this transactional data, they can produce better results. The results generated by training AI models with such qualified data can be used in systems and applications of various sorts.

Let's now explore the improvements that may be possible through using decentralized databases.

Building better AI models using decentralized databases

With more data about to reside on the blockchain, it is safe to assume that AI modeling becomes easier and more ethically aligned. Training AI can be enhanced by transactional data confirmed with private keys and fees paid by users. Such data need not be inherited from third parties but, instead, could be accessed from blockchains such as Ethereum and secondary decentralized database networks such as the **InterPlanetary File System** (**IPFS**). This also empowers current models, such as predictive analytics models, in detecting fraudulent attempts and Sybil attacks in an effective manner.

Immutability of data – increasing trust in AI training and testing

Clean and structured data has been in demand by data science for almost a decade now. In the midst of data scandals, getting legitimate access to perfect data is almost always complicated, due to compliance issues in following some of the cross-border data-harboring rules. By using blockchain, a **Public Key Infrastructure** (**PKI**) inherently comes to our rescue, protecting the privacy of user data with a joint signature between data vendors and users. This may serve as **proof of consent** and maintains accountability in the AI industry to build accurate but ethical models.

Better control of data and model exchange

Projects such as Ocean Protocol, which will be discussed in the upcoming section, have been proactive in establishing fair and open markets for data providers as well as consumers. Blockchain enables these transactions or the purchase of data in an ethical manner, without consciously giving away privacy elements.

Let's now explore more details on blockchain analytics in the following section.

Blockchain analytics

Most applications on public blockchains derive value based on the transactional transparency achieved by the network. Lately, this supporting feature has been leveraged by various institutions, ranging from for-profit entities to law enforcement agencies, to track user behavior. While some of the analytical capabilities have helped society, many others are considered as strategic **Intellectual Property (IP)** by corporations of all sizes to acquire market share by using these smart algorithms for better **User Experience (UX)**.

In retrospect, blockchain analytics practices have also attracted unwelcomed criticism on how they affect the privacy of the user by mining too deep into the transactions. Chainanalysis, Neutrino, and Elliptic are some of the early movers in this space that have an active community and customers.

In the following diagram, we can observe the application of blockchain oracles and decentralized databases to effectively run models:

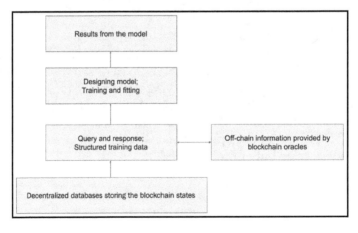

Fig 4.3: Blockchain data analytics with oracle

Let's now explore more about global decentralized databases in the following section.

Global databases

In this section, you will be introduced to some of the most popular decentralized databases. These databases use innovative cryptographic and networking techniques to address some of the key issues such as censorship, surveillance, and permissioned access to confidential information. Several efforts are being made by the projects outlined next to bring a new order to how data can be treated in the public sphere as well as the enterprise sphere.

Let's now understand some of the top global decentralized databases.

IPFS

IPFS is a distributed filesystem that allows users to host and receive content in a **peer-to-peer (P2P)** manner, eliminating any need for intermediaries, for storing or accessing data from any corner of the world. IPFS allows users to store and serve data in a censorless manner. The data remains persisted in the network as long as somebody in the network values the data. Although there may not be a monetary incentive for users who persist the data on their computers, the data may be valuable and reusable for other users in the network. Hence, data on IPFS can be virtually hosted forever, as long as the need for the data exists in the network. Notably, IPFS has been considered as one among the many *de facto* decentralized databases by DApp developers for their applications. Content accessed by anybody on IPFS is cryptographically verified, ensuring that information has not been tampered with.

IPFS has been used in many cases to circumvent transparency challenges, where access to global information was inhibited. Some of the notable uses of IPFS as a global database are listed as follows:

- The 2017 Catalan independence referendum document was hosted on IPFS, bypassing the High Court of Justice of Catalonia's order to block the original website.
- **Filecoin**, a decentralized storage network, uses IPFS to leverage unused storage space in computers and incentivizes users to host data for a fee. Fees are collected from users in the form of micropayments to serve smaller chunks of data from the hosted computer using the Filecoin token. These tokens are paid to the owner of the computer hosting the data with the help of smart contracts. Reportedly, Filecoin was one of the largest **Initial Coin Offerings (ICOs)** ever, grossing USD 250 million.

- Wikipedia was mirrored on IPFS when access to the online encyclopedia was restricted in Turkey on April 29, 2017. This circumvention provided access to Wikipedia without visiting the official website, which was blocked.

The following screenshot depicts how Wikipedia was inaccessible in Turkey:

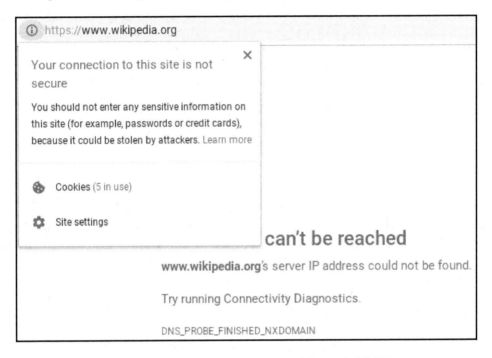

Fig 4.4: Screenshot of the Wikipedia page unable to be accessed in Turkey on April 29, 2017

You can check out this screenshot by Chidgk1 at the following link: `https://upload.wikimedia.org/wikipedia/commons/1/18/Wikipedia_from_Turkey_in_Chrome.png`. Here is the license to the screenshot, `https://commons.wikimedia.org/wiki/File:Wikipedia_from_Turkey_in_Chrome.png`.

The following diagram depicts the internal components of IPFS and the dependencies among them to provide storage and access to data:

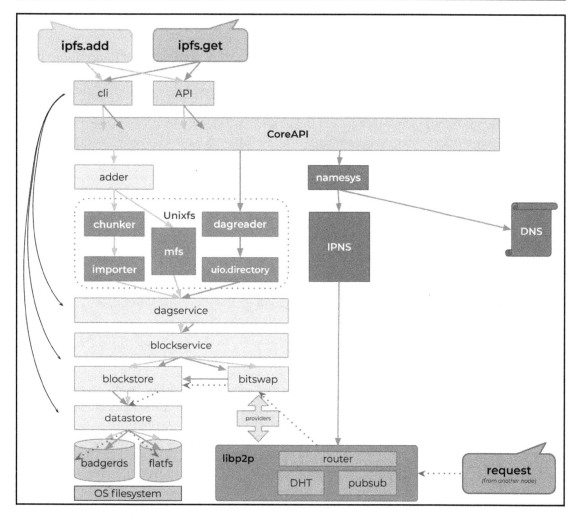

Fig 4.5: All the internal components and dependencies of IPFS

You can check out this diagram using the following shortened link: `https://git.io/Jf03g`.

To understand more about the underlying protocols supported by IPFS, visit the official documentation of IPFS, available at `https://docs.ipfs.io/`.

With a basic understanding of IPFS, let's now understand MóiBit.

MóiBit

MóiBit is a personal decentralized secure storage network with the power of immutability and provenance of blockchain systems. It offers software-defined decentralized file storage services and groundbreaking measures to reduce the unneeded cost of storing data on a blockchain, yet apps can store their data in a reliable and secure environment provided by IPFS. Simply put, MóiBit extends some of the enterprise features to IPFS, thereby enabling swift development and integration of apps into MóiBit, in just the way you would integrate an app with a cloud database.

Unlike IPFS, MóiBit offers permissioned networks by deploying a group of nodes that cannot be discovered and used by public networks. This allows enterprises to dedicate an infrastructure and enjoy the technical benefits of IPFS with their stakeholders in a federated manner. MóiBit also supports client-level encryption and many other flexible features through its **Software Development Kit (SDK)**.

To understand more about MóiBit, visit the official website at `https://www.moibit.io/`. MóiBit API documentation is also available at `https://apidocs.moibit.io/`.

Solid

Solid is a clever combination of the three powerful words in the age of the internet—**social linked data**. Solid is a decentralized data store, converging some of the key concepts of decentralization such as, identity, ownership of user data, seamless integration with applications, and offering backward compatibility. Notably, the project is led by Sir Tim Berners-Lee, the inventor of the **World Wide Web (WWW)**. Solid's aim to give back users control of their data is made possible by the powerful combinations of P2P networking and linked data.

All data pertaining to a user is stored in a **Personal Online Datastore (POD)**. PODs can be hosted on a PC, an on-premises server, or a **Virtual Machine (VM)** managed in the cloud. This decision is at the discretion of the user. Applications depending on the user's information need active consent from the user to access personal data. Some examples of personal data are health records, financial information, and so on.

To understand more about Solid, visit the official website at `https://solidproject.org/`. Solid's detailed specifications are also available at `https://github.com/solid/specification`.

Ocean Protocol

Ocean Protocol is a decentralized protocol with services for users to consume storage and compute. The protocol exhibits a trust framework that offers services to share user data in a safe manner, enabled by traceability and privacy. Similar to the global databases discussed previously, users are offered granular control over their personal data. In simple terms, users can provide access to their data and earn revenue, and consumers access data by buying the data.

Notably, Ocean Protocol also offers a wide range of third-party marketplaces and services that allow users to commercialize their data. This means that interested nodes can become a data provider by consent and earn revenue from data consumers. All these commercial activities are made possible through keeper smart contracts. The data marketplace and services are enabled by a tokenized layer that offers compute, storage space, and consented user data for sale.

To understand more about Ocean Protocol, visit the official website at `https://oceanprotocol.com/`. Detailed documentation on Ocean Protocol is also available at `https://docs.oceanprotocol.com/`.

Storj

Storj, pronounced as *storage*, is a decentralized cloud-storage platform that claims to be censorless, with no user monitoring or downtime. The Storj platform serves normal users as well as developers through the Storj API. The platform is powered by the Storj protocol, a P2P storage smart contract wherein a vendor willing to share an unused amount of storage can lend their system's storage to any Storj customer for a price, without having to know each other. The contract, once signed on a mutually agreeable price for the storage, regularly monitors whether the information is still available in the host. The storage host can respond along with verifiable cryptographic proof to ensure the contract that data is made available, as agreed. If the response is valid, the user pays the node owner, all of which is automated through a smart contract.

Storj also has a network of nodes that are willing to help the storage host by replicating and serving the same data in the expectation of a reward. This opens up huge potential for a free market for smaller storage providers. Similar to other cloud data service providers, Storj also provides an API for developers to integrate their applications with Storj in order to store application and user data for a fraction of the price in a flexible manner, compared to complicated lock-in contracts from a majority of the traditional vendors.

To understand more about Storj, visit the official website at `https://storj.io/`. Detailed documentation on Storj is also available at `https://documentation.storj.io/`.

Swarm

Swarm is an Ethereum native distributed data storage platform. The intention of the Swarm project is to facilitate the persistence of Ethereum's historic public data and enable storage for DApps. Similar to the Ethereum network, Swarm also allows anyone to participate in the network by pooling storage resources. In return, the individuals hosting nodes in the Swarm network will be incentivized with **Ether** (**ETH**) tokens, in return for dedicating their infrastructure.

Swarm claims its P2P storage network to be **Distributed Denial of Service** (**DDoS**)-resistant and fault-tolerant, as well as censorless. Its protocol, similar to `http://`, is denoted by `bzz://`. Users can access the network through the Swarm public gateway. Swarm banks on the thriving Ethereum network for its adoption and growth.

To understand more about Swarm, visit the official website at `https://swarm.ethereum.org/`. Detailed documentation on Swarm is also available at `https://swarm-guide.readthedocs.io/en/latest/`.

Data management in a DAO

A **Decentralized Autonomous Organization** (**DAO**) is a computer program representing a group of stakeholders and entities and is not influenced by external environments. A DAO is programmed by a set of rules and governance protocols to ensure that transactions occur between parties without the chance of any conflict. Dash and BitShares are some of the earliest implementations of a DAO. In the past few months, many more DAOs have been launched on blockchains such as Ethereum and Bitcoin.

Aragon

Aragon is an open source DAO running on the Ethereum blockchain network. Aragon leverages Solidity smart contracts for business logic, and IPFS for decentralized files and governance record management, thereby creating a truly P2P operating system for a whole new generation of organizations, called **aragonOS**. Users can perform operations and govern their DAOs using the **Aragon Network Token** (**ANT**).

Aragon has integrated IPFS very closely into its **command-line interface** (**CLI**) program. The IPFS daemon can be initiated through Aragon's CLI and manages pinning operations to ensure the reliable storage of critical components and files.

To understand more about Aragon, visit the official website at `https://aragon.org/`. Detailed documentation on using IPFS in Aragon can be found at `https://hack.aragon.org/docs/cli-ipfs-commands`.

Bisq

Bisq is a DAO running on the Bitcoin blockchain network. It offers a P2P cryptocurrency exchange service with no company or institution in control. Users and contributors vote on proposed updates. Governance decisions are made to the DAO by the BSQ token holders. A Bisq DAO is made sustainable by the following two approaches:

- Revenue distribution by sharing trading fees with contributors with the BSQ token. This makes the contributors a partial owner of the network and balances the power between traders and contributors.
- Decision-making through voting by the owners of the BSQ tokens—the traders and contributors. Since they are both in charge of the issuance collectively, there are no centralization vectors that can help either side achieve a majority.

At the time of writing, the Bisq community was making initial efforts in using the decentralized storage IPFS for hosting software binaries, documentation, network, and trading statistics. Proposals were also made on storing the governance proposal data to ensure that the access to DAO information is consistently available without a single point of failure.

To understand more about Bisq, visit the official website at `https://bisq.network/`. Current efforts on using IPFS in Bisq can be observed at `https://github.com/bisq-network/bisq/issues/2845`.

With a fundamental understanding of why DAOs can use decentralized databases, let's now understand some of the emerging patterns to be applied across a few domains.

Emerging patterns for database solutions

Very few companies have been able to both converge technologies and address key issues in the respective industries. In this section, we will explore the key issues of respective domains and explore patterns to solve them, along with ideal examples.

Let's now understand the current issues in the enterprise software domain and explore the emerging patterns applicable.

Enterprise

Enterprises and large organizations have been successfully scaling, thanks to scalable systems such as **Enterprise Resource Planning (ERP)** software, **Knowledge Management Software (KMS)**, and **Inventory Management Software (IMS)**, to name a few. However, growing requirements and a groundbreaking revolution in how data is managed have led to a path of blockchain applications and AI technologies.

Technical impediments

The enterprise software domain is facing new challenges in managing huge amounts of data among stakeholders in a reliable manner. Here are the top three challenges that could render enterprise software irrelevant, if they are not resolved any time soon:

- **Data protection**: Many ERP software architectures dump the organization's information into a centralized data management platform. There are also either weaker or unused applications of access management modules. This could lead to severe risks, such as insider corporate espionage, malicious attacks, ransomware, or backdoor vulnerabilities. Reportedly, we may recall the notorious WannaCry malware attack in May 2017 apparently costing the United Kingdom's **National Health Service (NHS)** more than GBP 50 million to fix the system. Similar attacks could easily target ERP data, potentially impacting stakeholders, organizations, and millions of consumers who have been depending on the system for a long time.

- **Interoperability and transparency**: More than 1,000 large-scale organizations use ERPs to handle their operations across manufacturing, accounting, inventory management, logistics, **Customer Relationship Management (CRM)**, and reporting. These operations in a large-scale organization have been handled by more than one software vendor and, hence, data interoperability has to be achieved. This is made possible by the APIs and other backend software programs developed to optimize these situations. This creates too much complexity within the organization among the IT team, as well as the operations team, to work together on making key decisions.

- **Reporting:** Reporting through ERP systems has streamlined management and enabled decision-making in an integrated manner. Reporting also provides management with good visibility on upcoming trends in the operations and guides them toward preparations. However, a lack of transparency and clarity can lead to clouded judgment and ineffective decision-making.

Summary of the emerging pattern

After delving into some of the key issues in the current enterprise software landscape, we will now observe some of the design patterns approaching these issues, leveraging AI, blockchain, and decentralized databases. Converging these technologies together has been an art of symphony, with the key goal of deriving meaningful business outcomes for organizations. AI should be applied to data originating from decentralized databases, with provenance supported by blockchains. Such patterns can introduce new efficiency in decision-making among stakeholders.

Financial services

Financial services and the entire **Banking, Financial Services, and Insurance (BFSI)** industry support the transactional economy of most industries. Hence, BFSI can be considered as the financial backbone of the economy.

Technical impediments

The following are the top three issues with regard to BFSI software:

- **Lack of full transparency**: Although efforts have been made to bring more transparency to the services made available to individuals and companies alike, the process still needs more revamping. Transparency in various programs in BFSI, such as fees and the status of loan applications, are a few day-to-day activities where more transparency by BFSI institutions may attract a more loyal following from customers.
- **Delays in settlements**: Although businesses and individuals alike are at the forefront of experimenting and adopting new technologies, BFSI is more conservative in applying new technologies and practices in a more frequent manner. Cross-border payments and trade transactions end up adding more days to the turnaround time of business processes. The delays have a large impact on businesses as well as individuals.

- **Faulty compliance reports**: The BFSI industry has been one of the victims of fraud and is well known for malpractice, failing to render services and report anomalies on time. These has led to hefty fines on financial institutions by local regulatory authorities. However, the application of technology has seldom been seen as a major force in changing the tailwind into a constructive headwind for the industry.

Summary of the emerging pattern

AI applications and blockchain technologies can help BFSI organizations organize their risk components in a much more transparent manner, streamline transactions, and ensure quality customer service. Many attempts have been made to decentralize processes among BFSI organizations to ensure a smoother experience for users and more productivity in the workspace.

Supply chain management

Supply chain management completes the curve of value delivery for all stakeholders in an industry with predictable costs and agility to respond to ever-changing demands. However, supply chains across various industry verticals have been facing multiple challenges, blocking the stakeholders from achieving the best value for their end consumers.

Technical impediments

The following are the top three issues with regard to supply chain software:

- **Lack of deeper visibility**: Recent solutions in the supply chain space have aimed to facilitate real-time transactions, but there are issues concerning how to persist such large volumes of transactions. Public blockchains are quite costly to persist such large volumes of data in the long term. However, using public blockchains helps achieve finality and helps maintain its integrity in the long term. Private blockchains can only do the same with a lesser, and predictable, cost but carry far less value unless the consortiums are large enough, as well as distributed enough.

- **Costs are not predictable**: With dynamic demands and ever-changing requirements, the supply chain industry has struggled to operate at fixed costs. Although variables are optimized in the planning process, the international regulatory landscapes and climate deeply affect the planned costs. This is due to a lack of intelligence in the planning stage. Although climate conditions are almost always predictable, not all logistic systems have the capacity to adjust to the situation and respond with recourse in a similar cost range. Apart from the changing operational costs, the stakeholders of the supply chain also suffer from insufficient insurance in cases of loss of goods due to a calamity or unexpected natural circumstances.
- **Lack of full agility**: External factors such as climate conditions, regulatory impacts, and changing customer requirements cannot be controlled in supply chain operations. However, it is imperative to keep the system flexible enough to sustain and continue operations. Few operations in the supply chain adopt cutting-edge technologies to ensure agile support for the dynamics involved here.

Summary of the emerging pattern

A smarter supply chain powered by AI, global datastores, and blockchain can improvise existing processes, resulting in achieving more flexibility to demands and also driving new business values. Exceptional visibility across the networks can be achieved by migrating transactional data to off-chain large-scale global databases such as IPFS, MóiBit, or BigchainDB. This enables full visibility to relevant stakeholders, enabled by the audit trail of changes, signed by the entities on the blockchain. Through this, AI models can be applied to the copious amount of historic transactional data to predict costs, and interruption, and achieve agility.

Healthcare

Innovation in healthcare is gradually shifting from proprietary medicines to open, research-based initiatives. This approach can be strengthened by exchanging critical information, ranging from personal health information to lab test results. In the past few years, health data exchange practices have faced serious criticism in the industry. However, it is important to note that the interoperability of information is key to the growth of the healthcare industry. With interoperability, the industry welcomes a range of issues, discussed next.

Technical impediments

The following are the top three issues with regard to healthcare software:

- **Controlled versioning**: There is a need for a transparent system which can create snapshots for all changes to medical records. Proper tracking of health records also serves as a piece of fit evidence for insurance claims, thereby leading the path for effective automation and a better experience for beneficiary patients.
- **Identity problems**: Dissemination of the patient's identity during a treatment or drug trials can cause trepidation in the ecosystem and hinder momentum. Hence, identities pertaining to medical data must be dealt with seriously with proven approaches, and actively monitored by standard bodies.
- **Centralization**: A few agencies and institutions benefit by forming alliances for health data exchange, leaving the rest of the industry behind. This could also potentially lead other stakeholders to create double standards in the near future, persisting health data on individual silos. These practices naturally favor data theft, espionage, and hacks.

Summary of the emerging pattern

Anonymized and encrypted health care records, and medical data pertaining to treatment and drug trials, can be persisted on decentralized databases to ensure common access among all the relevant stakeholders in the healthcare industry. Also, the patient is the self-owner of their medical data. This means that the patient can control and limit access to their personal health information by signing transactions on the blockchain, requiring the recipients to verify themselves before attempting to access the data. Hence, this emerging pattern could establish privacy at an atomic level, along with tightly enforced practices.

Summary

In this chapter, we have looked into the realm of storage by introducing you to the concept of centralized, distributed, and—finally—decentralized databases. Further, we have also contrasted the data consumption patterns between Web 2.0 and Web 3.0 apps. We have also understood more about the core motivations and the need for using decentralized databases in applications and DAOs. Finally, at the end of this chapter, we have explored various emerging patterns that can be analyzed and applied.

In the next chapter, we will observe how these emerging patterns are applied to build smart applications for the decentralized economy, with the help of blockchain and AI.

Empowering Blockchain Using AI

5

"Combining trust and intelligence for a better internet era"

This chapter explores multiple approaches and design patterns that are used to elevate the quality of blockchain solutions by leveraging **artificial intelligence** (**AI**) models and techniques. You will see how AI is applied along with blockchain across multiple verticals. Also, you will be able to identify white spaces, address them with guided approaches, and design solutions by using blockchain and AI. In this chapter, we will cover the following topics:

- The benefits of combining blockchain and AI
- About Aicumen Technologies
- Combining blockchain and AI in pandemic management
- Combining blockchain and AI in social finance
- Combining blockchain and AI to humanize digital interactions
- The democratization of AI with decentralization

The benefits of combining blockchain and AI

Simply put, the business benefit of using AI is the reduction of costs, and the business benefit of using blockchain is that transparency is enabled in processes. When both technologies are used together, you can apply a new class of solutions to a wide variety of problems in today's world that lack transparency and cost efficiency. In the following sections, we will observe products and solutions that use blockchain and AI together to solve real-world challenges. I would consider the following products and solutions the first generation of applications that use both technologies; there's probably more to come in the next wave of digital transformation.

About Aicumen Technologies

Aicumen Technologies (`www.aicumen.com`) is a leading digital innovation studio with a vision to empower value creation in the digital economy by building trusted **Decentralized Intelligent Applications** (**DIApps**) using blockchain and AI, and was established in 2017.

One of the key challenges in delivering solutions using emerging technologies is the ability to implement meaningful solutions to real-world problems. This challenge is more pronounced in step-changing technologies such as blockchain and AI. To address this challenge, Aicumen has developed a unique digital reimagination process that is both innovative and viable, to deliver meaningful, valuable business solutions using disruptive technologies such as blockchain and AI.

The digital reimagination process is a bottom-up process that is technically defined by cohesive layers of protocols, decentralized networks, intelligent transports, and adaptable applications. The protocol developed and consumed throughout the process is the **Krama Intelligent Protocol** (**KIP**). Decentralized networks such as MóiBit and MoiFi are built on top of KIP, embedding intelligent transports such as **Social Trust Quotient** (**STQ**) to create DIApps such as FINETs, Tracy, and REBECA.

This process can also be customized and reused for other blockchain and AI technologies that together form a digital reimagination technology stack.

In the following sections, you will be learning about some of the products built by Aicumen that are powered by blockchain and AI.

Combining blockchain and AI in pandemic management

In recent times, we have experienced a new pandemic called **COVID-19** that has impacted many lives. The global economy is almost at a halt, due to the fear of infection. In order to revive our economies, we need to manage current infections and prevent them from occurring again. This is a challenging task for governments, authorities, and citizens who are expected to abide by a new class of rules in these uncertain times. Hence, pandemic management software is emerging as an important enabler to revive economies in a responsible manner.

Current issues in digital contact tracing

While governments and authorities are doing their best to manage the recent COVID-19 pandemic with the help of contact tracing applications, there are some key issues we can observe:

- **Lack of user privacy**: Although contact tracing applications are helping in restoring normalcy, the privacy of the users is put at grave risk. This could result in data leaks in the short term and escalate to social inequality in the long term.
- **Low-quality data**: Inefficiently designed contact tracing applications have led to poor-quality data. In some cases, we can also see that location spoofing and other forms of trickery are being executed in order to fool the authorities. This is possible because the users lack a **Public Key Infrastructure** (**PKI**) and the apps are using traditional client-server models.
- **Longer times for verification**: With the unstructured data collected by such applications, it will take more time to decide whether a citizen or a community is at risk of infection. Without accurate and high-quality data points, it is difficult to arrive at a decision as to whether to quarantine an area or not. Delays or false negatives can further lead to devastating consequences and social unrest.

With a fair understanding of the current limitations in digital contact tracing, let's look at how one product named Tracy is overcoming these challenges.

 Case study: **Tracy** is a privacy-preserving app for pandemic management and safe movement that digitally enables governments, citizens, and medical professionals to live in an **anxiety-free** and **risk-mitigated** model. Tracy is customizable as per the needs of the local region. You can learn more about Tracy at `https://www.gettracy.app/`.

Let's now observe the products using blockchain and AI in social finance.

Combining blockchain and AI in social finance

Today's co-operative finance world needs to aim for a more inclusive approach to fund the people who need capital the most. In a post-COVID-19 era, access to capital beyond borders can help in creating an equilibrium between the rich who are interested in lending and the people who need capital.

Current issues in financing

While many applications are striving to work toward inclusiveness and intelligence-driven decisions, here are some of the key issues they are facing:

- **Lack of access to capital by the underbanked and unbanked**: In the post-COVID-19 era, many people have lost their jobs. Also, many small and micro-size business owners are unable to continue the day-to-day operations of their business due to a lack of capital.
- **Inability to personalize lending and borrowing**: Although some countries may have launched stimulus packages to support entrepreneurship and grow economies, the rates at which central banks and financial service institutions lend might be ineffective for the borrowers. Hence, there is a need to directly connect a lender to a borrower, where each can agree to terms and conclude the financing.
- **Inability to measure the intent and ability of the borrower to pay back**: Socially verifiable data can serve as proof to create a lending score. AI can measure the borrower's intent and their ability to pay back the loan. We lack this feature in many lending platforms, while some platforms may practice this at an extreme level, thus harming the borrower's privacy. Hence, there is a need to strike a balance between the borrower's privacy and the applications' abilities to track their ability to clear the loan.

With a fair understanding of the current limitations in social financing, let's observe how one product is overcoming these challenges.

 Case study: FINETs is India's first **Decentralized Finance (DeFi)** application specializing in co-operative finance models, which enable normal people in India to participate in a decentralized world. As part of the same DeFi initiative, Aicumen has also been developing assets and local currency-based DAO to support financial inclusion through rupee-backed stablecoins (RuCoin). You can learn more about FINETs by visiting their website at https://www.finets.us/.

Let's now look at some products using blockchain and AI to humanize digital interactions.

Combining blockchain and AI to humanize digital interactions

As several implementations of blockchain and AI models are helping the world to get better, there has always been a spirit in the decentralized software community of striving to design the most efficient decentralized protocols, networks, and software. This revolution of thought and technology has recently been fueled by an unprecedented amount of research in the past 10 years across the AI and blockchain fields.

Current issues with digital interactions

While the research for a better blockchain is still on, here are some of the key issues faced by blockchain technology in maturing and humanizing digital interactions:

- **Scalability**: Most decentralized networks are expected to operate in large numbers. Hence, the ability of a network to operate in its best form is hampered by a growing number of nodes in the network.
- **Lack of context**: Although most blockchain protocols and frameworks are inspired by the decentralization movement, they fail to capture the context needed to gauge the value generated by the network. This has created a barrier in understanding and interpreting the value of the tokens created by most of the traditional blockchain networks.
- **Application is limited by the network**: The behavior of the network severely limits the scope of the application. This limitation has discouraged a lot of large-scale adoption of blockchain, due to the rigid structure.

With a fair understanding of the current limitations with digital interactions, let's see how one product is overcoming these challenges.

 Case study: Aicumen is leading the research and development of **Krama Intelligence Protocol (KIP)**, an initiative trying to humanize the internet and give power and control back to the users. You can learn more about KIP by visiting the website at `https://www.kip.foundation/`.

With an understanding of how Aicumen is applying AI and blockchain in their products, let's now observe the application of blockchain and decentralized databases to decentralizing AI.

The democratization of AI with decentralization

In the past 10 years, we have seen progress and disruption in equal parts in AI, and the same goes for blockchain. With access to large amounts of user data, tech companies are now able to offer in-house AI-driven assistants to their customers. Banks and insurance companies are using chatbots to reduce operational costs and retain customer engagement. Investment companies and trading apps are using robo-advisors to get the latest buying and selling trends of stocks in the share market. Similarly, we have seen the introduction of virtual assistants such as Amazon Alexa, Google Home, and Apple's Siri. These virtual assistants are no longer installed on mobile phones exclusively. Recently, these assistants have become closely integrated with several third-party services to fulfill user commands in external apps.

With a single voice assistant or a chatbot technology integrated across many services for the user, there is a need to maintain the quality of the AI's response for each separate context. To ensure consistent response quality in these assistants and chatbots, I proposed a better testing model.

As introduced in `Chapter 2`, *Introduction to the AI Landscape*, AI is also software, and as such, it requires rigorous testing to ensure software quality. One of the earliest methods of testing AI was proposed by Alan Turing. He called it the Turing test.

In a Turing test, a human evaluator is tasked with scrutinizing two sets of text. The evaluator is told that one of the two pieces of text comes from a machine, and the other from a human. In the original idea of the Turing test, the interrogation would be limited to text only. If the evaluator cannot reliably determine the human-generated text and the machine-generated text, the machine is said to have successfully evaded the evaluator and has passed the test. It is important to note that the test does not focus on AI's ability to give correct answers to questions. The test only focuses on how closely the text resembles what a human might produce. I highly recommend that you learn more about the Turing test by reading the Wikipedia article: `https://en.wikipedia.org/wiki/Turing_test`.

Based on this, I was able to build an updated interface that suited the growing chatbot developer community in 2016 and 2017. This led to the development of the open source framework **Turing Test EXtended Architecture** (**TEXA**) as explained in the following section.

Case study – the TEXA project

This original version of the Turing test has faced several criticisms from many experts in the field of AI and philosophical thinkers of artificial psychology. These criticisms can be summarized as follows:

- **Non-quantification of the machine intelligence:** The original Turing test doesn't provide a **gradient of intelligence** exhibited by the machine under test. This criticism needs to be addressed in order to qualify an AI, which is based on sorting its functions into sections, and scores into levels.
- **Non-quantification of the human experience:** The original Turing test doesn't provide an **open knowledge base** of the interrogators who perform and operate the test. This criticism needs to be addressed in order to ensure the worthiness of the test as well as the potential of both the human intelligence and the AI involved in the instance.

 Artificial psychology: Although the term artificial psychology has many meanings, it is generally described as the study of the **mental processing** of AI. Such studies can help us understand how machines comprehend objects, data, and patterns.

To interact with, evaluate, and assess newer AI models in recent years, an enhanced framework was required in order to address criticisms that were relevant to recent developments of chatbots and voice assistants. The two criticisms mentioned previously are relevant to the current state of cutting-edge AI development because many products using such AI models are targeting users who are tied to multiple applications, which creates a rich context.

While some testing frameworks attempted to provide comprehensive testing capabilities to developers, there also exists a need to maintain the transparency of AI's performance. This will prevent companies from making audacious claims about the safety and quality of their AI algorithms in a context-rich environment. In conclusion, we need a comprehensive testing framework that can also maintain the transparency of test results. These requirements are fulfilled by the TEXA framework.

TEXA is a novel testing and benchmarking framework backed by simple mathematical theory. It can be used to interact with, evaluate, and assess AI that works in multi-context environments. In simple terms, TEXA enhances the concept of Turing testing by allowing the tester to assign a binary score to each and every interaction with the machine. This will allow us to quantify the quality of our models and compare their performance in multiple contexts.

This testing framework is based on new mathematical models that allow testers to provide their feedback on the AI's performance at a granular level. Each interaction between the AI and the tester can be scored. The score provided by the tester is in binary format, meaning 1 or 0. These scores are called **quantum scores**. Each quantum score represents the satisfaction of the tester with an interaction with the AI. The addition of quantum scores in the TEXA framework is a feature that can help quantify the experience of the user in a subjective manner.

Apart from quantum scores, the TEXA framework also provides the opportunity to test AI across multiple contexts. Let's assume that a chatbot is built to address the requirements of making suitable recommendations to traders dealing with capital markets, derivatives, and stocks. This chatbot might be plugged into a data interface that can provide insights to three different types of users. All these users require critical information without any delay or confusion. Hence, it is important that the chatbot does not mistake a stock-related query for a derivatives-related query. Under traditional testing circumstances, three separate testing sessions would be created to test the implementation. However, we must understand that only one chatbot instance will be running in production, supporting three types of users. Hence, anomalies are difficult to observe if testing is isolated. To observe anomalies during context switching, the TEXA framework allows the tester to create **slabs**. Basically, the slab is a parameter that represents the context of an interaction between the interrogator and the AI. During the interaction testing session, the tester can provide granular targeted feedback by selecting the appropriate slab before assigning the quantum score for the AI's response.

The quantum scores assigned to each interaction belonging to a slab are used to calculate scores and compare the AI's responsiveness and accuracy.

Once the testing session is complete and the scores are submitted, the test scores are computed and stored on the local database. Once stored on the local database, the test scores are published on the public **InterPlanetary File System** (**IPFS**). Once published, a public link is generated for the tester to check the results data. Subsequently, the **Content Identifier** (**CID**) returned by the public IPFS network is used to sign a transaction on the Ethereum blockchain's Kovan testnet. The transaction link is also generated and returned to the tester. The transaction is public data with an audit trail that's accessible to the general public and interested enthusiasts. This enables a transparent community for the development and testing of AI, with fewer chances of anyone meddling in the process of scoring and ranking AIs in the future.

The TEXA project offers a simple and interactive UI environment for uploading chatbot data and allows the user to interact with, evaluate, and assess the uploaded chatbot in an integrated flow. You can learn more about the functionalities of TEXA by reading the documentation available at the following GitHub link: `https://github.com/TexaProject/ texa-docs/blob/master/TEXA%20-%20Project%20Report.pdf`.

Functions of TEXA

With a basic understanding of TEXA theory and the features and functions it offers to chatbot and voice assistant developers, let's observe its functionalities at work step by step:

1. The person testing the AI implementation is called the interrogator or tester. The interrogator uploads the chatbot data on the welcome screen:

Fig 5.1: Screenshot of the TEXA web application asking the interrogator to upload the chatbot data file

2. Once the upload is done, the framework asks the tester to identify their AI with a name:

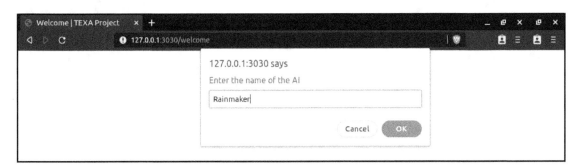

Fig 5.2: Screenshot of the TEXA web application asking the interrogator to give a name for the AI being tested in the session

3. Once the name has been provided, an acknowledgment is printed on the screen. A button is available at the bottom of the acknowledgment screen to continue with the testing:

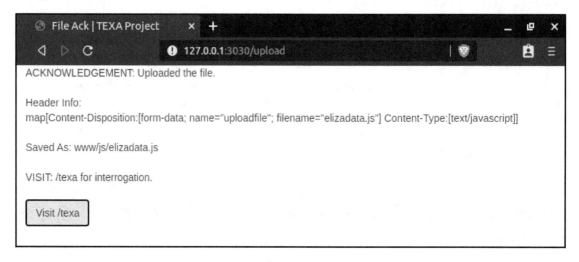

Fig 5.3: Screenshot of the TEXA web application acknowledging the storage of the chatbot data in the local server

4. Now, the framework asks the tester to enter the total number of slabs or categories in which the AI implementation needs testing:

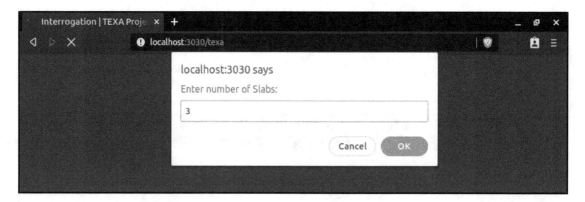

Fig 5.4: Screenshot of the TEXA web application requesting the user to enter the number of slabs

When the number of slabs is quantified, the tester is asked to enter the name for each slab.

5. Once the names are entered, we enter the main interrogation window. The screen offers a simple interface that allows the tester to communicate with the AI across many contexts. In the following screenshot, you can observe that we are testing a chatbot to respond to three contexts, called **Stocks**, **Derivatives**, and **Capital markets**:

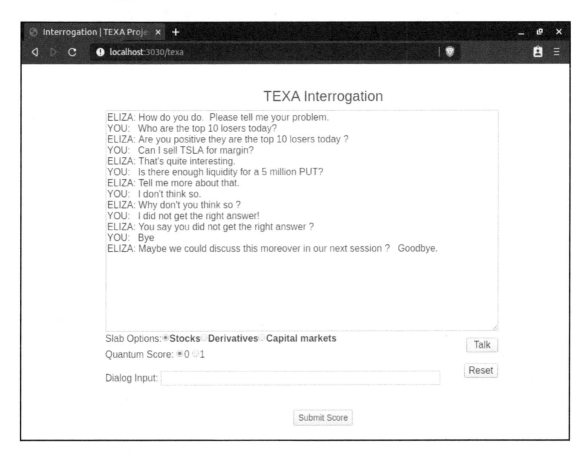

Fig 5.5: Screenshot of the interrogation window in the TEXA web application, where the interrogator interacts with the AI

The tester will now interact with the uploaded AI and evaluate each interaction by choosing the right context and assigning a score based on their satisfaction.

6. Once the testing is complete, the scores are submitted. Now, we receive an acknowledgment from the framework that the scores have been computed and published to public IPFS. The link to access the result data is given. Also, the link to the blockchain transaction is given:

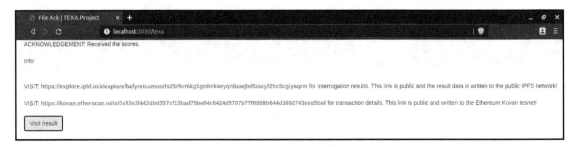

Fig 5.6: Screenshot of the TEXA web application acknowledging the publication of the results data to IPFS, and the blockchain transaction link

7. By clicking the first link, we can observe the results data:

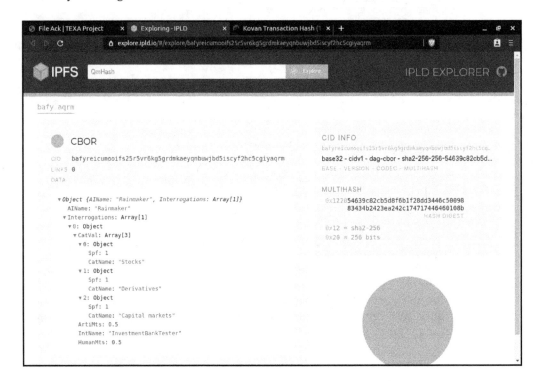

Fig 5.7: Screenshot of the IPLD explorer displaying the result data stored on IPFS

In this screenshot, you can observe the name of the AI, the name of the tester, and the results from the test session calculated by the TEXA framework.

8. By clicking the second link, we can observe the transaction and the signed data:

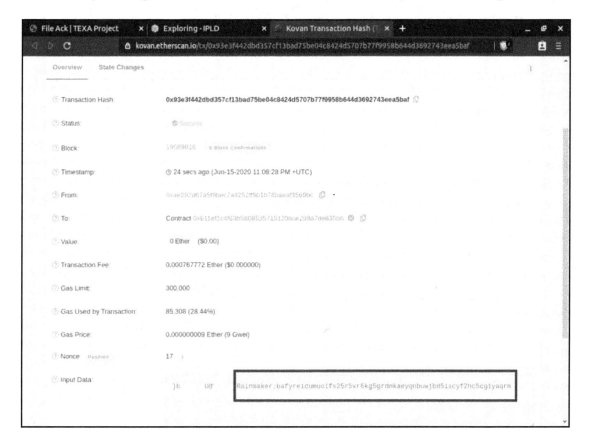

Fig 5.8: Screenshot of the Ethereum blockchain explorer displaying the CID hash value signed in the transaction as an input data

In the preceding screenshot, you can see that the name of the AI and the CID of the result have been provided as the input data. This is immutable data available on the public blockchain to establish proof that a test was conducted.

9. Finally, by clicking the **visit /result** button on the results screen, you can get to the following table:

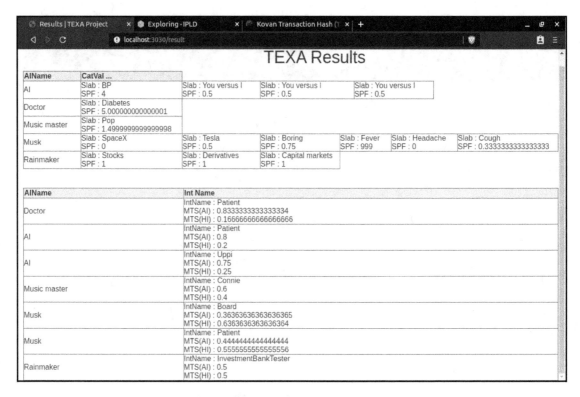

TEXA Results

AIName	CatVal ...					
AI	Slab : BP SPF : 4	Slab : You versus I SPF : 0.5	Slab : You versus I SPF : 0.5	Slab : You versus I SPF : 0.5		
Doctor	Slab : Diabetes SPF : 5.000000000000001					
Music master	Slab : Pop SPF : 1.4999999999999998					
Musk	Slab : SpaceX SPF : 0	Slab : Tesla SPF : 0.5	Slab : Boring SPF : 0.75	Slab : Fever SPF : 999	Slab : Headache SPF : 0	Slab : Cough SPF : 0.3333333333333333
Rainmaker	Slab : Stocks SPF : 1	Slab : Derivatives SPF : 1	Slab : Capital markets SPF : 1			

AIName	Int Name
Doctor	IntName : Patient MTS(AI) : 0.8333333333333334 MTS(HI) : 0.16666666666666666
AI	IntName : Patient MTS(AI) : 0.8 MTS(HI) : 0.2
AI	IntName : Uppi MTS(AI) : 0.75 MTS(HI) : 0.25
Music master	IntName : Connie MTS(AI) : 0.6 MTS(HI) : 0.4
Musk	IntName : Board MTS(AI) : 0.36363636363636365 MTS(HI) : 0.6363636363636364
Musk	IntName : Patient MTS(AI) : 0.4444444444444444 MTS(HI) : 0.5555555555555556
Rainmaker	IntName : InvestmentBankTester MTS(AI) : 0.5 MTS(HI) : 0.5

Fig 5.9: Screenshot of the TEXA web application displaying the tabulated results of all the chatbots interrogated locally on the server

The preceding screenshot shows the results of all the chatbots I have tested on my local PC. You may not see all the entries but only see one row in each table. That is expected behavior as the table reads the data from a local database.

To run this application on your local machine, you can follow the instructions in the documentation at the following link: `https://github.com/TexaProject/texa/blob/master/README.md`.

Summary

In this chapter, we have looked at how applications are empowered using blockchain and AI techniques. You have been introduced to Aicumen Technologies, which was one of the first companies to work on innovative solutions to problems using blockchain and AI. You have been introduced to challenges in several domains, such as pandemic management, social financing, and humanizing digital interactions on the internet. We have also covered applications that address some of these problems using blockchain and AI. You have been introduced to the concept of the Turing test and its application in testing chatbots. You have also been able to see the application of blockchain in the chatbot testing framework TEXA.

The examples demonstrated in this chapter should help you to analyze the benefits of AI and blockchain in bringing about transparent and robust applications in the next generation of internet applications.

In the next chapter, I will introduce you to the application of AI in cryptocurrency, and you will be able to experiment with some of the new techniques in crypto trading.

6
Cryptocurrency and Artificial Intelligence

"Bringing crypto closer to us with AI."

In this chapter we will focus on the application of cryptocurrencies in trading, and the application of proven **Artificial Intelligence** (**AI**) techniques in cryptocurrency trading. We will also identify solutions addressing existing market white spaces in the industry. You will learn more about the benefits of cryptocurrency transactions in wallets with various types of alternative coins. You will learn how to apply AI, predictive analysis, sentiment analysis, and **Auto Regressive Integrated Moving Average** (**ARIMA**), among others, in cryptocurrencies and the cryptocurrency economy. Finally, you will gain more experience with a case study related to AI applications in cryptocurrencies.

In this chapter, you will cover the following topics:

- The role of AI in cryptocurrency
- Cryptocurrency trading
- Making price predictions with AI
- Market making
- The future of cryptocurrencies in India

Technical requirements

This chapter requires you to be capable of analyzing the applications of AI and blockchain, based on their crucial abilities in the mentioned application domains.

A WORD OF CAUTION FOR YOU: In contrast to traditional financial markets, cryptocurrency markets are highly unregulated markets and are therefore deemed by many nations as high-risk for retail investors. The techniques identified in this chapter should NOT be considered as financial advice. Before experimenting with these techniques, it is imperative that you understand the trading strategies, along with their pros and cons. We do not recommend you use any of these techniques without financial advice. Without consulting your financial advisor, executing any of these trade strategies could lose your principal investment amount, and may also cause unexpected corrections in the markets. The author and the publisher will not be responsible for any financial losses accrued by experimenting with the techniques mentioned in this chapter.

The role of AI in cryptocurrency

Cryptocurrencies have enabled users across the globe to carry out commercial operations in a personal capacity as well as in an institutional capacity. This has reduced dependencies across the value chain, and, in some cases, has disintermediated the role of the stakeholders. Cryptocurrencies such as Bitcoin, Ethereum, and Ripple (under some constraints) have enabled a large number of people to disintermediate or explore new white spaces in the economy, including concepts such as **Non-Fungible Tokens (NFTs)**, an **Initial Coin Offering (ICO)**, and a **Decentralized Autonomous Organization (DAO)**.

AI, on the other hand, has been utilized in the **Banking, Financial Services, and Insurance (BFSI)** industry to reduce operational risks across borders, thereby leading to effective profit-making among institutions. The convergence of both technologies can be mutually beneficial to AI and to the cryptocurrencies.

Before we delve deeper into the role of AI in cryptocurrency, let's briefly observe the emerging need for cryptocurrency in the world with the following table of contrasts:

Fiat currency	Cryptocurrency
Most of these are minted by the government under the Fractional reserve banking or quantitative easing models.	Minted by the miners or validator nodes under a voted scheme of the network fee model.
Not all fiat currencies are in digital form, hence difficult to trace and appropriate taxes.	Most cryptocurrencies are digital, with transparent transactions, and this helps pave the way for ideal tax compliance.
Usually regulated by a national-level federal bank through active monetary policies.	Cryptocurrencies are decentralized. Hence, it is challenging to regulate them all of them by a country.
Money transfers and settlements may take days.	Monetary transfers are near-immediate, followed by finality within a few minutes.
Digital money may not be highly secure, due to centralization, and hence are vulnerable to cyber threats.	Effective in managing consistency. Hackers may not be able to hack all the nodes hosting the open ledger.
May not be highly volatile compared to cryptocurrencies.	Highly volatile compared to traditional currencies and money markets, due to speculation.

With a brief understanding of the potential benefits of using cryptocurrency, let's now understand how cryptocurrencies are used today.

Cryptocurrency trading

Trading cryptocurrencies has become a global alternative to wealth creation, apart from offering liquidity in the space for users in the respective blockchain platforms. Several entities, ranging from small crypto exchanges to billion-dollar hedge funds, offer wealth management services both directly and indirectly for their clients, in the form of trading services.

With well over 2,000 cryptocurrencies floating on multiple blockchains, and access to purchase, use, and trade, the holding of cryptocurrencies has never been easier over the internet. With the highest market capitalization of all the cryptocurrencies crossing 500 billion **US Dollars (USD)** in 2018, cryptocurrency has been regarded as an alternative wealth creation medium in the long term.

Let's now understand how crypto trading actually works. The following diagram is helpful:

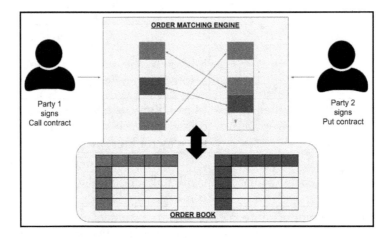

Fig 6.1: Working illustration of cryptocurrency trading in a decentralized exchange

The preceding diagram is a generic demonstration of how two users in a cryptocurrency exchange perform trading to buy or sell tokens. **Party 2** is willing to sell a cryptocurrency or a token at a predetermined cost on a particular date and at a particular time. This information, along with the number of tokens the party is willing to sell, is mentioned when placing a **PUT** option. Similarly, **Party 1** is interested in purchasing the corresponding cryptocurrency asset for a desired rate that is placed in a **CALL** option. Both options are received by a matching engine, which is an algorithm run by every exchange to help parties execute the trade based on identifying mutually agreeable buy and sell prices. Hence, matching engines are efficient and effective enough to perform the best trade in a short period of time.

With a basic understanding of how cryptocurrency trading works, let's now move forward and understand the issues the technology inherits.

Issues and special considerations

Although there has been an impressive growth in wealth creation using cryptocurrency trading, the market is still inefficient due to the following reasons:

- Difficulty determining sharp volatilities in the market
- Lack of an intelligent order-matching engine that allows users to estimate the right values for their holdings

- Inability to calculate predictable risks due to mixed responses in the market
- Weak cybersecurity strategy in protecting wallets from attacks, leading to more than a billion USD worth of crypto being lost to hacking

Benefits of AI in crypto trading

Several AI techniques such as **Machine learning** (**ML**) and **Deep Learning** (**DL**) based on quantitative (time series and so on) and non-quantitative (news, social reputation, and so on) data can be applied in the field of crypto trading. The benefits are that it can help investments toward more success, with a sharper ability to detect anomalies in trading trends, react quickly without human intervention to critical situations using trading bots, and establish an aggregated signal that represents the emotions of buyers and sellers. Also, the application of AI can bring remarkable security enforcements in password generation, detecting physical characteristics such as iris, retina, and other biometric identities to protect wallets organized and managed by the cryptocurrency exchanges or hedge funds. This means that user funds are also safe from anomalies in logins.

With an overview of cryptocurrency trading and the potential benefits, let's now move toward making price predictions in cryptocurrency markets.

Making price predictions with AI

Traditional markets, as well as the cryptocurrency market, are considered efficient if the growth of market capitalization increases gradually over time. One dimension of the market that deserves more attention in making margins has always been **price prediction**. Predictive analytical concepts have been put into practice in traditional markets for money making through algorithmic trading.

Several timestamped datasets serve as an input to a model that is able to classify whether a stock or a cryptocurrency price has increased or decreased based on dynamics such as news, announcements, and also reactions of the market to any regulatory actions made to a specific cryptocurrency.

Let's now try to understand some of the top issues faced by price prediction markets in cryptocurrencies.

Issues with price prediction

Let's look at the top two issues with regard to price prediction of cryptocurrencies. They are detailed as follows:

- Unable to adjust the algorithms to crypto market sentiments
- Unable to maintain and measure liquidity

There is a growing application of AI techniques such as neural networks in predicting the price of a publicly traded cryptocurrency. In contrast to price prediction in stock markets, crypto markets are highly volatile, with various attributes such as technical advancements, announcements, and emerging competition affecting the price with relatively higher sensitivity. Hence, ML may not be effective in these scenarios.

Although the data features used to train models are similar to traditional stock markets, the preceding factors are considered while choosing DL techniques. We will explore the application of an artificial **Recurrent Neural Network (RNN)** in an architecture generally called **Long Short-Term Memory (LSTM)**.

The following diagram is a representation of an LSTM cell, along with a depiction of how functions are applied to it:

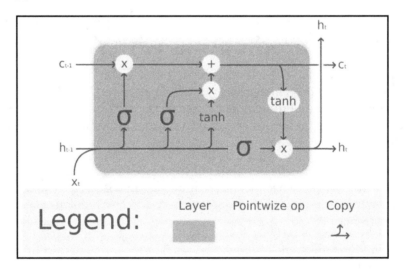

Fig 6.2: The repeating module in an LSTM cell contains four interacting layers

You can check out the diagram by Guillaume Chevalier at the following link: `https://en.wikipedia.org/wiki/Long_short-term_memory#/media/File:The_LSTM_cell.png`. Here is the license of the link, `https://creativecommons.org/licenses/by/4.0/`.

With the LSTM approach, the cryptocurrency trading data is grouped under basic common attributes such as open price, close price, high price, low price, and volume, detailed as follows:

- **Open Price** refers to the price of the cryptocurrency at the beginning of the day.
- **Close Price** refers to the price of the cryptocurrency at the end of the day.
- **High Price** refers to the highest value recorded versus the USD on that particular day.
- **Low Price** refers to the lowest value recorded versus the USD on that particular day.
- **Volume** refers to the total number of units traded on that particular day.

The preceding five attributes can be extracted for any given day from most of the cryptocurrency exchanges through the OpenAPI specification. The extracted information can be pruned into a dataset based on different styles preferred by individuals or tools. Generally, the dataset has to be split into three parts: 60% of the data points for training, 20% for validation, and 20% for testing. The LSTM model has a unique capability of identifying the patterns while processing the data, and also forgets any unnecessary information in the dataset. This information is now fed into the LSTM cells, along with the necessary activation functions, through multiple gates.

Let's explore an example of the application of LSTM in price prediction of cryptocurrencies. The following example is the work of Abhinav Sagar, a research assistant at **Vellore Institute of Technology** (**VIT**) (`https://github.com/abhinavsagar/Cryptocurrency-Price-Prediction`). The model is comprised of the three basic layers: an input layer, a hidden layer, and an output layer. So, the neural network will be composed of these layers with a linear activation function. The model is compiled using Adam as the optimizer and **Mean Squared Error** (**MSE**) as the loss function.

The following graph shows the output from the LSTM-based price prediction algorithm for Bitcoin:

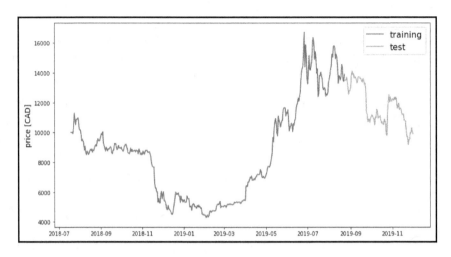

Fig 6.3: Cryptocurrency line plot based on the dataset

You can check out this graph at the following link: `https://github.com/abhinavsagar/Cryptocurrency-Price-Prediction`.

The following graph compares the predicted price values of Bitcoin with the actual price of the Bitcoin over the same timeline:

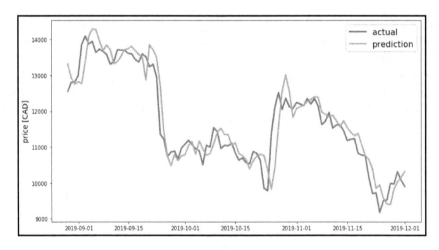

Fig 6.4: Actual versus predicted prices by applying the LSTM model

You can check out this graph at the following link: `https://github.com/abhinavsagar/Cryptocurrency-Price-Prediction`.

With a basic understanding of LSTM and how it could be used in price prediction, let's understand the benefits in the following section.

Benefits of AI in prediction

The application of classification models and predictive analytical practices on transactional data can offer traders well-trained decisions and help achieve efficiency. It can also help traders reap profits from better market making, notably in crypto trading, which runs 24/7 globally, similar to traditional high-frequency markets such as **Foreign Exchange** (**Forex**).

With a basic understanding of how LSTM can be beneficial for price prediction, let's now explore time series.

Introduction to time series

A time series is a series of data points indexed over time, graduating at discrete levels versus the price of a cryptocurrency. This idea is not novel or exclusively applicable to cryptocurrencies. In fact, tick databases exist in the traditional finance industry. This approach has been borrowed by the crypto industry to leverage the benefits of applying quantitative finance (also referred to as algorithmic trading) to reap higher rewards in crypto.

The following graph represents a price time series of the Bitcoin cryptocurrency from one of its longest rallies in the market:

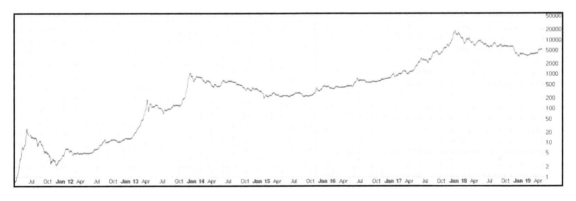

Fig 6.5: Time series information of Bitcoin price versus USD in logarithmic scale, before the crash happened

You can check out this graph at the following link: `https://commons.wikimedia.org/wiki/`
`File:BitCoin-USDollar_2011-19_(Bitstamp,_Mt._Gox).png`.

Time series are generally stored in the form of tick data and are represented in the form of charts. Data obtained from the time series can also be used to analyze non-quantitative price trends of commodities.

Now, let's explore the application of AI in time-series forecasting.

Time-series forecasting with ARIMA

Since cryptocurrency prices are affected by various factors, it is not easy to analyze and predict prices using simple ML models. Hence, the ARIMA model is used to predict the price. Consider the time-series example of Bitcoin, as depicted in the previous diagram. We cannot attribute changes to one single parameter and develop a linear regression model that satisfies our requirement of price prediction independently. Hence, ARIMA is widely used so that we can apply the model, make a note of the error in prediction, retest the model after making the necessary changes, and calculate the MSE again.

Generally, ARIMA models provide reasonable price prediction with an error rate ranging from 3% to 5%. The key advantage of ARIMA is that the model is fairly simple to calibrate, and this encourages data scientists to drastically reduce the mean error between the expected values and predicted values of cryptocurrency prices.

The following graph is a sample output from a calibrated ARIMA model to predict Bitcoin prices:

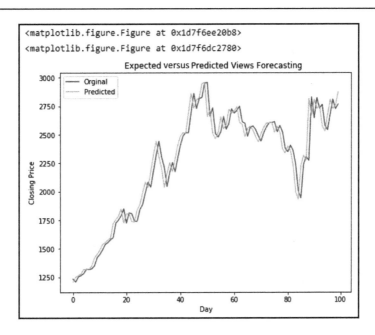

Fig 6.6: Bitcoin price prediction using ARIMA

You can check out this graph at the following link: `https://www.kaggle.com/ayushi2/bitcoin-price-ar-ma-and-arima`.

Let's now explore other applications of AI in high-frequency trading environments.

Applications of algorithmic or quant trading in cryptocurrency

Did you know that a significant number of trade calls happening around the world are not made by humans? Instead, they are programmed and automated to a certain extent by operations. This type of trading involves a keen eye on profits over a large number of calls, resulting in good profits over a very short term. This is called algorithmic trading. As the name suggests, the trade calls made by these machines are optimized to look at profits that humans cannot sense by reading charts and reports. These calls take place in a split sub-second and are predicted to take over finance as we know it.

Let's now understand some of the basic applications of algorithms optimized to make profits in cryptocurrencies.

Arbitrage

In case you are not active in finance, the term **arbitrage** refers to the practice of leveraging different prices of the same asset in two different locations in order to profit from the difference in the economic values of the asset in trade transactions. Simply put, arbitrage is a trading strategy that exploits the different economic values of the same asset in two or more markets. You can buy it in the market where the price is cheaper and sell it to markets with higher demands.

The history of arbitrage dates back to 650 BC (`http://www.sfu.ca/~poitras/EQF_ARB%24%24.pdf`), wherein it was a common practice to buy silver coins at a cheaper price in Persia and sell them at a premium in Greece.

It is important to note that the strategy is not novel to cryptocurrencies. Arbitrage was applicable to traditional financial instruments dating back to as early as the 1980s in modern finance. It is actively pursued as a trading strategy, even today.

Before we delve into how the application of algorithmic trading helps in the arbitrage of Bitcoin, let's understand some basic context. At the time of writing, Bitcoin—often referred to by its ticker symbol, **Bitcoin (BTC)**—is listed across more than 100 exchanges (`https://coinmarketcap.com/currencies/bitcoin/markets/`), with slight differences in prices at different exchanges.

In the following screenshot, you may observe two different prices for Bitcoin across multiple exchanges:

Fig 6.7: USD price of one Bitcoin across 10 different exchanges recorded on February 26, 2020

You can view the preceding screenshot at the following site: `https://coinhills.com/`.

You can simply apply basic math to understand the potential opportunity to profit USD 2 if there is a way to instantaneously purchase Bitcoins in exchange 1 and sell the same bitcoins to trading users in exchange 2. However, it is naive to assume that both the transactions can occur near-instantly in order to profit from this trade. If this trade can be achieved successfully, a crypto/fiat arbitrage has been successfully established.

However, it is important to remember that fiat withdrawals from exchanges depend on the ease of business in the respective countries. Hence, we need to understand that these trades may not always be instantly profitable.

Algorithms have been developed to enable instantaneous arbitrage transactions between two kinds of cryptocurrency. Assume that 1 **BTC** costs 50 **Ethers** (**ETH**) in exchange 1. Assume that the same quantity of 1 BTC costs 60 ETH in exchange 2. Algorithmic trading in this scenario would identify the best-fitting cryptocurrency trade pairs that can return maximum profits and execute the trade, thereby profiting 10 ETH in less than a few seconds. If such a trade can be achieved successfully, a crypto/crypto arbitrage has been successfully established.

San Francisco Open Exchange (**SFOX**) is a YCombinator-backed trading platform that has been serving more than 175,000 traders since 2015. The platform has a gross transaction value of nearly 11 billion USD over the course of years, exploring arbitrage opportunities for its customers across more than 20 markets. SFOX offers industry-leading algorithmic trading, such as the following:

- **Tortoise**: An optimized order routing suitable for trading lower numbers of bitcoins, but comparatively slower than the rest of the algorithms.
- **Hare**: Better price goals than Tortoise without any compromise in speed.
- **Gorilla**: Optimized to execute large trade orders with suitable controls on market fluctuations to make sure that the market does not move.
- **Polar Bear**: Optimized to execute hidden orders optimized for price, triggered by the best limit set by the user. Once the algorithm identifies the best price in the order book, it will immediately execute the order at that price without going too deep into the order book.

Although there are well-supported algorithms suitable for arbitrage, it does not always ensure a low-risk trading strategy. Algorithms must also be efficient enough to capture opportunities in a split second to make up for the total fees for all the trades carried out across multiple exchanges in different markets, as these are considered as the hidden-margin costs by some experts.

Let's now explore how AI could be leveraged to improve market making.

Market making

Market making is a crucial process in the crypto trading business, with the important goal of offering liquidity to cryptocurrencies in the market. Let's explore this in detail, as follows: buying parties in the markets place a bid (the **bid**) for purchasing a particular crypto asset. A seller with an intent to sell the same type of crypto asset may place their asking price (the **ask**) for the asset. Usually, the values from the buyer and seller do not match because the buyers usually quote for less value and the sellers quote for more value. This can create a gap between the expectations between both parties, thereby creating a **spread**.

When the disagreement on the mutual price grows, the spread value widens and creates an illiquid token or cryptocurrency. Illiquid tokens are basically non-tradeable since expectations are not matched. Hence, lower trade volumes create a slowdown for the token and reduce the market capitalization of the respective token. This is detrimental to the business. Hence, there is a need for liquidity providers who can help both buyers and sellers meet in the middle.

Market makers address this problem by acquiring huge tokens and offering liquidity to traders across multiple markets.

The following diagram is helpful for you to understand the market-making cycle:

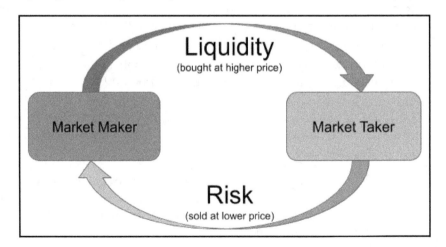

Fig 6.8: Generic illustration of a market-making cycle

Simply put, market making is a process of buying the tokens of an ICO wholesale and offering them a retail value for smaller investors. The revenue model for market makers is constructed by buying tokens in bulk at lower prices and selling at higher prices to takers in the future.

Again, market making is not a novel concept for cryptocurrencies. This is a huge operational business applied to almost every traditional financial instrument across multiple markets.

Although this model is fairly profitable in traditional finance, it is a huge challenge to identify the liquidity demands in the crypto trading landscape as there are more than 1,000 cryptocurrencies actively traded without borders or time zones. Hence, it has been imperative to apply some of the DL techniques such as evolutionary algorithms to identify all possible scenarios where liquidity may be in demand for a particular targeted list of cryptocurrencies.

With a basic understanding of market making, let's now go through the issues faced and how AI can solve them.

Issues and special considerations

One of the major issues faced by market makers is that the captured data lacks full context in traditional systems.

Benefits of AI in trading data

The application of AI on semi-structured data from blockchain transactions can pave the way for better analysis and provide deeper insights into making efficient trade decisions. Real-time high throughput from multiple blockchains can be analyzed by applying AI models to make informed decisions across different blockchain realms.

The future of cryptocurrencies in India

India has long been one of the few developing countries with an uncertain position on cryptocurrencies. A circular from the **Reserve Bank of India** (**RBI**) dated February 12, 2018 advised all the banks and RBI-regulated institutions against supporting any individual or entities involved in virtual currencies. This was considered as a blanket ban on all activities pertaining to cryptocurrencies, although exchanges in India were unable to support deposits or withdrawals associated with bank accounts.

On March 6, 2020, the Honorable Supreme Court of India's verdict quashed the RBI circular, thereby striking down RBI's ban on financial institutions rendering services to these exchanges and traders alike (`https://main.sci.gov.in/supremecourt/2018/19230/19230_2018_4_1501_21151_Judgement_04-Mar-2020.pdf`).

Although this is a temporary relief to the crypto trading industry and a role model to many other developing countries and economies, there are larger uncertainties looming around the ecosystem. At the time of writing, RBI has reportedly filed a review petition to challenge the verdict given by the country's Apex court. It is also notable that **Anti-Money Laundering (AML)** and **Know Your Customer (KYC)** regulations are to be updated in order to support these businesses without harming the country's economy.

Striking a balance between regulations and empowering the industry with the right education could help India blossom in this industry and emerge as a global leader of the next wave of the digital economy. Until then, such uncertainties in India remain open.

Summary

This chapter has highlighted the role of AI in cryptocurrencies and their emerging economies. Starting with the key differentiation between fiat and cryptocurrencies, we have introduced you to various practices in the cryptocurrency market such as trading, prediction, arbitrage, and market making. We have not only introduced you to the basic concepts but also identified the key issues faced by traders in the industry. Finally, we have introduced some approaches to solving the problems using AI and aiming for better, more efficient, and higher-profit-making models using several AI techniques such as ARIMA, LSTM, and so on.

We hope this chapter enabled you to identify the key white spaces of applying AI techniques into the crypto markets by analyzing some of the common approaches practiced today. In the next chapter, we will understand the formal software development life cycle required to build and deploy such applications.

3
Section 3: Developing Blockchain Products

In this last section of the book, we will learn about the DIApp architecture, understand how to develop a DIApp, and observe some of the example use cases for further research of the convergence of Blockchain and AI. We will also mention some key internet resources and community links that can further help you technically.

This section comprises the following chapters:

- Chapter 7, *Development Life Cycle of a DIApp*

- Chapter 8, *Implementing DIApps*

- Chapter 9, *Future of AI with Blockchain*

- Chapter 10, *Appendix – Moving Forward – Resources for You*

Development Life Cycle of a DIApp

7

"Fast. Good. Cheap. Choose any two."

- Unknown; used by many software project managers

In this chapter, we will explore a broad set of new patterns that can be used in the **Software Development Life Cycle** (**SDLC**) of blockchain and AI-enabled applications. It will help you to build modern applications addressing the problems faced by various industries discussed in the previous chapters. Before introducing the SDLC aspects, we will also compare traditional blockchain applications with the next wave of intelligent decentralized applications. We will also explore the architectural aspects of the new types of applications that can be built under the revised SDLC.

In this chapter, we will cover the following topics:

- Applying SDLC practices in blockchains
- Introduction to DIApps
- Comparing DIApps and DApps
- Designing a DIApp
- Developing a DIApp
- Testing a DIApp
- Deploying a DIApp
- Monitoring a DIApp

Technical requirements

This chapter requires you to be capable of analyzing the benefits of the application of AI techniques along with the application of blockchain technology in the software development process across several application domains.

Applying SDLC practices in blockchains

With more than 10 years since the advent of blockchain technology, there is a need for newer emerging patterns that can apply blockchain technology and AI techniques to address the growing demands from the ever-expanding internet, and effectively manage the software development practices across various industry verticals.

Let's now explore all the major aspects of SDLC step by step in the following sections.

Ideation to productization

Many ideas for building new applications on top of blockchain exist. However, fewer ideas are converted into designs. Although efforts are made to design decentralized applications, only a few designs are practical enough for the real world. This is due to the mismatch between product expectations and the readiness of technology at the developer's disposal. In some cases, the technology and features may become available, but they may not be supported well enough due to the recent and unstable growth of these blockchains. Hence, it is a commonly perceived problem that not all ideas in blockchain can be converted into a product.

Apart from the limitations of the platforms themselves, there is also a tendency to **blockchain-ify** every existing solution, due to the **Fear of Missing Out (FOMO)** on opportunities. Some companies want to try it even when it may be unsuitable for their purpose, and this can lead to issues as well.

Based on my experience from the past three years of active development in the blockchain and AI spaces, these issues could be resolved by taking some of the following steps:

1. **Understand the business process**:

   In most of the blockchain-based use cases I have come across, a clear understanding of the business process is crucial since a majority of blockchain solutions will be affecting the operational as well as financial aspects of a business. Therefore, it is important to educate all stakeholders about the business process in greater detail before dangerous assumptions can be made on the intricate steps involved or the method required.

   For example, if a new solution is being developed to digitally transform a dairy firm using blockchain and AI, everyone on the team must have a comfortable understanding of the end-to-end process of bringing milk from the cattle farm to the table.

2. **Establish clear requirements**:

   It is a common observation in any emerging technology that most of the efforts are often hyped, thereby lacking the objective clarity needed to build apps. Before we can identify potential points of integration, we must have clarity on what pain points are being addressed by the application of blockchain or AI in the solution. All stakeholders must do their best here to clearly communicate the functional and non-functional requirements. This can be helpful in managing expectations in the future.

   For example, the decision makers or owners of the organization may establish the need to achieve better transparency and accountability from the local cattle centers that produce raw unprocessed milk. The owners may also identify the need to analyze the current sales trends for all their dairy products in order to ensure that milk is made available for further processing to manufacture the necessary dairy products according to demand.

3. **Identify critical checkpoints in the business processes**:

   Once the requirements have been identified and clarified, it is crucial to not jump straight into design in the case of blockchain. We must identify the current implementations and understand the critical business components and the checkpoints where technology must be applied and integrated.

For example, identifying each cow in the cattle herd could be one of the most basic and foundational checkpoints for the team. Also, it is crucial to understand whether the volumes of raw milk collected at the local producers are manually inputted into the system or automated through a digital weight scale. In the case of maintaining a certain amount of milk as a reserve for other dairy products, it is important to understand who makes the decision or approves the manufacture of dairy goods out of the reserve milk.

4. **Check whether technology integration is feasible**:

Once the checkpoints are identified, we can now identify various technical approaches to solve the problem and check whether the approach fits in the larger process. A lot of the time, unlike traditional solutions, blockchain developers are limited, either by the infrastructure and platforms, or by the lack of technical stability of the features supported by a given blockchain platform.

For example, let's assume that we want to identify each cow in the cattle herd by a **Radio Frequency Identification (RFID)** tag. Now, each cow tagged with an RFID tag must be virtually represented in the blockchain through a state variable. Here, it is imperative that the developers do not assume that the value of the RFID tag will be persistable on a blockchain. Most blockchain platforms have serious constraints on the type of data that can be stored. They also impose serious restrictions on the length and range of the data types that could be persisted in a blockchain through a smart contract, due to the blockchain's decentralized nature. In this case, we may want to identify the structure of an RFID tag and try to store it in a secondary storage network such as MóiBit to identify all cows in the herd.

Similarly, in the case of measuring the volume of milk produced, it is imperative to identify whether a digital weight scale is capable of making a smart contract call in the blockchain. If the milk is collected from very remote areas, it is important to identify such operational impediments also.

Finally, it is also very crucial to identify how the application of AI models on the information gathered on the blockchain can be harnessed to address user requirements. That is, designers, architects, and developers must be aware of the blockchain's transactional information and its data structure. Initial efforts must be made to understand that the transactional information can be processed in such a way as to ensure that an AI model can be trained sufficiently to predict the sales trends and set aside necessary milk reserves for milk-based dairy products.

5. **Establish technical dependency across affected components**:

> Once we identify potential integration points, we should carefully establish the technical dependencies. These dependencies can be either internal dependencies or external dependencies. Technical dependencies are internal if the development of a solution depends on its design, architecture, user stories, or acceptance criteria. The poor design of a given solution or information flow can cause many issues. Incomplete architectural decisions can also lead to issues in implementation.

The following diagram summarizes the need for better clarity in all aspects to build the ideal solution using blockchain and AI:

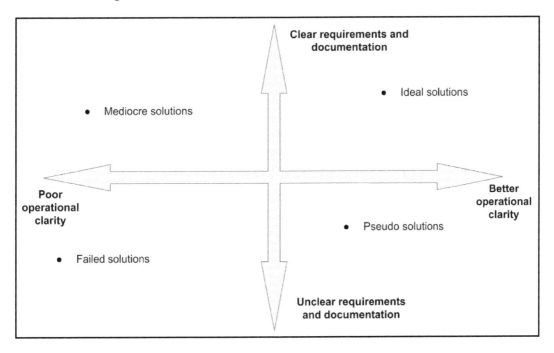

Fig 7.1: A diagram representing various outcomes and the quality of solutions

To summarize, as mentioned in the preceding diagram, ideal solutions can be achieved only when the requirements are very clear and specific, along with having the upper hand in technical capabilities. However, if the requirements are not fully documented, understood, nor communicated, the outcome is a partial solution that does not propose addressing the complete set of problems. The two other types of solutions in the left-side quadrants are poor and ineffective due to the lack of technical capabilities in establishing the dependencies with some room for ineffective documentation of requirements.

With a basic understanding of what must be considered before the development of blockchain or AI solutions, let's now move forward and understand how these solutions are defined.

Introduction to DIApps

Before understanding what we mean by a **DIApp**, let's first understand what a decentralized application really is. **Decentralized applications** or **dApps** (also written as **DApp** or **Dapp**) are user applications that run on a platform hosted by a number of nodes in a distributed manner. DApps emerged as a solution architecture on top of blockchains wherein custom business logic could be programmed in a particular language of support. Once the logic is interpreted into code, we deploy this code on the respective blockchain platforms. Once the logic is deployed on the platform, we further integrate the logical program with frontend applications for user interactions.

In contrast to DApps, a **Decentralized Intelligent Application (DIApp)** is an enhanced pattern of a DApp that facilitates the application of AI wherever applicable, on top of a blockchain platform, in a much more robust manner that provides value to all stakeholders. Although the concept of slapping AI on top of solutions is not an unusual thing, **DIApps** are an understandable approach and a novel pattern that makes more sense for future generations of solutions built using both blockchain and AI.

As the name suggests, a DIApp is an application offering both decentralized and intelligent capabilities. Since it is a pattern inherited from DApps, it is decentralized by default, thanks to the implementation currently followed by all the blockchain platforms. However, DIApps have the exclusive capability of being more intelligent. This is made possible by an intermediary off-chain database that gives DIApps the ability to store big data from an application or the users through the application running on the blockchain.

The following diagram providers a general schematic of a DIApp as explained in this section:

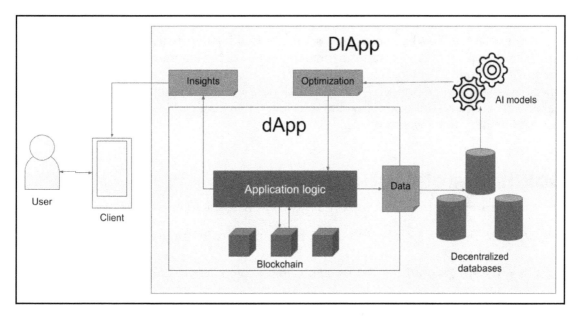

Fig 7.2: Composite view of the DIApp pattern

The preceding diagram depicts the composite view of a DApp within a DIApp pattern. The pattern is depicted in this fashion to help you understand the enhancements that are made to the existing pattern such that the application of AI can be facilitated.

With a basic understanding of both the DApp and DIApp design patterns, let's now contrast them, weighing the pros and cons between the patterns.

Comparing DIApps and DApps

In this section, we will outline the issues faced by enterprises in developing and using DApps. Further, we will outline the solution architecture of both the DApp and DIApp patterns in the enterprise scenario and outline the key differences.

Challenges in the enterprise

Although several blockchain platforms represented new waves of experimental approaches, most of these approaches radically focused on the full disintermediation of all the entities involved in a business process, thereby making the solutions purely peer-to-peer. The reason for the full disintermediation in most of the emerging patterns is due to the maximalist nature of blockchain to decentralize the world. In contrast to this ideology, enterprise solutions fundamentally rely on maintaining accountability among key stakeholders without full disintermediation. Hence, there is a need for an enhanced pattern that is fit for adoption by enterprises.

Solution architecture of a DApp

The solution architecture of a DApp primarily comprises the following key points:

- The business logic is written in a **Domain-Specific Language** (**DSL**) in a smart contract.
- The smart contract is deployed on a blockchain network, identified by an address.
- The smart contract will acquire a new address if the business logic is to be updated in a majority of the blockchain platforms.
- A web or mobile application is developed as a client to access and carry out operations on the business logic.
- Almost all the critical data is stored on top of the blockchain, with little or no scope for analytical capabilities.

Solution architecture of a DIApp

The solution architecture of a DIApp primarily comprises adding technical capabilities to make the pattern more approachable by enterprises. Here are the key highlights:

- Business logic is usually written in any high-level language such as C, Python, Java, or Golang, among others supported by the **Low-Level Virtual Machine** (**LLVM**) compiler. Also, normal smart contract languages can be used.
- The majority of smart contracts are upgradeable, meaning that the code can be updated without having to change its address.

- Traditional client applications can also integrate with these types of smart contracts as there is less need for integrating it with newer middleware.
- Critical business data is not only stored in blockchain networks but also in decentralized data storage systems to ensure better integrity of the data.

Key differences

With a deeper dive into the aspects of the DIApp pattern, let's now identify some of the key differences between the two patterns.

The following table offers a high-level comparison of both the patterns that you must be aware of:

DApp	DIApp
An application deployed on a blockchain platform with all the core logical elements.	Core logical elements are deployed on a blockchain platform, but are also powered by AI-driven insights in parallel.
Data is mostly sitting on the blockchain platform, making it costly in terms of expense and time for retrieval.	Critical provenance data resides on the blockchain, but the remaining data is persisted on a cheaper off-chain storage system.
Not all DApps are upgradeable, hence a new address is required for every update to the logic. This could break systems.	Most applications can easily be upgraded without making changes to the address, hence nothing breaks in the system.
Data is rarely analyzed due to the cost of read-writes in a blockchain platform, and also due to the lack of structured data required to train AI models.	Data can be easily structured in an off-chain storage system and tightly coupled back to the blockchain platform as well as the AI models.

With a detailed understanding of both the patterns, let's now explore the life cycle of DIApps across the stages of design, development, testing, and deployment.

Designing a DIApp

The design aspects of DIApps have been often considered to be somewhat challenging and dictated by the technical complications introduced in the constant waves of change seen in almost all blockchain platforms. It is also a common perception that the solution space lacks a common structure to define key components, resulting in an inconsistent design strategy for applications.

For example, the tools required by the user of an Ethereum-based DIApp are very distinct from that of Hyperledger Fabric, and subsequently, that of EOS. This is due to the distinct design of the respective blockchain's UI/UX framework, which is deeply dependent on its own design paradigms. Hence, it is important to identify the design constraints of the application before commencing the future steps.

Before carving out a design for the DIApp, we must understand the research efforts explained in the following section.

Research

Before choosing which blockchain technology or platform you will use, it is critical to understand the user requirements, analyze them, and perform better research at an early stage of design. Instead of asking which blockchain technology can help address the requirements, consider these scenarios:

1. Does the solution demand full decentralization over a public network for peer-to-peer interactions?
2. Does the solution need to be implemented in a private network due to the extreme sensitivity of the data and minimal exposure of the business logic?
3. Can the solution be implemented on a public network with all the sensitive data encrypted on a public decentralized storage system?
4. Can the same solution be implemented on a public network with all the sensitive data stored in a private virtual decentralized storage service?
5. Does the solution require a permissioned network of authorized nodes across multiple stakeholders of a consortium?

Based on the preceding pointers, we can undertake the following analysis. For scenario 5 in the preceding list, you are better off choosing a blockchain such as Hyperledger Fabric. However, in the cases of scenarios 3 and 4, you will need the **InterPlanetary File System (IPFS)** or an IPFS-based service provider who will encrypt the data and store it in a safe medium, offering security and redundancy with a secondary network. In scenario 2, you may be better off again with Hyperledger Fabric. Finally, in scenario 1, which might be the majority of cases, Ethereum might best fit your solution requirements.

Conceptualization

Formulating the **Proof of Concept** is an essential step in the development of solutions using emerging technologies. The development of proof of concepts for decentralized applications is also important, as they ensure alignment between the requirements and delivery of the solution. This helps maintain functional and design conformity right from the early days of development.

Also, it is notable that the proof of concept specifications may change due to the waves of design and architectural change in the blockchain landscape. Hence, proof of concepts should focus more on the functional viability of compatible patterns available to the developers.

Product-market fit

Developing the proof of concepts and prototyping the critical aspects of an application form a recursive practice until we are able to see a product-market fit. The definition and constraints of the product-market fit for DIApps cannot be general since each DIApp may target a specific problem in a specific domain. However, a few common attributes could help assert the product-market fit of a DIApp.

They are as follows:

- Does the DIApp solve a unique problem faced by various stakeholders in the industry?
- Does the DIApp disintermediate a current entity that is inefficient in the current process, or bring more order to the process?
- Can the benefits of DIApps be achieved only by utilizing the combination of blockchain and AI?
- Does the DIApp facilitate users to derive insights by using the DIApp with the help of AI models?

By answering the preceding questions, we may be able to identify whether the DIApp has achieved a suitable product-market fit. It is also important for you to identify other key indicators apart from the preceding general attributes to identify the product-market fit for your DIApp.

With the basic knowledge and key points on the design aspects under our belts, let's now understand the key highlights of the development aspects of the SDLC in the next section.

Developing a DIApp

The development of a DIApp can be tricky. Since AI and blockchain are yet to see the limelight in development, some practices in the industry are not yet visible to all. In this section, we will highlight the key development aspects of a DIApp.

Before exploring the technical aspects, let's understand a fundamental aspect of development capabilities in an organization. As blockchain and AI are on the bleeding edge of innovation, it is an open truth that many organizations are still in the process of building combined expertise in the respective technologies. Having said that, it is also essential to set up a team of members with complementary skill sets in smart contract development, web or mobile application development, and finally AI or data science modeling. The following section provides an overview of an ideal DIApp team.

Team formation

In a corporate setup, I recommend the following team format for proof of concept development. It is assumed that the team members are enabled with regular technical and solution expertise:

- Two smart contract developers with good hands-on knowledge of the Solidity, Rust, and Golang programming languages are essential. Knowledge of Haskell is also preferred, since a few blockchains offer smart contracts based on functional programming languages. One smart contract developer may be able to focus on feature development and another smart contract developer could work on bug fixes, internal auditing, code quality reviews, and so on.
- One full-stack web developer with basic knowledge of blockchain to develop the frontend web application. If the target audience is on mobile, you might choose a mobile application developer accordingly.
- One SMACK-stack developer may be required to set up the analytics platform needed for building AI capabilities in the solution.
- One machine learning or deep learning engineer may be required to build the required models. If an application requires deep learning or a neural network, you should make your choice accordingly.
- Finally, you may need one DevOps engineer to orchestrate the infrastructure and deploy all the necessary components across vendors or cloud platforms through a well-defined **Continuous Integration/Continuous Delivery (CI/CD)** pipeline.

An all-star team of six members with complementary skill sets can help develop the proof of concept and establish the needed technical features. The two smart contract developers can be replaced by one senior smart contract developer with end-to-end experience.

With a proper team setup, we shall discuss one of the best project management practices for delivering the proof of concept in the following section.

Agile development

Once the team is set up and the requirements are neatly documented, I recommend establishing a clear release plan for the proof of concept and the subsequent builds as much as possible. As mentioned earlier in the *Designing a DIApp* section, the technical aspects of blockchain technologies change very frequently. In order to match the pace of change, it is important to manage client expectations. Otherwise, it could lead to another level of complication on top of technical issues.

Let's look at the following diagram:

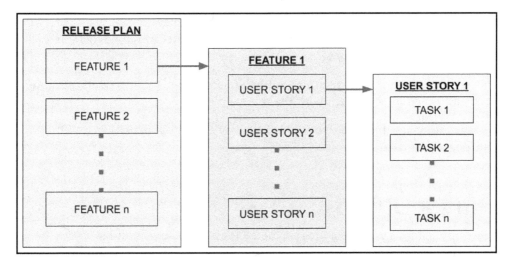

Fig 7.3: Schematic of breaking down the release plan into workable tasks for the team

As shown in the preceding diagram, the requirements need to be documented very specifically and broken down into items across three levels. Managers and product owners both work on features in a release plan, whereas the product owner alone specifies the requirements for each aspect of the proof of concept or any release in the form of a user story. Once the user story is documented with an expected output, the team can collectively break it down into many work items or tasks. You can also break down the task into multiple sub-tasks for a large project beyond the proof of concept release for a better and more granular documentation of efforts. The tasks can be assigned to individuals and can be either blockchain-related or AI-related.

If the requirements are documented clearly, you can organize **sprint planning**. As per agile development, you can organize a sprint for at least 2 to 3 weeks. A proof of concept release can be planned across one or many sprints. At the end of each sprint, the team must organize a **retrospective meeting** to review the progress and reflect on the current practices.

Compared to retrospectives of traditional apps, you could also identify the risks or issues created by the components. Since the ecosystem is still under development, the observed deficiencies can be converted into issues. The issues can be segregated and filed at the repositories on the respective dependencies. Most of the dependencies reside on GitHub. So, the developers must have sufficient awareness of the platform to navigate it, collaborate with others, and resolve the issues.

The process repeats across many sprints until all the features, requirements, and bug fixes have been addressed in alignment with the release plan.

With a basic understanding and overview of the key aspects of developing a DIApp, let's now consider testing DIApps.

Testing a DIApp

Since these applications will most likely manage high-value assets and sensitive information, testing DIApps is a crucial step in the process before and after the deployment of all the modules in the network. Ensuring the correctness and lasting service of the application is critical for businesses and hence, it is a very important aspect of the development life cycle to bring back rigorous testing practices into the process.

Let's now go through the key highlights of the testing and deployment processes for a DIApp.

Authoring the test cases

Before the software can be deployed, we can try to ensure the correctness of the software and also confirm the fitness of the runtime environment by running a few crucial tests. Usually, these tests are implemented within the source code, in the form of unit test files containing dummy input values being passed to the functions, later checked through assertion to ensure the correctness of the software in the relatively new environment. Each test case represents a scenario for the logic to perform and provide a predetermined output scenario. We will explore more about the generation of unit test cases in `Chapter 8`, *Implementing DIApps*, in a hands-on practical.

Test cases are executed across two levels of testing: unit testing and integration testing.

Unit testing

Each component in the DIApp pattern delivers an exclusive value to the solution. Hence, it is important to ensure the correctness of each component in the solution. This can be made possible by performing **unit testing**. Under unit testing, we can test the core functionalities of each module before integrating it with the other modules. Unit testing helps in formally verifying the correctness of these modules by comparing the real output to the desired output. This process repeats for each change made to the module, thereby preserving the correctness of the module each time a change has been made.

Once the modules are unit tested and integrated, we can perform integration testing, as explained in the following section.

Integration testing

As explained in the previous sections, a DIApp is a hybrid composition of many technologies. Hence, it is important to test the behavior of each heterogeneous component in order to ensure that they provide accurate results. This is achieved by performing **integration testing**. Once the components are integrated, we can run a few test cases that can formally verify the correctness of a few critical components that rely upon one or more heterogeneous components to provide output.

Testing AI models

Although traditional software can be tested by unit tests and integrations tests, we need different measures and methods to test AI systems. Testing AI models and capabilities can be split into two phases. One phase of the testing is before the model reaches production. The other phase of the testing is applied post-production. Before bringing the AI model to production, testing can be performed by verifying the correctness and completeness of the training data. Similarly, once the AI models are deployed, we can test them frequently for accuracy and availability. Turing tests can also be performed to understand whether the AI model has sufficiently been able to replace a human response to the task.

With a fundamental understanding of testing in DIApp development under our belts, let's now go through the deployment process for a DIApp.

Deploying a DIApp

In this section, we will discuss the common practices for deploying blockchain-based applications in hybrid environments. Unlike other emerging technologies, blockchain platforms demand a relatively larger stretch of time to set up the network and make the whole ecosystem functional. Accordingly, several blockchain platforms have understood the need for DevOps as an integral part of developing those platforms. Hence, it is also important to note that DevOps knowledge is also essential in using these platforms for developing applications and deploying solutions.

Scaling the application for production

Deployment of the DIApp is the final crucial step in the life cycle. Apart from correctness, it is imperative that the application is designed, architected, and developed in a manner supportive for the deployment of the application in a scalable manner. The scale is not only measured in terms of the number of users, but also depends on the cost, form factors, and other economic attributes that may directly affect the operations.

Several tools such as Docker, Kubernetes, Ansible, Terraform, and Mesos are available for deploying DIApps and their dependencies. We will be exploring DevOps tools further in `Chapter 8`, *Implementing DIApps*, with some examples.

Monitoring a DIApp

In this section, we will discuss the common practices used by many to monitor transactions of applications in blockchains.

Explorers

Most of the decentralized solutions are deployed on a public blockchain network or digital ledger. In most of the public networks, blockchain explorers are available to look up information concerning a transaction or block. However, if the DIApp solution is implemented in a private or permissioned environment, these public blockchain explorers may not be able to provide information on transactions belonging to a private network or private ledgers. Hence, we must be able to deploy existing blockchain explorers and plug them into the endpoints of a private service. This is the only way to facilitate users' monitoring of their transactions in a private environment. Several open source implementations of blockchain explorers are available, which could be downloaded and connected to private services.

Some examples of public blockchain explorers include Etherscan, EthStats, and BlockScout. We will discuss them in our next chapter. For example, BlockScout is an open source explorer that you can use to create a specific explorer for your private Ethereum network.

Summary

In this chapter, we explored the basic definition of a DApp and a DIApp. We also contrasted both the solution architectures and design patterns of these two technologies. Based on the advantages of DIApps, we further explored the SDLC aspects of DIApps from ideation to release or deployment. The new economy of blockchain and AI requires a redefined SDLC that is inclusive of the new technologies involved. We have outlined the steps and processes to be considered before developing a DIApp.

In the next chapter, we will focus on applying the development aspects of the SDLC by developing sample applications on various blockchain platforms, along with common AI techniques.

Implementing DIApps

8

"Blockchain and AI are the binary stars in IT. They are here to help save humanity from an invisible virus."

With it being more than 10 years since the advent of blockchain and AI, there is now a whole new range of solutions that can be built by combining both technologies. By combining these two technologies in a new way, we can address some tough problems. In this chapter, we'll propose a better pattern for application development that leverages the combination of AI and blockchain. This is a hands-on chapter where you will learn more about using blockchain and AI techniques to build a smart application that could potentially save us from further outbreaks of COVID-19, along with other agents of infection. By the end of this chapter, you will be able to identify the benefits of **Decentralized intelligent application (DIApp)** as you build a sample contact tracing application using the DIApp design pattern.

This chapter will cover the following topics:

- Evolution of decentralized applications
- Building a sample DIApp
- Testing the sample DIApp
- Deploying the sample DIApp
- Retrospecting the sample DIApp

Let's get started!

Technical requirements

While following the tutorials in this chapter, please ensure that the following software is installed on your system:

- Just (v0.5.11 and above): `https://github.com/casey/just#installation`
- Python (v3.6.9 and above): `https://www.python.org/downloads/`
- Node.js (12.18.2 LTS and above): `https://nodejs.org/en/download/`
- Brave browser (v1.5.123 and above): `https://brave.com/download/`
- Jupyter Notebook: `https://jupyter.org/install`

With the preceding software dependencies installed, we have tested the code on Linux (Ubuntu) and macOS (Mojave) to ensure it works.

In order to understand and appreciate the content in this chapter, you must be familiar with the basic concepts of the DIApp design pattern, as explained in `Chapter 7`, *Development Life Cycle of a DIApp*.

This chapter also assumes that you are familiar with the basic concepts of blockchains, as explained in `Chapter 1`, *Getting Started with Blockchain*. It is also assumed that you are familiar with the basic concepts of AI, as explained in `Chapter 2`, *Introduction to the AI Landscape*.

To appreciate the connection between these two technologies and apply them in this chapter, you are also expected to understand the benefits of decentralized database technologies, which were articulated, along with examples, in `Chapter 4`, *AI and Blockchain-Driven Databases*.

Evolution of decentralized applications

Let's begin this chapter by quickly refreshing our memory about the current state of decentralized applications in a chronological manner. The following diagram shows how applications have evolved over the past three decades:

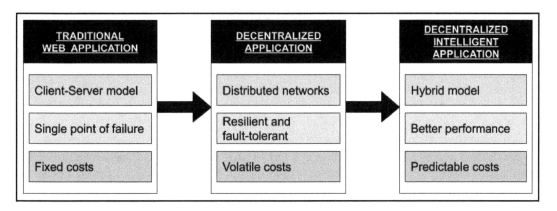

Fig 8.1: Evolution of applications since the dawn of the internet

Here, we can observe three major shifts in the application design pattern. We can also observe the three major aspects of how applications evolve over time.

We will discuss each in the following sections.

Traditional web applications

Although prominent work for the foundation of the internet was laid out in the 1970s and the 1980s, it was the World Wide Web that made a significant leap in how information can be shared easily among nodes in a network. Traditional web applications such as blogs, chatrooms, and e-commerce websites emerged since the advent of the public internet in the mid-1990s. The majority of internet traffic is still driven by such applications, offering information and services to internet users.

Most of these applications started with a simple web server in the backend. Servers were hosted to accept limited client connections across the world but easily crashed after reaching the desired threshold. Now, the majority of these applications have moved toward an n-tier architecture.

The currently used **n-tier architecture**, also called **multi-tier architecture** or **multi-layer architecture**, is used to manage large-scale web applications such as e-commerce websites, social media sites, chatrooms, blogging platforms, and so on. Dedicated infrastructures are managed on the cloud in order for companies to facilitate transactions performed by users. Compared to the primitive version of the client-server model, the n-tier model separates the functions into many layers (hence the name). This also means that the n-tier model is serving as a better version of the client-server model in terms of handling failures and managing the liveness of traditional web applications. Companies manage their own infrastructure, such as servers, which is needed to provide services to users. Most of the infrastructure used by companies can be purchased or rented from cloud providers for a short period of time. This means the costs of operating traditional web applications are almost fixed.

Now, let's try to understand how decentralized applications have evolved on the internet over the past 10 years.

Decentralized applications

The foremost characteristic of a decentralized application is the fact that it is not controlled by a single entity. Another important characteristic is that it facilitates a common bar of entry to use the app. By textbook definition, Napster and BitTorrent were some of the earliest decentralized applications that could be used to host and share various files of sorts in a peer-to-peer format.

Some of you might be wondering whether blockchains were used to build these apps. It is partially true that these peer-to-peer file sharing protocols used the fundamental cryptographic and networking technologies we use in blockchains today.

 At the time of writing, in 2020, we associate decentralized applications mostly with business logic running on blockchains such as Bitcoin and Ethereum. We must understand that decentralized applications are also a design pattern that existed long before the invention of Bitcoin.

Comparing decentralized applications with traditional web applications, we can see that decentralized applications run on more than one server or computer. Also, such computers are not necessarily owned and operated by a single entity or individual. They usually consist of interested parties who are willing to run the software for a benefit or an incentive. Hence, it is safe to conclude that most of the decentralized applications run on a peer-to-peer network. Unlike traditional web applications, these applications do not experience a single point of failure.

These peer-to-peer networks are defined by a protocol and are usually fault-tolerant to protect the users from many attack vectors. Compared to a client-server model, it is very difficult to compromise a peer-to-peer network due to its distributed topology. Incentivization and penalties in a blockchain protocol make it more difficult to compromise the network as the cost of an attack is much higher than the returns gained from such an attack.

Although decentralized applications address the two aforementioned problems, the cost of running business and mission-critical applications is challenging due to the volatility associated with token prices. At the time of writing, efforts are being made to reduce this volatility in terms of signing the transaction on behalf of the user or paying the user in advance for the transactional costs.

So far, we have learned that traditional web applications and centralized services offer predictable performance at a fixed cost, whereas decentralized applications offer independent services without risking the network, vendor, or user. However, we have also learned that, in achieving independence using decentralized applications, we invite some degree of uncertainty in terms of fees. Finally, we have also observed that users opt for centralized models to achieve performance and security in an internal environment.

Now, let's try to understand how decentralized intelligent applications are evolving on the internet.

Decentralized intelligent applications

Now that business models are leaning toward transparency and efficiency, there is a need for a new design pattern that favors a combination of traceability, decentralization, and predictability. Decentralized intelligent applications can use reliable infrastructure in a peer-to-peer network. This network is composed of nodes operated by more than one entity that may have vested interests in serving users and growing their businesses. Also, transactions on this kind of network are usually confirmed in a very short period of time at significantly lower fees. Similar to large public networks, it would be costly to attempt to compromise the network due to the deficit between the benefit of the attack and the cost of performing an attack.

A key differentiator between this pattern and others is the closer integration of AI models with the help of decentralized databases. This makes it possible to build mission-critical and business-centric applications with traceability and insights as first-class features.

Now, let's summarize our analysis of all three models.

Contrast and analysis

We can summarize our learning and decide the right design pattern by weighing the benefits of each pattern against its trade-offs.

In the case of traditional web applications, we may observe better performance when using a centralized and dedicated infrastructure. The transactions will achieve near-immediate finality at a reasonable and fixed cost for the company developing the app. However, this design pattern may lack some security and traceability features offered by other design patterns.

In the case of decentralized applications, we may observe reasonable performance and traceability at the expense of variable transaction costs. Compared to traditional web applications, the speed of transactions may be impacted.

In the case of decentralized intelligent applications, we may observe predictable costs and near-immediate finality for most of the transactions. Apart from better cost, speed, security, and performance, the pattern also provides decentralized storage for building privacy-preserving applications that can be used to derive actionable insights with ethical usage of AI models on user data.

Now that we've analyzed the three major patterns, let's end this section with a table summarizing their differences:

	Traditional web application (App)	Decentralized application (DApp, dApp, or Dapp)	Decentralized intelligent application (DIApp)
Network	The client-server model is used with n-tier architectures.	A distributed network topology is used to allow anyone to join the network.	A distributed network topology is used to allow anyone to join the network.
Security	Single points of failure are very likely. Data can be hacked or leaked due to weak encryption or centralized control over data.	The user is the owner of the data. All the data and operations are secured by a unique key pair. Limited data can be stored.	Users can store and operate on larger sizes of data with the same key pair security in order to own their own data.
Cost	Fixed costs in managing a dedicated infrastructure throughout the year.	The costs of transactions are volatile since the costs depend on the price of the native token in the blockchain.	Prices are relatively stable in smaller yet decentralized groups of nodes.

Transparency	Apps and data operations are not transparent to the user or other stakeholders.	The logic of the app and most of the operations are transparent. Private transactions are optionally allowed.	Logic and operations are transparent, with options to use privacy without harming security.
Performance	A large number of transactions can be processed with immediate finality	The throughput is low due to the large distribution of nodes. Finality is slower.	Transaction throughputs are higher. Finality is also achieved quickly.
Privacy	Complete privacy and the anonymity of user data is seldom practiced by companies while harnessing insights as data is hosted on a centralized or distributed database controlled by organizations.	Anonymity is practiced through wallets, but data management on blockchain networks is a costly affair. The privacy of the user depends on the application's policies. AI models are not used regularly.	DIApps aim to provide complete privacy and anonymity to users while providing meaningful and actionable insights using AI in a fair manner, without hampering the anonymity of the user.

The preceding table shows the benefits and drawbacks of different application patterns.

Now that we have had a quick recap of the evolution of apps, let's build a sample DIApp that addresses real-world challenges.

Building a sample DIApp

In this section, we will cover the problem statement, find a solution to the stated problem, come up with a technical architecture as per the DIApp design pattern, and observe how to develop all the deliverables needed to launch the DIApp.

Let's begin by understanding the problem statement in the following section.

Problem statement

A novel coronavirus that goes by the name of **Severe Acute Respiratory Syndrome coronavirus 2 (SARS-CoV-2)** has created a new pandemic outbreak called **Coronavirus Disease 2019 (COVID-19)**. At the time of writing this chapter, the virus has infected over 11 million people globally through various modes of transmission, tragically taking the lives of more than 500,000 people: a sad page in the history books of humanity. Although efforts have been made by local governments to reduce these infections, some virus carriers appear to be asymptomatic. This means that a person may be carrying the virus without knowing it. Sometimes, the prescribed checkups could also fail to recognize the virus in its early stage of incubating inside the patient's body.

Current challenges

This virus has introduced humanity to new challenges. Let's take a look at the two major challenges that are, at the time of writing, being faced.

- **Detecting the virus in asymptomatic patients**: As discussed previously, the SARS-CoV-2 virus poses a new challenge to medical professionals in terms of identifying infections in a human body that fails to show any symptoms. Such people may be allowed to continue their daily life, thus risking the wellness of the entire community they belong to. This leaves a gaping hole in security checks, which may allow asymptomatic people to access public services or interact with people who may potentially contract the virus from the patient.
- **Tracing the transmission of the virus**: Although it is difficult to detect the virus in its early stages for a few people who are asymptomatic, symptoms do surface over time. Once they do, and the person tests positive, it is important to trace back all the actions of the diagnosed patient in order to contain the infection. This is difficult to achieve without an accurate history of the patient's activity over the past couple of weeks. Any efforts to jot it down will need time and will remain inaccurate due to human errors.

To contain such infections, medical professionals resort to contact tracing. We'll learn more about contact tracing in the following section.

Contact tracing

Contact tracing is a process of identifying all the people involved in the patient's activities over the past few days or weeks since the diagnosis of the infection. This is a process carried out by health department officials in coordination with law enforcement agencies.

A generic workflow of contact tracing is as follows:

1. The doctor has diagnosed the patient as positive for SARS-CoV-2.
2. A contact tracer is assigned to the case.
3. The contact tracer interacts with the patient to identify the activity of the patient.
4. Depending on the jurisdiction/country, the contact tracer is responsible for collecting accurate information about the patient's whereabouts for a designated number of days or weeks. For example, a patient that tests positive in India might be asked to share their activity for the past 14 calendar days.
5. Based on the input provided by the patient, the contact tracers may verify some information.
6. If the information shared by the patient is convincing, more contact tracers are hired to identify the first-degree people infected by the patient.
7. Once this manual search is over, the people who have been contacted are tested for the virus.
8. Depending on the jurisdiction, the people who have been contacted may be placed under mandatory quarantine for up to 14 days to check whether symptoms develop.
9. The quarantined people are tested for the virus periodically.
10. If there are no signs of the virus, the suspected people are released. However, if they test positive, the same process repeats.

Although you may find this process to be tightly planned and sophisticated, most of the steps mentioned here are manually carried out by many countries. Although some countries have opted to automate contact tracing with the help of digital technologies, they do not consider all the agents of infection.

Issues with contact tracing

As we discussed previously, contact tracing is an arduous process. Although some countries have successfully been able to automate this process digitally, it is very difficult to track infections from non-human sources.

We tend to forget that a significant number of hypotheses claim that the origin of the virus leads back to bats, animals that live in forests and rural and urban areas. It has also been observed by many researchers that the virus can remain on many forms of surfaces for a few hours. Modern supply chains are so advanced that goods can be transferred from one point to another in just a matter of hours. Unfortunately, this velocity of the supply chain provides a potential window for the virus being transmitted from one container to another while the cargo is airborne. Such infections not only risk the supply chain of normal goods but could also infect a wide range of people who may use these products without effective sanitization. Assessing the risks of infection before delivering goods to the public should be considered. Similarly, we want to protect our pets and other important species of animals.

Hence, it is imperative to consider monitoring animals and non-living objects for infections of the SARS-CoV-2 virus. As such, there is a need for a digital contact tracing algorithm that can address the possibility of infections among these two agents in the ecosystem.

With the need for digital contact tracing for animals and objects clearly established, let's try to formulate a solution approach.

Solution approach

Since we are developing a sample application to track potential infections from animals and non-living objects, I would like to name the solution **Decentralized Intelligent Contact Tracing for Animals and Objects (DICTAO)**. As discussed in the preceding section, there is a need to track animals and objects. We must be able to track down the infection status at a granular level for the sake of transparency. A public blockchain with a decentralized and open ledger can offer this feature. Similarly, we must understand that the global supply chain is a busy world of its own. Manually tracking down all potential contacts is virtually impossible. Similarly, it is very difficult to identify potential contacts between animals. Hence, there is a need for an automated but intelligent way of identifying the potential infections and separating them from the noise. Thus comes the need for blockchain and AI in tracing animals and objects.

In the following sections, we will see how DICTAO can be built.

Choosing the blockchain technology

As discussed previously, blockchains are essential in maintaining the transparency of the status of animals and objects. Since this is a tutorial to building a sample DIApp, I am going to keep the context very simple and accessible to everyone.

The Ethereum network has many testnets for developers to deploy and test their applications in a sandboxed test environment. One of the most famous test networks is called the **Kovan** testnet. Kovan is a **Proof of Authority** (**PoA**)-based Ethereum blockchain network. It is maintained by the Ethereum developer community. The Kovan testnet is known for its speed of execution, reliability, and free access to test ethers made available through a faucet. You can read more about the Kovan testnet here: `https://kovan-testnet.github.io/website/`.

Faucet is a piece of software used by smart contract developers and users to acquire testnet tokens for free, without the need for mining them on their local PCs. Most of the blockchain testnets have their own respective faucets.

I have chosen Kovan to only help you understand and get along with blockchains as easily as possible. Kovan is a test network, so it is not intended to be used for any production-grade Ethereum applications. If you wish to deploy this example for a live use case, I recommend that you either use the Ethereum mainnet or prefer sidechains such as Matic. If you wish to deploy it live, you can learn more about the Matic sidechain here: `https://matic.network/`.

Choosing a decentralized database

Digital contact tracing often involves collecting data. To enable accuracy and provide high-quality predictions, more data could be collected at a high frequency. Over time, data can become very large. Such data should not be stored on a blockchain directly since it incurs a high cost. Also, storing huge amounts of data can often lead to bottleneck issues and may hamper the performance of a blockchain. Hence, there is a need to store the activity of the animals or objects in a decentralized database.

I will be using the MóiBit REST API as the decentralized database for this sample DIApp. MóiBit offers a developer-friendly API environment, which makes it an easy choice.

Since MóiBit is an IPFS-based decentralized storage service, each change to a new file or an existing file generates a new hash. Similar to blockchains, each new hash represents a successful state change. However, updating the data on MóiBit will be cheaper and faster compared to blockchains. Since it is driven by hashes, the file's integrity is also secured and easily verifiable.

To learn more about MóiBit's APIs, visit their documentation at `https://apidocs.moibit.io/`.

Choosing an AI technique

Tracking innumerable objects and animals across an area – even a small one – will lead to a humongous quantity of data points. It is virtually impossible to perform contact tracing manually on these data points. Due to some low-quality data points, the efforts of a manual contact tracer could easily go to waste. As the number of positive cases increases, more pressure mounts on the manual contact tracers to close a case and move on to the next one. This could also lead to inaccurate identification of infections.

In order to reduce errors and automate the process of cleaning, ordering, grouping, and predicting the infections, we can leverage AI techniques.

As discussed previously, contract tracing usually involves the process of analyzing the activity of the infected person/animal/object. It is safe to assume that snapshotting the location data, along with a timestamp of when it occurred, will provide enough insights into potential contact cases. Therefore, we will be analyzing geolocation data.

We'll use geospatial analysis to identify some anomalies in the data points. Specifically, we will be using the **Density-Based Spatial Clustering of Applications with Noise (DBSCAN)** algorithm to perform geospatial analysis to identify potential infections among animals and objects. It is a data clustering algorithm used to effectively group data points in a range under a cluster and drop the outliers that cannot be reached by other data points.

To learn more about the DBSCAN algorithm, consult the following Wikipedia article: `https://en.wikipedia.org/wiki/DBSCAN`.

Now that we have decided what technologies and techniques will be used in the sample DIApp, let's try to formalize it in the form of a reference technical architecture by borrowing it from the DIApp design pattern.

The technical architecture of the sample DIApp

In this section, I will be proposing the technical architecture of the sample DIApp. Based on the decisions made in the preceding sections, I have compiled all the solution components into one diagram, as follows:

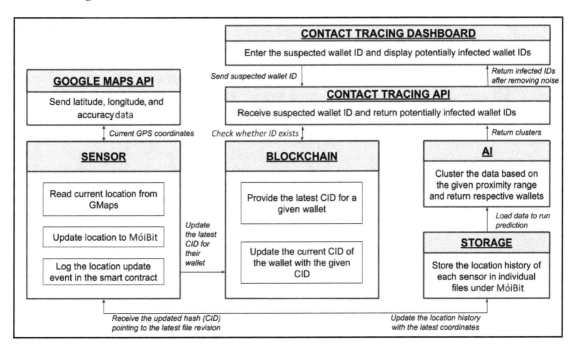

Fig 8.2: DIApp reference architecture of our sample application

In the preceding diagram, we have represented all the solution components as per the DIApp reference architecture proposed in the DIApp design pattern. Now, let's examine each component:

Sensor: A sensor is a hardware device attached to the animal or object that needs to be tracked in case of infection. Each sensor is identified by a unique wallet address that is recognizable on the Ethereum blockchain. Also, it is important to note that each sensor gets a dedicated file on MóiBit where the location history of the corresponding sensor can be stored.

An application will run inside the sensor. This application is expected to automatically read its location and update the location to its dedicated file on MóiBit. The current location of the sensor can be accessed by making a call to a geolocation API. In our sample DIApp example, we are using the Google Maps API to retrieve the current location of the sensor. When called, the Google Maps Geolocation API returns the latitude, longitude, and accuracy of the coordinates back to the sensor.

For the sake of simplicity, we will be ignoring the accuracy value returned by the Google Maps API and uploading the rest of the data to MóiBit. Since the example DIApp is trying to demonstrate the convergence of AI and blockchain technologies, optimizations are not given priority in this book. Handling the accuracy of the data while predicting infections will take us out of the scope of this book. However, I look forward to solving that problem with you offline.

Now, once the sensor receives the response from the Google Maps Geolocation API, the data is restructured and uploaded to the dedicated location history file on MóiBit. We will discuss the design and structure of the client application in the *Developing the client code for sensors* section.

Smart contract in the blockchain: The significance of the smart contract in this sample DIApp is to maintain proof for each location update performed by every sensor. Every time a sensor updates its location history on MóiBit, a new function call is made to the smart contract to update the **Content Identifier** (**CID**) value for the corresponding wallet designated for the sensor. We will discuss the design and structure of the smart contract in later sections.

Contact tracing dashboard: The contact tracing dashboard is a simple Express-based Node.js web application that spawns a local server to host a single HTML file. Through the dashboard web page rendered by the Node.js application, users can enter the suspected wallet ID. The web application performs basic form validation and returns a list of potentially infected wallet IDs, if any. We will discuss the design and structure of the contact tracing dashboard in later sections.

Contact tracing API: The user input to track a suspected wallet ID is received by the contact tracing API. This is a backend API that also predicts the infected IDs in order to return them to the dashboard. We will discuss the design and structure of the contact tracing API in later sections.

Developing the smart contract

In this section, we will discuss the design and structure of the smart contract used to record the proof each time the location history is updated. As discussed in the previous section, we will be using the Ethereum blockchain and therefore I will be showing you how to develop the smart contract in the Solidity language.

 If you are not familiar with the Solidity programming language, I suggest that you take a look at their website for more technical details, know-how, and documentation: https://solidity.readthedocs.io/. It is important that you understand the semantics of the Solidity programming language to understand this section and learn the benefits of a smart contract in the proposed DIApp solution.

Let's start by identifying the actors. We know that the solution aims to trace infections that originate from animals and objects. Hence, we understand that a tracking device or sensor is necessary. Let's assume that each sensor can be identified by a unique Ethereum wallet address. Apart from sensors, we also have end users such as medical professionals and enforcement teams who may want to identify the potentially infected actors from a given animal or object:

1. Each time the sensor has a new location to update on MóiBit, it makes the necessary update and receives a hash back from MóiBit. We are using that hash and the wallet address from the calling sensor to maintain a mapping on the smart contract. Each time a new location coordinate is updated by a sensor, the corresponding value of the sensor's wallet address needs to be updated. Hence, we need to define a mapping to record any changes that are made to the location history of each sensor. We can do this with the following mapping:

   ```
   mapping(address => string) private deviceIDToLatestCID;
   ```

   From the preceding mapping, we can see that the address serves as a unique key to an updated string value, which is basically the CID received from MóiBit when the location of the corresponding sensor is updated.

2. Apart from the preceding mapping, we will also need another mapping to track all the sensors by their addresses to confirm whether they have ever updated their location. We can achieve this by persisting a list of all the wallet addresses in the following mapping:

   ```
   mapping(address => uint256) private deviceIDExists;
   ```

From the preceding mapping, we can see that every sensor that has ever updated its history will be recorded in this mapping. We will learn more about the reason behind this soon.

3. Finally, we will record the address of each and every sensor that has ever updated its history to this smart contract with the following array of wallet addresses:

```
address[] private deviceIDs;
```

From the preceding array declaration, designated users can access the list of all the addresses that have ever updated their location history in the smart contract. Do not confuse the `deviceIDs` array with the `deviceIDExists` mapping. The array is used to directly access each and every sensor's wallet address, whereas the mapping is used to check whether a sensor has already updated the location history before.

Before we move on to the functional aspects of this smart contract, we have two more declarations: a modifier and an event.

4. A modifier is a conditional instruction that must be fulfilled before executing a function. If the conditions of a modifier for a function are not satisfied, that function call will not happen. In our case, we use a modifier to control who can update the location history mapping: `deviceIDToLatestCID`. As you may have observed, this mapping needs to be updated with the CIDs pointing to the latest location history of a sensor. But we also need to make sure that only the sensor can update its own value. Other sensors, users, or developers should not be allowed to update the location history of an unknown sensor. This important design decision will prevent other rogue actors from corrupting the reputation of a good standing sensor on the blockchain.

To achieve this, we can use the following modifier:

```
modifier onlyBy(address _account) {
    require(
        msg.sender == _account,
        "Sender not authorized to update this mapping!"
    );
    _; // The "_;"! will be replaced by the actual function body
when the modifier is used.
}
```

From the preceding modifier declaration, we can observe that a function with the preceding modifier is executed only if the caller is the same as the address whose location history is being updated in the blockchain. We will understand the implication of this `onlyBy` mapping when we understand how the location is updated by the `setLatestCID` function. But before that, let's quickly go through one last declaration of an event.

5. Events are very helpful when working on complex use cases. As a user who may be depositing some ethers or other tokens to a wallet, we wait for the transaction receipt as confirmation. For confirmation of some logical execution, we can't just wait for transaction receipts. There may be other sub-components that may have to be triggered, depending on the successful execution of the logic. Events come to our rescue here. Events in Solidity are a logging feature that helps non-blockchain applications take a cue point and continue with their execution.

We'll declare one event in our smart contract, as follows:

```
event MappingUpdated(address deviceID, string latestCID);
```

From the preceding event declaration, we can see that an event can be emitted with the wallet address of a sensor, along with its latest CID. This event is emitted every time the mapping is successfully updated with the new CID pointing to the latest location history of a sensor on MóiBit.

6. We will learn more about the application of this `MappingUpdated` event by looking in the `setLatestCID` function body, as shown here:

```
function setLatestCID(address deviceID, string memory latestCID)
    public
    onlyBy(deviceID)
{
    deviceIDToLatestCID[deviceID] = latestCID;
    if (deviceIDExists[deviceID] == 0) {
        deviceIDs.push(deviceID);
        deviceIDExists[deviceID] = 1;
    }
    emit MappingUpdated(deviceID, latestCID);
}
```

As you can see from the preceding function declaration, `setLatestCID` is a setter function that allows each and every sensor to update its own location history by passing its wallet address, along with the CID pointing to the latest history on MóiBit. The `address` and `string` types are used to define the `deviceID` and `latestCID` input parameters. `deviceID` is the wallet address of the sensor, which is calling the function, while `latestCID` is the hash pointing to the latest history of the corresponding sensor on MóiBit. The `public` keyword defines that the function can be called by anyone globally. Thereafter, we see the `onlyBy` modifier being used to validate the function call. It takes the same input argument, `deviceID`, and checks whether the caller intending to update the location history is the sensor itself. If the modifier conditions are validated to be true, the remaining function body is executed. Otherwise, the transaction will be reverted. Now that we have a fair understanding of the `setLatestCID` function's header, let's understand its body.

Inside the function's body, we can observe that the `latestCID` value is assigned to `deviceID` immediately. Once the mapping is updated, it checks whether the sensor had previously updated its location. This is made possible by checking the status bit for the corresponding sensor's wallet address in the `deviceIDExists` mapping. If no entry exists for the given wallet address, it is added to the `deviceIDExists` mapping and the corresponding status bit value is set to 1. Simultaneously, we can also observe that we are appending the `deviceIDs` array to the new array. Updating this array under this condition ensures that the wallet address is not added to the array again as a duplicate. This means that the `setLatestCID` function only appends the wallet address when a new sensor is onboarded to the smart contract. Finally, once the location mapping is updated and status bits are managed, the `MappingUpdated` event is emitted by the function. You can see that the input parameters have been supplied in the parentheses to log the event for corresponding values. This summarizes the details of the `setLatestCID` setter function. Now, let's take a look at some of the other `getter` functions in the smart contract.

7. Once we set the location history mapping with a new CID for a given sensor, we may have to read the mapping in case we need the details of a sensor.

Hence, we will define a `getter` function to read the latest CID of the sensor from the mapping, as follows:

```
function getLatestCID(address deviceID)
    public
    view
    returns (string memory latestCID)
```

```
    {
        return deviceIDToLatestCID[deviceID];
    }
```

As you can see, the `getter` function, `getLatestCID`, reads one input parameter. The `deviceID` input parameter represents the wallet address of a sensor, with the Solidity type address. Since anyone should be able to read the proof that a sensor is updating its location from time to time, we have to make this `getter` function accessible globally. This is possible by using the `public` keyword. Also, since this is a function that only fetches the data from the blockchain and does not intend to make changes, it is also required to use the `view` keyword. This ensures that the `getLatestCID` function has read-only powers. Since we want anybody to be able to call the function, we do not have modifiers for this function. In the function's body, we can only see one line of instructions, and that is to return the CID value of the corresponding sensor from the `deviceIDToLatestCID` mapping. Since the returned value is a string that has been defined in the mapping, the function's header also defines the same. This summarizes the `getter` function, `getLatestCID`.

8. Now, let's look at the peripheral functions required by the backend scripts.

   We'll continue with one more `getter` function, as defined here:

   ```
   function getDeviceIDsLength() public view returns (uint256) {
       return deviceIDs.length;
   }
   ```

   As you can see, `getDeviceIDsLength` is a getter function that does not take any input, but simply returns the current length of the `deviceIDs` array. Since we need to call this from a backend program, we have set the visibility of this function to `public` too. Similar to our previous function, this function is also a read-only function returning an unsigned integer value. Hence, `view` and `uint256` are used in the function's header. This summarizes the `getter` function, `getDeviceIDsLength`.

9. Now, let's take a look at the last function in the contract:

   ```
   function getIDByIndex(uint256 index) public view returns
   (address) {
       return deviceIDs[index];
   }
   ```

As you can see, `getIDByIndex` is a `getter` function that returns the wallet address by the index value from the `deviceIDs` array. Since it is complicated to return composite values in Solidity directly, I have resorted to reading them one by one. If you are a sophisticated Solidity developer, you may eliminate this function and read the whole array directly at the client side without spending too much on gas costs.

 The complete Solidity smart contract code is available at the following GitHub link: `https://github.com/PacktPublishing/Hands-On-Artificial-Intelligence-for-Blockchain/tree/master/Chapter08`.

Now that we have a way to manage proofs of location updates, let's go ahead and develop the client code for sensors, which can make location history updates on MóiBit and call this contract.

Developing the client code for sensors

In this section, we will discuss the design and structure of the sensor application. The application is used to get the current location of the sensor in a periodic manner and update the location history to MóiBit. Once the location history is successfully updated, the new CID or hash received by MóiBit is used as proof that the sensor is in good standing by updating its location in a periodic manner. The applications will now call the appropriate blockchain function to maintain its reputation.

 I have chosen to implement this application in the Python language since it is a well-known language for reference implementation across the fields of **AI**, the **Internet of Things (IoT)**, and blockchain. It is important that you understand Python in order to make sense of this section. I suggest that you enroll yourself in a Packt micro-course to understand the basic concepts of the Python language: `https://subscription.packtpub.com/interactive-courses/data/introduction-to-python`.

My implementation is a single Python script. First things first, the following `import` statements are required to make the necessary calls in the Python script:

1. Please make sure that you install the third-party libraries mentioned in the `import` statements using the `pip install` command:

```
import requests
import os
import datetime
import calendar
```

```
import time
import json
from web3 import Web3
import http.client
```

2. There are some important variables that I'll be using throughout the script. They are as follows:

```
url = 'https://www.googleapis.com/geolocation/v1/geolocate'
myobj = {'key': os.environ['GMAPS_API_KEY']}
```

From the preceding code block, you can observe that `url` is a string variable with the URL to Google Maps' Geolocation API. `myobj` is a request object that I'll be passing to the Geolocation API during requests. Since the Geolocation API is protected by an API key registered by the user, I need to pass it along with every request I make to Google Maps' Geolocation API. Inside the `myobj` variable, you can observe that `key` is mapped to `API KEY`, which is set inside the shell and accessible through `os.environ['GMAPS_API_KEY']`. Basically, it fetches the value of the `GMAPS_API_KEY` environment variable and uses it as the corresponding value to `key`. We will observe how to set the value for `GMAPS_API_KEY` in later sections.

3. Now, let's understand some of the common variables I use for MóiBit operations:

```
conn = http.client.HTTPSConnection("kfs2.moibit.io")
moibit_url = 'https://kfs2.moibit.io/moibit/v0/'
moibit_header_obj = {
    'api_key': os.environ['MOIBIT_API_KEY'],
    'api_secret': os.environ['MOIBIT_API_SECRET'],
    'content-type': "application/json"
}
```

As you can see, `conn` is a variable that represents the HTTPS connection that's been established between the sensor as a client, and MóiBit as a server. `moibit_url` is a string variable that points to the base URL of the MóiBit API. Furthermore, `moibit_header_obj` is a JSON object that I need to pass as part of the request header. Since the MóiBit API is also protected by an API key and API secret, I need to pass these two values in order to authenticate my requests with the MóiBit network. These are represented by the `api_key` and `api_secret` fields, respectively. Both fields are, again, mapped to the `MOIBIT_API_KEY` and `MOIBIT_API_SECRET` environment variables, respectively. `os.environ` fetches the value of the corresponding environment variables from the shell.

Finally, the `content-type` field represents the metadata of the request header. Since it is a JSON object, we use `"application/json"` as the corresponding value.

4. Now, let's look at the variables related to blockchain interactions within the script:

```
blockchain_url = 'https://kovan.infura.io/v3/' + \
    os.environ['WEB3_INFURA_PROJECT_ID']
```

From the preceding code block, we can observe that the `blockchain_url` string variable points to the URL of the Ethereum Kovan testnet, which is accessible via the service provider Infura. Since Infura's API is also protected, we need to pass a project ID that's been created under an Infura user account. This is observed as we append the string with the value of the `WEB3_INFURA_PROJECT_ID` environment variable that we read from the shell using `os.environ`.

5. Since we interact with a smart contract on the blockchain, we also have to define its corresponding **Contract Application Binary Interface** (**ABI**) in our script, as follows:

```
abi = """[{"anonymous": false,"inputs": [{"indexed":
false,"internalType": "address","name": "deviceID","type":
"address"},{"indexed": false,"internalType": "string","name":
"latestCID","type": "string"}],"name": "MappingUpdated","type":
"event"},{"inputs": [{"internalType": "address","name":
"deviceID","type": "address"},{"internalType": "string","name":
"latestCID","type": "string"}],"name": "setLatestCID","outputs":
[],"stateMutability": "nonpayable","type": "function"},{"inputs":
[],"name": "getDeviceIDsLength","outputs": [{"internalType":
"uint256","name": "","type": "uint256"}],"stateMutability":
"view","type": "function"},{"inputs": [{"internalType":
"uint256","name": "index","type": "uint256"}],"name":
"getIDByIndex","outputs": [{"internalType": "address","name":
"","type": "address"}],"stateMutability": "view","type":
"function"},{"inputs": [{"internalType": "address","name":
"deviceID","type": "address"}],"name": "getLatestCID","outputs":
[{"internalType": "string","name": "latestCID","type":
"string"}],"stateMutability": "view","type": "function"}]"""
```

Do not panic if you do not understand this. This is basically a serialized JSON representation of the contract's variables, functions, and input and output specifications.

 If you are not a Solidity smart contract developer, I suggest that you get acquainted with ABI by going to `https://solidity.readthedocs.io/en/v0.5.3/abi-spec.html`.

6. Now that we have defined every variable that's important to the functionality of the script, let's go ahead and understand the functionality of the following script.

As usual, the entry point to our Python script starts with the `main()` function, as defined in the following code extract:

```
if __name__ == "__main__":
    main()

def main():
    # Fetching the Tracking ID locally, or generating a new one
    Tracking_ID = os.environ['WALLET_ADDRESS']
    print("# Setting tracking ID: ", os.environ['WALLET_ADDRESS'])

    # Getting the current geo-coordinates of the device
    print("# Getting the current geo-coordinates of the device from
GMaps API")
    (latitude, longitude) = getGeoCordinates()

    # Reading the current UTC based Unix timestamp of the device
    print("# Reading the current UTC based Unix timestamp of the
device")
    timestamp = getCurrentTime()

    # Generate the JSON structure
    jsonData = Marshal(Tracking_ID, latitude, longitude, timestamp)

    # Updating the location history to IPFS-based MoiBit network
    print("# Updating the location history to IPFS-based MoiBit
network")
    latest_cid = updateLocationHistory(Tracking_ID, jsonData)

    # Publishing the proof to Ethereum
    print("# Publishing the proof to Ethereum")
    txnHash = CommitTxn(Tracking_ID, latest_cid)
    print("https://kovan.etherscan.io/tx/"+txnHash)
```

From the preceding code block, we can understand that when the `main` function is called, it reads the wallet address of the sensor from the `WALLET_ADDRESS` environment variable as `Tracking_ID`. Once it identifies its wallet address, the `getGeoCordinates` function is called to get the current latitude and longitude. Now that we have the current latitude and longitude, the `getCurrentTime` function is called immediately to get the current UNIX timestamp at that time. Now, all four variables – `Tracking_ID`, `latitude`, `longitude`, and `timestamp` – are expected to be formed as one JSON object. Hence, the `Marshal` function is called to marshal the four values into one JSON object under the `id`, `latitude`, `longitude`, and `timestamp` fields, respectively. The resulting variable, `jsonData`, is now ready to be updated in the corresponding location history file dedicated to that sensor on MóiBit. Now, the `updateLocationHistory` function is called by passing the wallet address variable, `Tracking_ID`, along with `jsonData`. Once the latest location data is updated in MóiBit, the function returns the latest CID back to the main function as `latest_cid`. This is now used to sign a new transaction on the blockchain via the smart contract. Once the transaction is signed and placed in the Ethereum Kovan blockchain, the transaction hash is returned as `txnHash`. The same hash is suffixed to an URL for preview purposes. The resulting URL can be used to review the status of the transaction. This summarizes the `main` function.

7. Since `main` needs the geocoordinates first, it calls the `getGeoCordinates` function, which is defined as follows:

```
def getGeoCordinates():
    res = requests.post(url, data=myobj)
    geoCordinates = res.json()['location']
    lat = float("{:.7f}".format(geoCordinates['lat']))
    long = float("{:.7f}".format(geoCordinates['lng']))   return
(lat, long) # Accuracy is not considered in the POC because
optimizations are out of scope
```

From the preceding code block, we can see that the `getGeoCordinates` function is making a POST API call to the Google Maps Geolocation API, along with the credentials. The API response, `res`, is parsed to extract the latitude and longitude. You can observe that we are rounding off the decimal degrees of both values to seven places. You can also observe that we are ignoring the `accuracy` field since optimizing this solution is simply out of the scope of this book.

8. Once the `main` function receives the `lat` and `long` values, it now captures the timestamp instantly by calling the `getCurrentTime` function, which is defined as follows:

```
def getCurrentTime():
    dt = datetime.datetime.utcnow()
    timestamp = time.mktime(dt.timetuple())
    timestamp = int(timestamp)
    return timestamp
```

As you can observe from the preceding code block, the `getCurrentTime` function simply captures the UNIX timestamp based on the local time of the sensor and returns it.

9. Now that we have all the necessary data, the `main` function needs it in a presentable format for MóiBit. Hence, it calls the `Marshal` function, which is defined as follows:

```
def Marshal(Tracking_ID, lat, long, timestamp):
    data = {"id": Tracking_ID,
            "latitude": lat,
            "longitude": long,
            "timestamp": timestamp
           }   return data
```

As you can see, the `Marshal` function simply takes the four values and returns the marshaled version of the data in JSON format.

10. With the new location data of the sensor ready to be updated, the `updateLocationHistory` function is called, which is defined at this link https://github.com/PacktPublishing/Hands-On-Artificial-Intelligence-for-Blockchain/blob/master/Chapter08/iot-client-code/python/main.py:

As you can see, the `updateLocationHistory` function checks whether a dedicated file for the sensor already exists on MóiBit by calling the `checkIfFileExists` function. Based on the status value returned by the `checkIfFileExists` function, a new file is created if a dedicated file does not exist for the sensor on MóiBit. Once created, the JSON marshaled data is uploaded to the newly created file and the CID of the file is returned to the main function as `latest_cid`. However, if a dedicated file for the sensor already exists on MóiBit, the current location history of the sensor is first downloaded, and then the newly marshaled location data is appended to it. Once appended, the updated location history is now uploaded to MóiBit. As a new update to the file, the CID hash of the file with the new location data is returned to `main` as `latest_cid`.

In case of any errors, suitable response error codes are printed, along with data from the response body and headers.

11. The `checkIfFileExists` function is defined as follows:

```
def checkIfFileExists(walletAddress):
    print("checkIfFileExists(): Checking if /dictao/" +
        walletAddress+".json exists.")
    pre_payload = {"path": "/dictao/"}
    payload = json.dumps(pre_payload)
  conn.request("POST", moibit_url+"listfiles", payload,
moibit_header_obj)
    res = conn.getresponse()
    responseObject = json.loads(res.read())
    if res.status == 200:
        if responseObject['data']['Entries'] == None:
            print("checkIfFileExists(): /dictao/" +
                walletAddress+".json does not exist!")
            return False, ""
        else:
            for fileObject in responseObject['data']['Entries']:
                if walletAddress+".json" == fileObject['Name']:
                    print("checkIfFileExists(): Found
/dictao/"+walletAddress +
                        ".json "+"with the hash
"+fileObject['Hash'])
                    return True, fileObject['Hash']
    print("checkIfFileExists(): /dictao/" +
        walletAddress+".json does not exist!")
    return False, ""
```

As you can see, the `checkIfFileExists` function sweeps across the entire `dictao` folder to check whether there is a dedicated file for a sensor. Since the name of the file is the same as the wallet address, it is easier to simply pass the wallet address of the sensor and check whether a dedicated file exists for the sensor on MóiBit. If the wallet address of the calling sensor is `0xABC`, then the dedicated file for this sensor on MóiBit would be `0xABC.json`. If a file is found under the root folder, `dictao`, of your respective MóiBit developer accounts, it returns the Boolean value `True` to the `updateLocationHistory` function. If such a file does not exist, it will return `False`.

12. Finally, once the `main` function receives the updated CID hash of the location data of the sensor, it needs to maintain the proof of this location update on the blockchain. Hence, it calls the `CommitTxn` function, which is defined as follows:

```
def CommitTxn(id, cid):
    print("CommitTxn(): Connecting to the ethereum network")
    w3 = Web3(Web3.HTTPProvider(blockchain_url))
    print("CommitTxn(): Initializing the live contract instance at "
+
            os.environ['PROOF_SMART_CONTRACT_ADDRESS'])
    contract = w3.eth.contract(
        os.environ['PROOF_SMART_CONTRACT_ADDRESS'], abi=abi)

    print("CommitTxn(): Creating a raw transaction to call smart
contract function setLatestCID()")
    nonce = w3.eth.getTransactionCount(os.environ['WALLET_ADDRESS'])
    setLatestCID_txn = contract.functions.setLatestCID(
        os.environ['WALLET_ADDRESS'],
        cid,
    ).buildTransaction({
        'chainId': 42,
        'gas': 3000000,
        'gasPrice': w3.toWei('1', 'gwei'),
        'nonce': nonce,
    })
    print("CommitTxn(): Signing the raw transaction with private
key")
    signed_txn = w3.eth.account.sign_transaction(
        setLatestCID_txn,
private_key=os.environ['WALLET_PRIVATE_KEY'])
    w3.eth.sendRawTransaction(signed_txn.rawTransaction)

    tx_hash = w3.toHex(w3.keccak(signed_txn.rawTransaction))
    tx_receipt = w3.eth.waitForTransactionReceipt(tx_hash)
    print("CommitTxn(): Sucessfully updated the CID in the
blockchain. Transaction receipt:\n", tx_receipt)
    print("CommitTxn(): Checking the new/latest hash for the wallet
from blockchain: " +
contract.functions.getLatestCID(os.environ['WALLET_ADDRESS']).call(
))
    return tx_hash
```

From the preceding code block, you can see that the `CommitTxn` function is taking the wallet address and the latest cid using `id` and `CID`, respectively. The function now creates a new `web3` object connected to one of the Ethereum nodes run by Infura. Once connected to the Ethereum Kovan blockchain network, it connects to the smart contract deployed on the blockchain by passing the contract address. The contract address is also fed into the shell as `PROOF_SMART_CONTRACT_ADDRESS`, which can be read by `os.environ`. Using this address, the contract variable is initiated and points to the smart contract instance on the blockchain. Now, a new transaction is created by using the input data; that is, `id` and `CID`. The transaction is created using the `buildTransaction` call that's offered by the Python `web3` library. The `chainId` field represents the network ID of the Ethereum Kovan blockchain.

 To find out more about each parameter passed to this function, I suggest that you go through the documentation of how to send raw transactions using `web3.py` here: `https://web3py.readthedocs.io/en/stable/web3. eth.account.html#sign-a-contract-transaction`.

Once the transaction has been built, sent, and verified by the network, a receipt is obtained as `tx_receipt`. We wait for this receipt and then send the transaction hash back to the `main` function as `tx_hash` for reference purposes. This summarizes the `CommitTxn` function.

Now that the location history data has been updated and proof is available on the blockchain, let's learn how to apply AI techniques in order to predict the potential infections.

Training the model

In this section, I will walk you through all the steps needed to build a contact tracing algorithm by leveraging AI techniques. We will go through the common steps in training an AI model to predict an outcome or a value. With the help of our sample DIApp, we'll understand the 10 common steps taken when training an AI model and reapply them to our use case. We will be using Jupyter Notebook to explain each step involved.

The steps to building our AI-based contact tracing algorithm are as follows:

1. **Preparing the training dataset**: As mentioned in the previous section, the location history of each sensor is stored in a separate file under MóiBit. Each file serves as a subset of the main DataFrame and will be used to identify potential infections. The DataFrame of an individual sensor looks as follows:

	id	timestamp	latitude	longitude
0	0xF161df29a8451D5d5Ae98E9eBF5f0DB6999E65F1	2020-06-28 19:52:26	12.880172	77.784798
1	0xF161df29a8451D5d5Ae98E9eBF5f0DB6999E65F1	2020-06-28 20:52:26	12.993111	77.596512
2	0xF161df29a8451D5d5Ae98E9eBF5f0DB6999E65F1	2020-06-28 21:52:26	12.975756	77.463615
3	0xF161df29a8451D5d5Ae98E9eBF5f0DB6999E65F1	2020-06-28 22:52:26	12.974606	77.615150
4	0xF161df29a8451D5d5Ae98E9eBF5f0DB6999E65F1	2020-06-28 23:52:26	12.997514	77.706261

Fig 8.3: Location history of an individual sensor captured in Jupyter Notebook using the pandas DataFrame view

To detect potential infections and cluster the infections in an intelligent manner, we are going to use the DBSCAN algorithm.

DBSCAN is a data clustering algorithm that separates high-density data points from low-density points. The algorithm was proposed by Martin Ester, Hans-Peter Kriegel, Jörg Sander, and Xiaowei Xu in 1996. Basically, the DBSCAN algorithm clusters a group of data points that are close to each other in a certain space and ignores the outliers as noise.

In order to understand the location history and its applicability in DBSCAN, we generated a training dataset with preset random IDs, a timestamp, and lat-long values. It is not easy or safe to assign random values by ourselves. Hence, we used the **JSON Generator** tool. JSON Generator allows users to generate JSON documents with random values in a customizable manner. This is made possible by programming the JSON generator to use specific values for a given field.

We used the following syntax to generate 100 JSON objects with random values for the ID, timestamp, latitude, and longitude:

```
1    ▼  [
2    ▼      {
3    ▼          'repeat(100, 100)': {
4    ▼              id: '{{random("0xA", "0xB", "0xC", "0xD", "0xE", "0xF",
     "0xG", "0xH", "0xI", "0xJ")}}',
5    ▼              timestamp: '{{random(1593373946, 1593377546, 1593381146,
     1593384746, 1593388346, 1593391946, 1593395546, 1593399146,
     1593402746, 1593406346, 1593409946, 1593413546, 1593417146,
     1593420746, 1593424346, 1593427946, 1593431546, 1593435146,
     1593438746, 1593442346, 1593445946, 1593449546, 1593453146,
     1593456746, 1593460346)}}',
6    ▼              latitude: '{{floating(12.8794001, 13.0693001, 7)}}',
7    ▼              longitude: '{{floating(77.4451001, 77.7982001, 7)}}'
8                }
9            }
10   ]
```

Fig 8.4: Schema required to generate a training dataset on JSON Generator

As shown in the preceding screenshot, the schema specifies all four attributes desired in the dataset. Since this is a dataset, the `id` attribute has a set of dummy wallet addresses. The `timestamp` attribute also has a set of UNIX timestamps ranging between 24 hours with at least a 1-hour gap between each other. Finally, the `latitude` and `longitude` attributes have also been specified to take any value between the specified minimum and maximum values at a precision of seven decimal places.

From the preceding schema, we can generate exactly 100 random JSON objects. However, this may not be enough. Hence, I regenerated some more random JSON objects to form a training dataset consisting of 1,000 JSON objects. I concatenated the 100 JSON objects that were generated by the preceding schema repeatedly 10 times. The resulting dataset is an array of 1,000 random JSON objects.

The resulting dataset can be viewed on Jupyter Notebook by executing the `head()` function of the `pandas` library, as follows:

```
In [1]: import pandas as pd

In [5]: df = pd.read_json('/home/username/folder/train_dataset.json')

In [9]: df.head()

Out[9]:
              id         timestamp      latitude   longitude

        0    0xE   2020-06-29 02:52:26   12.968631   77.524636

        1    0xG   2020-06-29 08:52:26   12.968631   77.524636

        2    0xA   2020-06-29 08:52:26   13.064601   77.537578

        3    0xA   2020-06-29 07:52:26   12.927443   77.724200

        4    0xD   2020-06-29 07:52:26   13.016827   77.640742
```

Fig 8.5: Output of the df.head() function call on Jupyter Notebook

From the preceding screenshot, we can see that a training dataset has been created and read on Jupyter Notebook.

2. **Analyzing the training dataset**: Now that we have created a training dataset with random values and loaded it into Jupyter Notebook, we shall analyze it a bit further to understand the dataset. This process is called analyzing the training dataset. This step helps us understand more about the nature of the data points and how they are distributed.

First, we begin the analysis by describing how to get topline information about the dataset. We do this by calling the `info` function:

```
In [7]: df.info()
        <class 'pandas.core.frame.DataFrame'>
        RangeIndex: 1001 entries, 0 to 1000
        Data columns (total 4 columns):
         #   Column     Non-Null Count  Dtype
        ---  ------     --------------  -----
         0   id         1001 non-null   object
         1   timestamp  1001 non-null   datetime64[ns]
         2   latitude   1001 non-null   float64
         3   longitude  1001 non-null   float64
        dtypes: datetime64[ns](1), float64(2), object(1)
        memory usage: 31.4+ KB
```

Fig 8.6: Output of the df.info() function call on Jupyter Notebook

From the preceding screenshot, we can observe that there are 1,001 entries in the dataset. The output of the `info` function call also lists all the columns in the DataFrame, including their types. It also checks whether there are any null values. Since our schema for JSON Generator was very specific, we do not have any null values in any rows of the DataFrame.

Next, we need to understand the distribution of the data points by tasking pandas with describing the dataset using the `describe()` function:

```
In [11]: df.describe()
Out[11]:
                  latitude      longitude
         count  1001.000000   1001.000000
          mean    12.973009     77.621612
           std     0.054532      0.101059
           min    12.879612     77.445554
           25%    12.925427     77.535446
           50%    12.973943     77.616680
           75%    13.019113     77.709591
           max    13.069226     77.798141
```

Fig 8.7: Output of the df.describe() function call on Jupyter Notebook

From the preceding screenshot, we can observe the statistical summary of the same DataFrame. We can see that `count` represents the total number of non-null rows in the training DataFrame, `df`. `mean` represents the average values of the latitude and longitude columns at around 12.973009 and 77.621612, respectively. `min` represents the minimum latitude and longitude value ever recorded in the DataFrame at 12.879612 and 77.445554, respectively. `max` represents the maximum latitude and longitude value ever recorded in the DataFrame at 13.069226 and 77.798141, respectively. Although `count`, `mean`, `min`, and `max` highlight the boundaries, they do not explain the distribution of data points. However, the distribution of the data points can be understood by the `std`, `25%`, `50%`, and `75%` parameters. Let's understand what they mean.

`std` numerically represents how far the latitude and longitude values are from the mean latitude and longitude value. In this case, the values are 0.054532 and 0.101059, respectively. The `std` values are so low in our training dataset because of the minimum and maximum value range we have entered into our JSON Generator schema. Although it looks like all the rows in the DataFrame are close enough, each of them is placed kilometers away from one another due to a change or shift in one decimal degree as well.

If the `df` DataFrame were to be sorted, the first 250 columns of the DataFrame would have latitude values ranging from 12.879612 to 12.925427. Similarly, the longitude values would be ranging from 77.445554 to 77.535446. This is represented by the resulting parameter, `25%`. The same can be interpreted for the remaining parameters – `50%`, `75%`, and `max` – by cascading 250 rows while analyzing.

It is also important to note that the summary is helpful in understanding whether the data points are distributed enough.

3. **Feature engineering**: Feature engineering usually involves identifying critical data points, transforming the data points, and grooming them for a better analysis. Since there are no missing values or NaN values in our dataset, we will not be performing any featuring engineering on our dataset.

4. **Exploratory data analysis**: Next, we will try to visually analyze our dataset. Since we are dealing with geographic data, it is better to understand the data points by plotting them against a real map. We are going to be using the Plotly library to plot the lat-long coordinates on a real map. By doing so, we'll obtain the following visualization:

```
In [42]: import pandas as pd
         df = pd.read_json('/home/username/folder/train_dataset.json')

         import plotly.express as px

         fig = px.scatter_mapbox(df, lat="latitude", lon="longitude", zoom=3, height=300)
         fig.update_layout(
             mapbox_style="white-bg",
             mapbox_layers=[
                 {
                     "below": 'traces',
                     "sourcetype": "raster",
                     "source": [
                         "https://basemap.nationalmap.gov/arcgis/rest/services/USGSImageryOnly/MapServer/tile/{z}/{y}/{x}"
                     ]
                 }
             ])
         fig.update_layout(margin={"r":0,"t":0,"l":0,"b":0})
         fig.show()
```

Fig 8.8: Graphical output of the datapoints on Jupyter Notebook using Plotly

From the preceding screenshot, we can see that all the data points are being plotted across many areas in Bengaluru city. This is because of the limits we have set in our training dataset. As you can see, we have manually set the limitations for the latitude and longitude in the JSON Generator schema. Hence, we cannot see any other data points beyond the city limits of Bengaluru. While trying out this tutorial, you may wish to change it as per your requirements and mention a city-specific lat-long range or keep it very wide open in your JSON Generator schema.

Apart from plotting the lat-long data on a map, we can also analyze the data points using a scatterplot. Under a scatterplot, we plot the lat-long values on a two-dimensional graph, with the x axis representing the latitude and the y axis representing the longitude.

Now, let's take a look at a simpler version of a scatterplot on our training dataset:

```
In [65]: import matplotlib.pyplot as plt
         import seaborn as sns
         %matplotlib inline
```

```
In [67]: plt.figure(figsize=(12,6))
         sns.scatterplot(x = 'latitude', y = 'longitude', data = df, hue = 'id')
         plt.legend(bbox_to_anchor = [1, 0.8])
```

Out[67]: <matplotlib.legend.Legend at 0x7f5e1c6cd890>

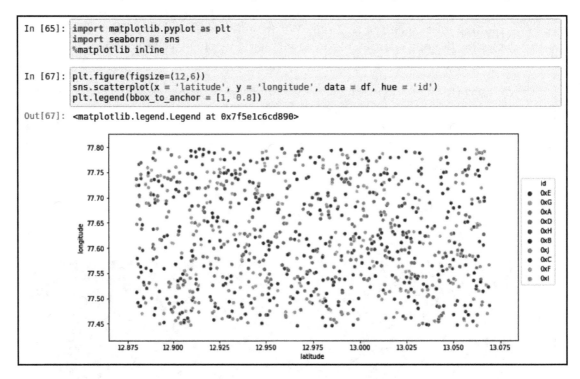

Fig 8.9: The scatterplot's output of the datapoints on Jupyter Notebook using Seaborn

From the preceding screenshot, we can observe the location history of all 10 IDs randomly scattered across the geographic space. Each color represents an ID, while all the colored dots on the graph represent its corresponding location history. You can get more creative by applying more parametric filters and also performing analysis using other charts, including, but not limited to, box plot, joint plot, heatmap, and so on.

To find out more about visualizing your training dataset, I recommend that you use Seaborn and Plotly. To learn more about Seaborn, visit `https://seaborn.pydata.org/`. To learn more about Plotly, visit `https://plotly.com/`.

5. **Splitting the training dataset**: Most of the time, we split the training dataset into two parts. One part is used to train the model, while the other part is used to predict the values and compare the predicted values with the actual values in the training dataset. Since we are clustering the data and not using regression-based models to actually predict a value, there is no need to split our training dataset.

6. **Selecting the model**: When it comes to performing digital contact tracing for animals and objects, one approach is to use clustering algorithms that can provide customizations as per the new-found medical data and approaches. Although there are many clustering approaches, such as K-means, hierarchical clustering, and density-based clustering, we chose density-based clustering in this sample application as it is simple to understand and also offers some customizations that can be applied for practical use cases.

K-means clustering is also easy to understand but it generally does not have a strong reputation when it comes to analyzing geocoordinates and spatial data. Although hierarchical clustering can help us analyze spatial data, it does not offer an easy learning curve like DBSCAN does.

We are going to use the DBSCAN algorithm for this, which is available under the scikit-learn machine learning library.

For more information about the features that are available, visit the following link: `https://scikit-learn.org/stable/modules/generated/sklearn.cluster.DBSCAN.html`.

7. **Training and fitting**: Now that we have created the training dataset, analyzed it, and visualized it, we need to use the training dataset to train our model using the DBSCAN algorithm to cluster the data points and identify them distinctly.

As per the medical norms accepted by many practitioners globally, it is a popular opinion that we can contract coronavirus if people are not maintaining the minimum safety distance of at least 6 feet. So, we are assuming the same accepted metric for physical distancing and creating our model so that it clusters data points that are connected to each other whose distance is less than or equal to 6 feet.

Based on the criteria we've discussed so far, we'll define the model using Jupyter Notebook as follows:

```
In [99]: epsilon = 0.0018288 # a radial distance of 6 feet, which is medically presribed
         min_sample = 2

         model = DBSCAN(eps=epsilon, min_samples=min_sample, metric='haversine').fit(df[['latitude', 'longitude']])
         df['cluster'] = model.labels_.tolist()

         labels = model.labels_
         fig = plt.figure(figsize=(20, 15))
         sns.scatterplot(df['latitude'], df['longitude'], hue=["cluster-{}".format(x) for x in labels])

Out[99]: <matplotlib.axes._subplots.AxesSubplot at 0x7f5e17c0f650>
```

Fig 8.10: Initiating the DBSCAN model with the training dataset

From the preceding screenshot, we can observe that a `model` has been initiated based on the DBSCAN algorithm. The inputs given to the DBSCAN algorithm are the training dataset, `df`, itself. Along with df, the `epsilon` variable is also sent. `Epsilon` is the maximum distance between any two given data points. We choose 0.0018288 as the value of the `epsilon` variable since it is the kilometer equivalent of 6 feet. This is a crucial parameter while setting up a DBSCAN-based model. Along with `epsilon`, the `min_sample` variable is also sent to the DBSCAN algorithm to initiate the model. `min_sample` defines the minimum number of data points that need to be present within the `epsilon` radius to form a cluster. We chose 2 as the value of the `min_sample` variable since it takes a minimum of two actors to spread the infection.

Finally, we need to choose the metric function, based on which the distance between the data points is calculated. Since we are working on geographic coordinates, we chose `haversine` as the metric function to calculate the distance between the data points to form the cluster.

> To find out more about the haversine geographic distance formula, visit the following Wikipedia article: https://en.wikipedia.org/wiki/Haversine_formula.

Once the model has been initialized, the clusters are formed and assigned to the respective data points by us adding the new column, called `cluster`, to the training dataset. You can now see that the same DataFrame is updated with one more column cluster, as shown in the following screenshot:

```
In [119]: df.head()
Out[119]:
```

	id	timestamp	latitude	longitude	cluster
0	0xE	2020-06-29 02:52:26	12.968631	77.524636	0
1	0xG	2020-06-29 08:52:26	12.968631	77.524636	0
2	0xA	2020-06-29 08:52:26	13.064601	77.537578	-1
3	0xA	2020-06-29 07:52:26	12.927443	77.724200	-1
4	0xD	2020-06-29 07:52:26	13.016827	77.640742	1

Fig 8.11: Reading the updated contents of the DataFrame with the new column cluster by using the df.head() function call on Jupyter Notebook

When the clusters are plotted on the graph with the *x* axis representing latitude and the *y* axis representing the longitude, this results in the following:

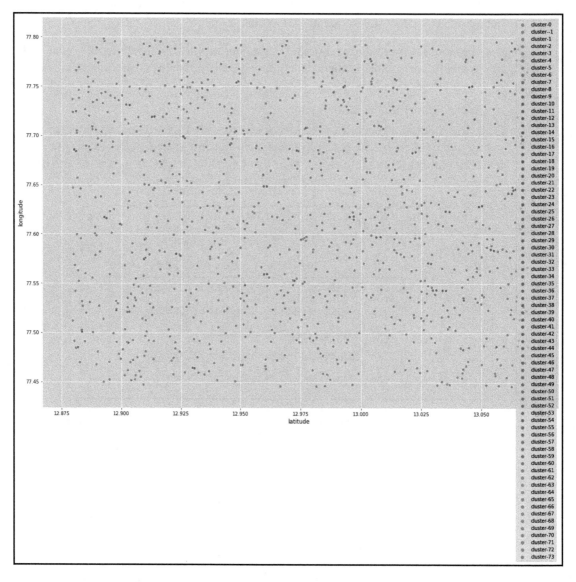

Fig 8.12: Scatterplotting all the clusters, including noise

From the preceding plotted graph, we can observe that there are 74 normal clusters ranging from **cluster-0** to **cluster-73**. It is also important to observe that there is one more cluster that goes by the name **cluster--1**, which represents all the data points that do not belong to any cluster. Such data points are considered **noise** and hence they are irrelevant to our further efforts in contact tracing. Noise data points occur if the sensors were attached to animals or objects that have likely been isolated and have not interacted with another animal or object wearing a sensor.

It is difficult to analyze the data since there's so much noise in the preceding graph, so let's go ahead and remove all the data points in the DataFrame that are considered noise.

We can remove the noise and replot the graph as follows:

```
In [131]:  epsilon = 0.0018288 # a radial distance of 6 feet, which is medically presribed
           min_sample = 2

           model = DBSCAN(eps=epsilon, min_samples=min_sample, metric='haversine').fit(df[['latitude', 'longitude']])
           df['cluster'] = model.labels_.tolist()
           ids = df[(df['cluster'] == -1)].index
           df.drop(ids, inplace=True)

           labels = model.labels_
           fig = plt.figure(figsize=(20, 15))
           sns.scatterplot(df['latitude'], df['longitude'], hue=["cluster-{}".format(x) for x in labels])

Out[131]:  <matplotlib.axes._subplots.AxesSubplot at 0x7f5e150848d0>
```

Fig 8.13: Removing the noise cluster before plotting again

From the preceding screenshot, we can observe that we have dropped all the rows that belonged to **cluster -1**.

The resulting graph is cleaner and can be observed as follows:

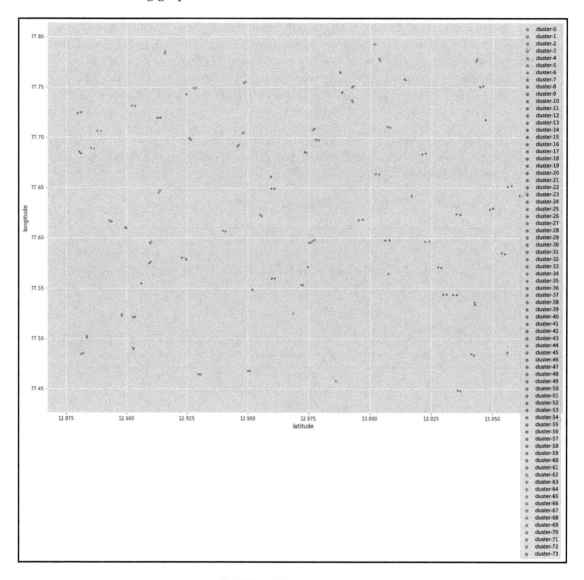

Fig 8.14: Replotting the clusters without noise

From the preceding screenshot, you can observe that the DBSCAN model has been successfully initiated with the configured parameters. Now, let's check the accuracy of the model.

8. **Evaluating the model**: Usually, prediction models use logistic regressors or classifiers. But in our sample application, we are not predicting any new values; we're simply using machine learning to split the data into smaller, customized clusters.

Now that we have been able to split the dataset into clusters of two or more data points, we need to check whether the clustering is working effectively. In simpler terms, we need to check the basic correctness of the model. In our case, we can perform a basic evaluation by checking whether the model is generating any false positives; that is, we need to check whether the model is clustering two or more data points whose haversine distance is more than the specified distance. If such data points are grouped under one new cluster, we can easily conclude that the model has its limitations with false positives. Similarly, we also need to check whether the model is prone to false negatives; that is, we need to check whether the model is clustering two or more data points whose haversine distance is less than the specified valid distance, but the model fails to recognize it as a potential infection by not clustering them together. Due to the limited scope of this book, we will conclude by making one observation that the current model seems to be generating false positives for data points up to 10 meters in haversine distance. As far as false negatives are concerned, we have not observed such anomalies or limitations.

9. **Tuning the parameters**: There are only three main input parameters that are required by the DBSCAN algorithm. They are `epsilon`, `min_sample`, and the haversine metric function. Apart from these parameters, you can also add some more parameters when you are trying this solution on your system.

 For more information regarding the other parameters, visit the documentation at the following link: `https://scikit-learn.org/stable/modules/generated/sklearn.cluster.DBSCAN.html`.

Due to the limited scope of this book, I will not be focusing on the optimization of the model since it does a decent job with clustering as-is.

10. **Predicting infections**: The model is now ready to take live data from MóiBit and predict the potential infections by clustering the data points using the preceding parameters. Of course, the model will be prone to some false positives for neighboring data points of up to 10 meters as it is not fully tuned. It is out of the scope of this book to only focus on optimizing the AI component of the sample solution.

All the screenshots in this section have been borrowed from Madhusudhan Kumble's Jupyter Notebook. The complete implementation of the notebook is available on his GitHub: `https://github.com/madatpython/PRANA/blob/packt/prana_contact_tracing_using_DBSCAN.ipynb`.

Now that we understand how to apply the DBSCAN algorithm to our use case and we have developed a fair understanding of its limitations, let's incorporate this model in the backend API.

Developing the backend

In this section, we will be discussing the design and structure of the contact tracing backend API. The backend API is responsible for performing contact tracing by reading a wallet address and returning the wallet addresses of any other potentially infected sensors.

Similar to sensor application code, I will be implementing the contact tracing backend API in the Python language as it is easier to bridge the language gaps between the AI, IoT, and blockchain communities.

As usual, we start by noting down all the `import` statements that are necessary for proceeding with the API's development:

```python
import os
import sys
import flask
from flask import request, jsonify
from web3 import Web3
import web3
import json
import http
from flask_cors import CORS
import datetime as dt
import pandas as pd
from sklearn.cluster import DBSCAN
```

Please make sure that you have all the external packages installed through the `pip install` command.

To develop the contact tracing backend API, I will be using the Flask framework. You can read more about the Flask web application framework here: `https://flask.palletsprojects.com/en/1.1.x/`.

We initiate the API by defining the `flask` web app, as follows:

```
app = flask.Flask(__name__)
CORS(app)
app.config["DEBUG"] = True
```

As you can see, the API is allowing any source on the internet to query the API. This is made possible by using `CORS(app)`. Also, I have set the app to debug mode to help you get more exposure to the API as you follow these instructions.

The entry point to this API script is made by using the following instruction in the script:

```
app.run()
```

For those of you who are not familiar with the Flask framework, this is equivalent to the `main` function, which we discussed when we looked at the IoT client code for sensors.

Similar to other programs, this API is also manifested in a single-file Python script. As such, we will have to use a few variables.

Let's look at them in the following code block:

```
blockchain_url = 'https://kovan.infura.io/v3/' + \
    os.environ['WEB3_INFURA_PROJECT_ID']

abi = """[{"anonymous": false,"inputs": [{"indexed": false,"internalType":
"address","name": "deviceID","type": "address"},{"indexed":
false,"internalType": "string","name": "latestCID","type":
"string"}],"name": "MappingUpdated","type": "event"},{"inputs":
[{"internalType": "address","name": "deviceID","type":
"address"},{"internalType": "string","name": "latestCID","type":
"string"}],"name": "setLatestCID","outputs": [],"stateMutability":
"nonpayable","type": "function"},{"inputs": [],"name":
"getDeviceIDsLength","outputs": [{"internalType": "uint256","name":
"","type": "uint256"}],"stateMutability": "view","type":
"function"},{"inputs": [{"internalType": "uint256","name": "index","type":
"uint256"}],"name": "getIDByIndex","outputs": [{"internalType":
"address","name": "","type": "address"}],"stateMutability": "view","type":
"function"},{"inputs": [{"internalType": "address","name":
"deviceID","type": "address"}],"name": "getLatestCID","outputs":
[{"internalType": "string","name": "latestCID","type":
"string"}],"stateMutability": "view","type": "function"}]"""
```

As you can observe from the preceding code block, we are using the same techniques as that of a sensor application in order to access the blockchain network and access the smart contract through the ABI.

Similarly, we also reuse the variables needed for interacting with MóiBit:

```
conn = http.client.HTTPSConnection("kfs2.moibit.io")
moibit_url = 'https://kfs2.moibit.io/moibit/v0/'
moibit_header_obj = {
    'api_key': os.environ['MOIBIT_API_KEY'],
    'api_secret': os.environ['MOIBIT_API_SECRET'],
    'content-type': "application/json"
}
```

As you can observe from the preceding code block, the same variables are used to access resources from MóiBit. Unlike the sensor application, the variables will be used in this script to read the location history of each sensor and build a dataset for further analysis. To summarize, all these variables are used for read-only purposes.

When the script is run, it procedurally falls back to the home function defined, as follows:

```
@app.route('/', methods=['GET'])
def home():
    return "<h1>DICTAO - Decentralized Intelligent Contact Tracing of
Animals and Objects</h1><p>This is a simple demonstration of applying
blockchain, decentralized storage and AI to solve the COVID-19 crisis.</p>"
```

As the name suggests, the `home` function is a handler function used to respond to the `GET`-based API requests made to the root of the API. In this case, I am returning simple HTML content.

To make sure that we send a proper response for any illicit request or invalid requests, we have defined the `page_not_found` handler function, as follows:

```
@app.errorhandler(404)
def page_not_found(e):
    return "The given ID could not be found", 404
```

As shown in the preceding code block, this function returns a string response along with an HTTP response code 404 back to the client, which means **file/resource not found**.

Apart from illicit or invalid client requests, we also need to cover some of the internal errors that may occur. This can be achieved by defining the `internal_server_error` function, as follows:

```
@app.errorhandler(500)
def internal_server_error(e):
    return e, 500
```

As shown in the preceding code block, when an `internal_server_error` function is called by the API program, along with an error or an exception, the same will be returned to the client, along with the HTTP response code 500, which means an internal error occurred on the server.

Now that we have covered the API by designing the contingent communications, let's focus on the main logic of the API program. Our API will respond to requests made by web clients at the `/api/v0/get_infections` endpoint. For example, if the API is hosted at `example.com`, then the API calls must be sent to the following URL: `https://example.com/api/v0/get_infections`.

Now, let's continue with the logic that supports such API calls. Here is the code link `https://github.com/PacktPublishing/Hands-On-Artificial-Intelligence-for-Blockchain/blob/master/Chapter08/backend-contact-tracing/server.py`:

A new app router is now set up for the `/api/v0/get_infections` endpoint. The type of API calls accepted by this router has been set to `GET`. This means that there is a response from the server being waited on by the web client. `get_infections` is the handler function responsible for handling the API calls landing at the said endpoint. As you may be able to predict from the code, `get_infections` is returning a list of potentially infected wallet addresses back to the web client.

 A wallet address is communicated as `ID` in this section as it aligns with the design of the backend and that of the dataset.

When the API receives the wallet address from the web client, it is checked for any possible corruption or loss of data. If the received ID is not an empty string, then the API makes the next move by retrieving all the wallet addresses registered on the smart contract. For each wallet address registered in the smart contract, the latest location history CID of each wallet is retrieved from the blockchain. Furthermore, each CID is used to retrieve the location history data of each registered sensor from MóiBit.

The corresponding code can be seen in the following code block:

```
def getLatestCID(id):
    w3 = Web3(Web3.HTTPProvider(blockchain_url))
    contract = w3.eth.contract(
        os.environ['PROOF_SMART_CONTRACT_ADDRESS'], abi=abi)
    cid = ""
    try:
        cid = contract.functions.getLatestCID(id).call()
    except web3.exceptions.ValidationError:
```

```
                print("ID does not exist!")

                return ""
        except:
            print("Some other error occured!")
            return ""
        else:
            print(cid)
            return cid
```

From the preceding code block, you can observe that the `getLatestCID` function is used to fetch the latest CIDs of the respective wallet addresses of the sensors, once the `get_infections` function retrieves each and every wallet address. The CID value read from the mapping in the smart contract is returned to the caller function, `get_infections`.

Now that the `get_infections` handle function contains the CID hashes of the corresponding wallet addresses of each and every registered sensor, it is used to retrieve the location history data from MóiBit, as follows:

```
def getJsonDataFromMoiBit(cid):
    pre_payload = {"hash": cid}
    payload = json.dumps(pre_payload)
    conn.request("POST", moibit_url+"readfilebyhash",
                payload, moibit_header_obj)
    res = conn.getresponse()
    if res.status == 200:
        responseObject = json.loads(res.read())
        print(
            "updateLocationHistory(): Appending the captured data to
historic data.")
        return responseObject
```

From the preceding code block, you can see that the retrieved `cid` from the `getLatestCID` function is passed along to the `getJsonDataFromMoiBit` function. This CID is used to retrieve the latest location history data of the corresponding sensors.

Now that the data is available for analysis, the AI-based contact tracing algorithm we designed in the previous section comes into the picture.

The AI model is incorporated in the following function:

```
def get_infected_ids(input_id):
    basePath = os.path.dirname(os.path.abspath('live_dataset.json'))
    dflive = pd.read_json(basePath + '/' + 'live_dataset.json')

    epsilon = 0.0018288 # a radial distance of 6 feet, which is medically
presribed
```

```
    min_sample = 2
  model = DBSCAN(eps=epsilon, min_samples=2,
metric='haversine').fit(dflive[['latitude', 'longitude']])
    dflive['cluster'] = model.labels_.tolist()

    input_id_clusters = []
    for i in range(len(dflive)):
        if dflive['id'][i] == input_id:
            if dflive['cluster'][i] in input_id_clusters:
                pass
            else:
                input_id_clusters.append(dflive['cluster'][i])

    infected_ids = []
    for cluster in input_id_clusters:
        if cluster != -1:
            ids_in_cluster = dflive.loc[dflive['cluster'] == cluster, 'id']
            for i in range(len(ids_in_cluster)):
                member_id = ids_in_cluster.iloc[i]
                if (member_id not in infected_ids) and (member_id !=
input_id):
                    infected_ids.append(member_id)
            else:
                    pass
    return infected_ids
```

As you can see, the `get_infected_ids` function can be called to fetch all the potentially infected IDs. When called, this function basically clusters the live dataset generated at runtime and checks whether the given ID exists in any of the clusters. If the IDs exist in the cluster, all the neighboring IDs are considered to be affected by the coronavirus infection. Each neighboring ID in the same cluster is appended to an array and the search for the potentially infected IDs continues until the function reaches the last cluster. Once the potentially infected IDs have been identified, they are returned to the caller function, `get_infections`.

Developing the frontend

In this section, we will discuss the design and structure of the contact tracing dashboard web application. In short, let's call it the dashboard. The purpose of the dashboard is to help us identify all the potentially infected IDs by entering the ID or wallet address of the suspected sensor that may be attached to an animal or an object.

The dashboard application is simply composed of two components: an Express server that hosts the static files and an index.html HTML file that reads the input from a user, calls the contact tracing API, and prints all IDs returned by the backend API.

The dashboard web server code is as follows:

```
const express = require('express')
const app = express()
const port = 3000
app.use(express.static('public'));
app.get('/', (req, res) => res.send('Welcome to DICTAO: Contact tracing web app!'))
app.listen(port, () => console.log(`DICTAO: Contact tracing web app listening at http://localhost:${port}`))
```

As you can observe from the preceding code block, this is a simple Express-based Node.js application that starts a web server locally at port 3000 and starts hosting the index.html file for users who visit the root of the server. The web server also logs all the requests made by the clients.

You can visit the markup code for the dashboard at https://github.com/ PacktPublishing/Hands-On-Artificial-Intelligence-for-Blockchain/blob/master/ Chapter08/frontend-tracking-dashboard/public/index.html:

From the preceding code block, we can observe that the markup code, index.html, is hosting a simple form to take the wallet address of the suspected sensor as input from the user. The input is confirmed when the user clicks the submit button. On clicking the submit button, the JavaScript getInfectedIDs function is called. Now, the getInfectedIDs function is responsible for performing basic form validations and alerting the user in case of any faulty inputs. If not, the function is responsible for calling the contact tracing backend API to retrieve the list of potentially infected sensors. If it receives a non-null response from the API, it populates the received IDs or wallet addresses in a table.

Now, let's go take a look at some of the testing tools available to test our sample DIApp.

Testing the sample DIApp

Unfortunately, due to the limited scope of this book, we cannot cover too much on testing, so I will point you to some relevant resources in this section.

- **Testing smart contracts**: Truffle is one of the most renowned toolchains for Solidity smart contract development. You can follow the test instructions mentioned in their documentation, which are available at the following link: `https://www.trufflesuite.com/docs/truffle/testing/testing-your-contracts`.

- **Testing sensor implementation**: The sensor application is implemented using basic Python programming skills. You may have already observed that the script interacts with the Google Maps Geolocation API, Ethereum, and MóiBit. Hence, I suggest that you heavily test the HTTP client code. I highly encourage you to perform unit testing with as many test cases as possible. You can learn all about testing basic Python code by viewing the Python documentation that's available at the following link: `https://docs.python-guide.org/writing/tests/`.

- **Testing the AI model for accuracy**: Testing the AI models with **Mean Absolute Error (MAE)** is pretty simple and straightforward. However, we are not using regressors or classifiers in our sample DIApp. Hence, I urge you to play with the dataset by adding new data points so that you can manually verify the results. You can check whether the model responds with a false positive or false negative in such edge cases. This is your opportunity to get fluent with geospatial analysis! Finding content for calculating the accuracy of unsupervised clustering algorithms is pretty rare in my experience.

  However, there are a few resources that are hidden gems. I recommend that you read `https://www.cs.kent.edu/~jin/DM08/ClusterValidation.pdf` to understand more about measuring the accuracy of clustering algorithms through various approaches. You can also visit the scikit-learn documentation, which highlights some aspects of clustering performance: `https://scikit-learn.org/stable/modules/clustering.html#clustering-performance-evaluation`.

- **Testing the contact tracing backend API**: Since we have written our API using the Flask framework, I highly recommend that you visit the official testing documentation of Flask for more information on testing Flask web applications: `https://flask.palletsprojects.com/en/1.1.x/testing/`. I suggest that you test each route with more than one test case for each route and handler function defined in the script.

- **Testing the web dashboard frontend app**: Finally, the frontend web application is a simple piece of implementation. As there isn't much to test on the Node.js side, I suggest that you test the inline JavaScript function in `index.html` to get better form validation, pagination, and other edge cases that can make the UX better while you're presenting it.

Now that you have a basic understanding of testing tools and techniques, let's deploy the sample DIApp solution.

Deploying the sample DIApp

So far in this chapter, we have been able to explain the problem statement, design a solution for addressing the problem, build the solution, and also make some recommendations regarding testing. The whole effort will be fruitful if you deploy this application on your own. Hence, in the following sections, I will be suggesting that you sign up for the appropriate services that are needed to deploy this sample DIApp. I will also instruct you to set up your local system with another important special piece of configuration management software required to run these programs.

Signing up for the Google Maps API

As you know, we use the Google Maps Geolocation API to get the current lat-long coordinates of the sensor. Hence, please follow the instructions in the following documentation and get yourself an API key: `https://developers.google.com/maps/premium/apikey/geolocation-apikey`. Make sure that you do not share your API key with anyone. It is also important that you do not disseminate the API key on open source code hosting platforms. If your API key is exposed and still valid, someone could exploit this credential, and this will surprise you with a fat invoice. If you think that your API key may be exposed, you can delete or disable it and regenerate a new one for our sample DIApp.

Signing up for MóiBit

As you know, we use the MóiBit decentralized file storage API to store the location history data of each sensor. Hence, you are required to sign up for the MóiBit API. The signup process for MóiBit is very straightforward. You can sign up for MóiBit at the following link: `https://account.moibit.io/#/signup`. Once you've verified your email address and your password, a new API key will be generated for you.

Using these credentials, you are expected to create a new folder under the root folder. Please create a new folder there and name it `dictao`, as it is hardcoded into our current implementation. This makes sure that all the files will be persisted in a dedicated folder. This will also help you use MóiBit for other applications without any hassle or clutter. Again, make sure that your API key is not visible or accessible to the public.

Signing up for Infura

We use Infura to connect to the Ethereum Kovan blockchain. You need to create a new Infura account and create a new project. Once you've created a new project, you will need to copy the credentials for the project and use them to get dedicated access to the blockchain using Infura's infrastructure. The registration process for Infura is also pretty straightforward. You can sign up for an Infura account here: `https://infura.io/register`.

Updating your local justfile

As you may have already observed, we use a lot of credentials in our sample DIApp. To ensure that these credentials are safely managed, I suggest that you manage an isolated file on the host that can privately share these credentials to the respective processes. To achieve this, we will be using the `just` command. You can install the `just` command by following the instructions available on GitHub: `https://github.com/casey/just#installation`. Please follow the installation instructions that fit your system the best, and make sure that you create a `justfile`, which is untracked by the `git` protocol. This is possible by adding the name justfile to the `.gitignore` file.

Fill in the necessary fields by replacing the question marks with the appropriate credentials for the services you have now signed up for:

```
export GMAPS_API_KEY := "?"
export MOIBIT_API_KEY := "?"
export MOIBIT_API_SECRET := "?"
export WEB3_INFURA_PROJECT_ID := "?"
export PROOF_SMART_CONTRACT_ADDRESS := "?"
export WALLET_PRIVATE_KEY := "?"
export WALLET_ADDRESS := "?"

run-client:
    python iot-client-code/python/main.py

run-web:
    cd frontend-tracking-dashboard && node index.js
```

```
run-server:
    python backend-contact-tracing/server.py

install-dependencies:
    pip install --user -r requirements.txt
    cd frontend-tracking-dashboard && npm install
```

Depending on where you write the source code, you may need to change the relative paths of the source code files as well. Just make sure that the justfile is in the root of a project folder where you manage all the source code for this chapter.

Now, your **justfile** is ready to launch the necessary applications, along with your credentials.

Deploying smart contracts

Paste the final smart contract code into `https://remix.ethereum.org/` and deploy the contract on the Ethereum Kovan testnet blockchain. If you are not very familiar with the Remix IDE or smart contract development, I recommend that you follow the instructions provided in the official Remix documentation, which is available here: `https://remix-ide.readthedocs.io/en/latest/create_deploy.html`.

Deploying client code into sensors

In this section, I will show you how to deploy the sensor application. You can deploy the sensor application by running the `just` command, as follows:

```
just run-client
```

If the credentials entered by you are valid and under the service quota, your client application will run. Also, make sure that the relative path to the Python script is updated in the **justfile**.

Deploying the backend API

In this section, I will help you launch the contact tracing backend API. You can deploy the contact tracing backend API by running the `just` command, as follows:

```
just run-server
```

If the credentials entered by you are valid and under the service quota, your backend API will run. Also, make sure that the relative path to the Python script is updated in the **justfile**.

Deploying the web dashboard

In this section, I will help you launch the frontend web dashboard, which can be used to query the backend for any potential infections. You can deploy the web dashboard application by running the `just` command, as follows:

```
just run-web
```

If the credentials entered by you are valid and under the service quota, your dashboard application will run. Also, make sure that the relative path to the Node.js script is updated in the **justfile**.

If you are confused about the setup process or the code, you can find the complete implementation, including the justfile template, at the following GitHub link: `https://github.com/PacktPublishing/Hands-On-Artificial-Intelligence-for-Blockchain/tree/master/Chapter08`. Add your credentials in the appropriate fields of the justfile, and you should be able to deploy easily. Feel free to raise an issue if you find difficulties in understanding the code or running it. You can also propose improvements to the branch by forking the repo and creating a pull request with your suggested changes.

Retrospecting the sample DIApp

In this section, we will try to analyze the pros and cons of the proposed sample DIApp.

Merits of the sample DIApp

Here are some of the merits of our proposed sample DIApp solution:

- It covers other agents of infection, apart from humans.
- It helps in restoring the global economy and normalcy.
- It allows insurance companies and organizations to assess supply chain risks.

However, there are some limitations in the sample DIApp we must acknowledge and understand.

Limitations of the sample DIApp

Here are some of the limitations in our proposed sample DIApp solution:

- The AI algorithm can be prone to some false positives. Optimization will be needed.
- Due to a lack of hardware precision, software accuracy, and a better approach to computational complexity, the current implementation of the DIApp cannot be used in production.
- The DIApp is unable to trace infections indoors as GPS is unable to identify the floor that the sensor is currently placed in. Other alternatives such as Wi-Fi, Bluetooth, a manual check-in register, and CCTV image analysis can be considered to boost the accuracy of the model.

Now, let's look at some future enhancements.

Future enhancements

I think that the proposed sample DIApp is simply the beginning of a new revolution. You can consider making the following enhancements to the code:

- Better precision with other modes of input, apart from GPS
- Better accuracy by optimizing the models to prevent false positives
- Better data retention management for preserving privacy
- Installing beacons to develop a heat map and assessing risks

You can always reach out to me on GitHub by creating new issues for each of the suggestions or by participating in existing issue threads.

Summary

Both AI and blockchain are major technologies that are catalyzing the pace of innovation. The combination of these two technologies is expected to redesign the whole industrial paradigm. This chapter has articulated how we can empower blockchain and its decentralized applications using various AI techniques and models. We covered the evolution of applications and contrasted different types. We also explained the latest problems caused by the COVID-19 pandemic and discussed how to tackle these problems by taking contact tracing as an example use case. We covered the problem statement, the solution approach, and the technical architecture in order to develop a sample contact tracing application using the DIApp design pattern. We also highlighted the tools needed to test each solution component and make it more robust. Finally, we explained how to sign up for each of the dependent services used by the solution. This chapter has enabled you to develop a paradigm of thinking where you combine both AI and blockchain technologies to bring about productive and robust applications aimed at the next generation of the internet.

If the DIApp tutorial in this chapter has inspired you, I highly recommend that you contribute what you've learned to a live use case called Tracy. Tracy is a privacy-preserving mobile application suite that offers many features to citizens, businesses, and government authorities so that they can handle the COVID-19 pandemic and beyond. To find out more about how you can contribute to Tracy, please join the telegram community at, `https://telegram.me/ProjectTracy`.

In the next chapter, we will cover some of the potential use cases of building DIApps, where blockchain, AI, and decentralized storage can be used to address challenging problems.

9
The Future of AI with Blockchain

"Let's walk the talk with blockchain and AI!"

In this final chapter of the book, we will take a peek at the future of both AI and blockchain technologies. We will examine how these technologies could be used together to solve some of the biggest problems affecting many industries and our planet. In this chapter, I have also made multiple suggestions that could be used as new ideas for academic projects by interested students and faculties. If you are a working professional or an enthusiast, you could still consider using the ideas as a side project and work with people who would like to brainstorm on new ideas in their leisure time.

In this chapter, we will cover the following topics:

- The convergence of AI and blockchain
- The future of converging AI and blockchain
- Converging AI and blockchain in enterprise
- Converging AI and blockchain in government
- Converging AI and blockchain in financial services
- Converging AI and blockchain in human resources
- Converging AI and blockchain in healthcare
- Converging AI and blockchain in supply chain management
- Converging AI and blockchain in other domains

Technical requirements

This chapter requires a basic conceptual understanding of blockchain and AI, articulated in Chapter 1, *Getting Started with Blockchain*, and Chapter 2, *Introduction to the AI Landscape*, respectively. This chapter also requires you to brainstorm on new ideas and speculate on outcomes that can be observed by reading Chapter 3, *Domain-Specific Applications of AI and Blockchain*, and Chapter 5, *Empowering Blockchain using AI*.

This chapter also requires you to reapply the design patterns learned from Chapter 7, *Development Life Cycle of a DIApp*. Finally, this chapter can help you to dive into blockchain and AI development by suggesting ideas in terms of building POCs that can address a number of real-world challenges. It would also be beneficial if you are able to build an intelligent application using blockchain and AI based on the steps articulated in Chapter 8, *Implementing DIApps*.

The convergence of AI and blockchain

AI and blockchain technologies are no longer buzzwords given that you have arrived at the end of this book. Billions of dollars' worth of assets are managed by innovative financial instruments on public blockchain networks such as Ethereum. AI is used in predictive healthcare, cancer research, and contact-tracing COVID-19 infections. Both technologies are serving humans in an indirect manner. As explained in Chapter 5, *Empowering Blockchain using AI*, the combined application of AI and blockchain is helping to solve a number of critical use cases today.

Now that you are equipped with the basic concepts and hands-on skills of both technologies, let's go through some ideas on converging AI and blockchain to address a number of real-world problems.

The future of converging AI and blockchain

Several experiments are being undertaken on building new waves of digital solutions where AI and blockchains can co-exist to deliver optimal solutions that enable faster decision making and provide the desired transparency to all stakeholders. Some companies have already released products and commercial solutions offering the convergence of both technologies to consumers and enterprise businesses.

It is important we understand that this convergence is just beginning, as we are yet to explore the best of AI techniques to blend with viable blockchain and decentralized storage networks.

In the following diagram, I have provided a general representation of the hybrid solution architecture of a DIApp:

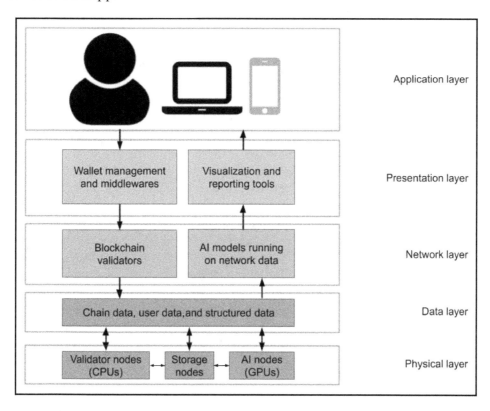

Fig 9.1: Reference solution architecture for a DIApp

The preceding diagram is a pictorial representation of reference architecture for the majority of DIApp solutions. I have identified all the major resources and stakeholders involved in the solution across five layers. I have depicted this in a layered format, similar to the **Open Systems Interconnection** (**OSI**) model to provide an understanding of the concept. We have understood how to use several blockchain platforms and AI techniques in Chapter 8, *Implementing DIApps*. In this chapter, we are presenting the same knowledge in terms of a solution involving all common stakeholders and major technical components.

OSI is a network model conceptualized in the late 1970s. It was published by the **International Standards Organization (ISO)** in 1984. The ISO model is made up of seven layers: Physical, Data link, Network, Transport, Session, Presentation, and Application.

Before we explore the real-world challenges, let's understand all five layers of the solution architecture from the preceding diagram.

These layers are as follows:

- **Application layer**: The application layer consists of end users and client software installed on mobiles, laptops, and devices. Users will sign transactions through the middleware and access data through reporting tools from the presentation layer. The application layer also represents a wider range of deployment facilities, and administration of the DIApp through special tools such as an **Identity and Access Management (IAM)** manager.

- **Presentation layer**: The presentation layer consists of backend functionalities manifested in the clients, which are not visible to end users. This layer includes all the supporting tools and software required to enable blockchain functionalities in an application such as signing a transaction, propagating a signed transaction, and receiving results. The layer also contains tools required to enable AI-related functionalities that can help users gain insights from the application, such as visualization and reporting.

- **Network layer**: As the name suggests, the network layer consists of service networks consisting of blockchain validator nodes running a software bundle designated for verifying user transactions and blocks formed by other nodes in the blockchain network. Similarly, the network layer also consists of several AI services based on **machine learning (ML)** algorithms and **deep learning (DL)** algorithms. Some of these AI services may also use **artificial neural networks (ANNs)**, **convolutional neural network (CNNs)**, and so on.

- **Data layer**: The data layer defines, persists, and provides the interface for applications to access user data, network data, and other processed data. The data layer is a connecting layer between the network layer and the physical layer. Applications, validation software, and AI models will access the critical information from this layer through proper authentication methods configured by administrators.

- **Physical layer**: The physical layer represents all the **Graphics Processing Unit (GPU)** nodes, **virtual machines (VMs)**, and storage nodes used to store the data and perform complex computations. This layer also addresses the core management of infrastructure, through a variety of DevOps practices.

Now that we understand the reference architecture in granular detail, let's go through some of the real-world challenges in the following sections. I will be providing ideas in these sections and you can use them to build POCs.

Converging AI and blockchain in enterprise

The global market size of **Enterprise Resource Planning** (ERP) software is expected to reach around USD 70 billion over the next 5 years. Over the past few years in the last decade, leading companies in the ERP software market, such as SAP and Oracle, have consistently pushed for the use of cloud and other emerging technologies. Several pilots were also launched in the interest of reducing costs and increasing overall productivity on the floor across various solution spaces, including **Customer Relationship Management** (CRM) and **Supply Chain Management** (SCM). There are a few niche use cases that could leverage the best of AI and blockchain technologies, along with other peripheral technologies, such as decentralized data management and **Decentralized ID** (DID) management.

Let's now explore some of the use cases that could enhance current enterprise software with blockchain and AI technologies.

Customer service

When it comes to customer service, it is somehow perceived that companies and brands from developing countries, including India, are not very great at serving their customers. This perception may be true, for the following general reasons:

- A lack of necessary talent
- A lack of proper staff training

There is also an issue with incentives and endless shifts that could prevent personnel from giving their best. This issue could be resolved by using a combination of blockchain and AI technologies.

Let's go through the current scenario of how customer service requests usually play out, especially in the electronics industry.

As-is scenario

Customer service agencies and call centers are usually plagued by issues including the following:

General lack of context: As a customer and user of a premium phone brand, you may want to visit their service center and get the whole picture on what is going wrong with your mobile phone. However, instead of simply scanning the mobile IMEI and pulling the latest records, the representative might ask you to fill in a form and include all the details pertaining to the current issue you are facing with your phone. This issue can be resolved very easily by bringing context to service desks.

Now, let's go through the to-be scenario for the same problem, addressed by AI and blockchain.

To-be scenario

Using the power of blockchain and AI, service desk personnel should be able to automatically identify and verify the owner of the phone. If the same could be authenticated successfully with a signature using the private key or through sophisticated **Zero-Knowledge Proofs** (**ZKP**), the same personnel should be automatically granted access to the phone log locally to perform basic diagnostics. I would also like to propose the use of decentralized data storage services such as MoiBit (`www.MoiBit.io`) to store the necessary diagnostic files. These files can be hosted by the mobile owner and used by personnel for further examination of the problem with strict sharing options set by the owner. MoiBit can also be used by the personnel to verify the ownership of the mobile through sale deeds or purchase receipts.

Now, let's go through some of the architectural ideas that can facilitate this scenario in the following section.

Possible solution

We can use **Decentralized Identifiers** (**DIDs**) to identify each mobile owner in the mobile company's retail side of the supply chain management software. Instead of a silo system, this supply chain would be a consortium of phone manufacturers, who could also recognize the owner of this premium phone, meaning that one DID could represent the ownership of one or more mobiles.

Now, in situations where persistence of documents and files are necessary, we can use MoiBit due to its ease of use and also the granular level of access control you could use to provide privacy to the owner of the mobile (before and after purchasing the phone).

This also means that we can use MoiBit to store the logs of the owner's phone securely in their own dedicated infrastructure or a common network without paving the way for centralization or illicit data mining activities. Once the phone is able to log all the data, we just need to apply predictive maintenance machine learning algorithms to ensure that customer service is available even before the user identifies the need for help.

The following diagram summarizes our approach in a compartmentalized reference structure to help you understand the solution better:

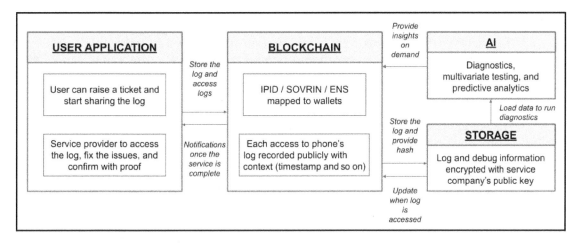

Fig 9.2: Reference solution architecture for addressing customer service issues

As shown in the preceding reference solution architecture diagram, the suggested solution is split across four components, with the following first:

- **User application**: There could be one application that enables users to raise tickets for an issue. The app can also request users to allow access to the logs in order to provide a secure backup, and access to the log on MoiBit's decentralized storage.

On the other hand, we could have another application that can provide the delegation of tickets to a service executive. The service executive can be notified of the new ticket assigned to them.

Both applications will require users to operate through a wallet, which is discussed in the following component.

- **Blockchain**: The user application should allow customers to share more details about the problem they are facing. The details relating to the problem may include product information and technical specifications. If the problem persists, the user should be able to share the boot log or any other sensitive information. To enforce transparency in audit and bring accountability to the access given to such sensitive data, we require all verified personnel to perform service-related operations through a specific wallet address. These wallet addresses can be further enhanced with the help of DIDs and name services such as the **Ethereum Name Service (ENS)**.

  The blockchain network will not only provide wallets for customers and service personnel, but also record each **read** and **write** operation, meaning that every update (**write**) made to the log will be recorded with a new hash embedded in a transaction. Similarly, every time a member of the service personnel accesses the user's log, a transaction is emitted along with a notification.

  Once the service ticket is resolved, the service personnel will provide suitable evidence and stake a resource in order to claim and verify that the service job is closed. If a majority in the network is unable to verify the claim with the given proofs, the stake can be diluted, causing an economic loss to the personnel who are acting dishonestly.

- **Storage**: We require a decentralized storage service that can securely log personal information and other proofs in order to support the aforementioned logic. We can use MoiBit to store the information, encrypting it only between the user and the service personnel. Service personnel can now use their designated wallet in order to access the logs, perform analysis, and provide suitable support. The specifics regarding analysis will be covered by the following component.

- **AI**: Now that the information is safely stored on MoiBit, we can build a simple model that can run basic diagnostics followed by multivariate testing on the data. The data can be made accessible by using the MoiBit API along with the service professional's credentials already registered on the ticketing contract in the blockchain. The API will not provide unwarranted access to data by service personnel or other users who are not assigned the ticket.

This idea could be applied across many products that require active maintenance, without harming user privacy or the company's IP. Hence, the scope can be expanded to automobiles, shop floor machines, 3D printers, mission-critical systems in the military as well as other consumer electronics, such as refrigerators, air conditioners, and security cameras.

Let's now explore another domain in the enterprise software landscape called performance management and try to address some of the real-world challenges.

Performance management

Enterprise companies require undivided attention from the board and its executives in managing various performance factors. These factors drive revenue and profits and they are communicated through **Key Performance Indicators (KPIs)**, which are used to identify any potential growth or pitfall in the business. As the company progresses toward achieving a number of business objectives, it is important to understand the potential issues coming their way. These issues could slow down the momentum needed to achieve the business objective or, in worst case scenarios, end up sabotaging the objective altogether.

Following this brief introduction to performance management in enterprises, let's understand some of the issues faced by enterprises today.

As-is scenario

Over the past few years in the previous decade, a considerable amount of **Research and Development (R&D)** has been undertaken in analyzing KPIs, enabling boardrooms to make effective decisions in less time. However, the quality of the data used to transform business models, or to optimize them, could be revisited. Every business process that is digitized today has both pros and cons. The pros are quite obvious in terms of automation, along with the reduced time and effort required to achieve an objective. However, the cons are a lack of transparency, among a wider range of issues associated with internal compliance with the process. There could be hidden blind spots in a digitized business process that may not be effective in churning out the critical data required over the longer term.

Let's take food delivery apps for example. There are multiple applications giving users the option to order food remotely and have it delivered in 30 minutes or less. The process of ordering the food from a user's app, to reaching the kitchen of a restaurant, to delivering the cooked food from the restaurant to the user's address, is already a digital process today. Quite certainly, nobody is taking your remote order with a pen and paper to keep track of things.

Many of these food delivery app companies would have established KPIs such as the **Number of cancelled orders**, the **Number of delayed deliveries**, and the **Number of orders placed**. These KPIs are internally dependent on the outcome of the process I have mentioned above, and AI is already being used in monitoring such KPIs through big data analytics.

A number of issues looming around limited data being gathered to analyze the business include the following:

Lack of incentivization: There are a few issues associated with plugging into data from the metrics alone. Consumer-facing apps will only sustain if they actively listen to the user. Let's all ask the question of how many times have we honestly rated a food delivery experience in the app? And even if we did take the time to provide valuable feedback, how many times were we incentivized by the app to do so? Most of us might answer here with a *no*, at least to the latter question.

Hence, there is a need to gamify this digital process to harness the real information from the end user and optimize the process for better outcomes.

To-be scenario

There is always a hunger in a consumer-facing company to grow and offer better customer service. In the future, apps should consider rewarding customers by paying them in cryptocurrency for each successful review submission. This will help incentivize users to provide genuine feedback for each service instance rendered by the app. In this process of collecting user reviews, companies would also be able to solve some of the current inefficiencies and cut the costs associated with a particular type of service and make business decisions.

Possible solution

You could consider building a novel food delivery app that not only handles normal operations, but identifies each user with a decentralized identifier DID. This is step 1 on the road to user privacy. With the DID, you could associate a wallet that is used to remit a digital currency for every successful review. You could also consider applying form validation and rate limiting techniques to ensure that bad actors are not gaming this system just to collect the rewards. If the rules of the app consider the review content compelling enough, a bot can be used to quickly remit the digital currency and also start a dialogue with the user, notifying them that the feedback is greatly appreciated.

Later on, the bot can also be used to communicate, if the user wishes, to brief a little more on the problem. This is called an **interactive feedback system**. Any extended information received by users via chatbot can later be tokenized and sent to models using narrative analysis and content analysis. Using this approach, the new enhanced versions of the app are poised to receive more feedback, elevate the quality of service, and also cut down costs as regards unnecessary components in the service.

The following diagram summarizes our approach in a compartmentalized reference structure to help you understand the solution better:

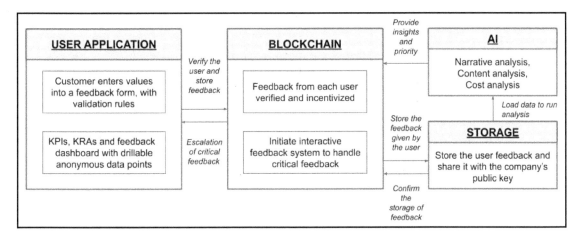

Fig 9.3: Reference solution architecture for gamifying the user feedback system in order to increase the performance of a product or service

As shown in the preceding reference solution architecture diagram, the suggested solution is split across four components, namely:

- **User application**: There could be one application or page within an existing application to facilitate a user feedback system. This system will ask users to provide valuable feedback on the product or service availed by the user, in exchange for a cryptocurrency. This is a new method of incentivizing a user with a liquid asset, compared to loyalty points that may come with strings attached. There could also be a need to develop a separate dashboard for companies and vested stakeholders of the product or service, who need to be given the topline information on the feedback. Apart from providing the topline information such as the KPIs and KRAs, the dashboard also needs to provide an interface to drill down on the feedback in order to better understand the context.

- **Blockchain**: In order to gamify the feedback process with cryptocurrencies and limit the bad actors and Sybil attacks, we need to use a blockchain network. The blockchain network will be used to designate a wallet for each user of the product or service who opts in to provide feedback. When the feedback is validated at the client level, the data needs to be signed by the user's designated wallet in order to verify and confirm their action. When the wallet is used to sign the data, the resulting transaction is then sent to the blockchain network. The network validates and executes an oracle or a webhook in order to store the feedback data in a secondary network. The storage aspects are covered in the following bullet point:

- **Storage**: We need a decentralized storage service that enables users to store their feedback data in a permissive manner. In most of the feedback systems we use today, the user loses control over the feedback data once it leaves the app. This needs to change in order to provide more control to the user. We can use any IPFS-based network, such as MoiBit, to persist the feedback in a permissive manner. The feedback data will be encrypted to the user and the company rendering said product or service. This data can now be used by companies in a permissive manner to assess, evaluate, and enhance their service to customers.

- **AI**: Once the feedback data is stored safely in MoiBit, and shared with the respective companies, you can build an AI model that uses the MoiBit API to fetch the data remotely with appropriate authentication. Once the data is loaded, we can use several NLP techniques, such as content and context analysis, in order to gain a preliminary understanding without any human effort. Once a priority is set by the model, we could use chatbots to initiate a resolution to the feedback. While the conversation is progressing, we can also use narrative analysis in order to gain a richer context of the situation. If the resolution is not achieved by a well-trained chatbot, we can provide the result of the entire analysis to a human representative in order to identify and rectify any gaps. The human representative will resolve the feedback by making a final decision based on the supporting data made available by the AI models.

Let's now explore another domain in the enterprise landscape called data security and try to address some of the real-world challenges.

Data security

Securing trade secrets, critical market data, and other sensitive information of a growing enterprise is of high importance in order to preserve the company's strategic and tactical position among its competitors. Although there were several items of special security software offered to enterprises in the previous generation, only a handful were able to protect the information from a new wave of attacks leveraging cutting-edge techniques.

The next wave of information or data security software could be powered by blockchain and AI in order to empower enterprises and reduce potential attacks as far as possible. We will explore this in the following sections.

As-is scenario

The traditional model of enterprise data management moved from on-premises **Knowledge Management Systems** (**KMSs**) to data warehouses. Later on, we saw more innovation happening on the cloud, wherein companies were encouraged to move from on-site infrastructure to a hybrid model of storing all the information remotely in servers managed by **Cloud Service Providers** (**CSP**) such as Azure and Amazon Web Services. Further to the adoption of the cloud, a more practical approach was proposed, wherein relevant pieces of data could either be stored on the cloud or on-premises (on-prem) to provide flexibility.

Although the cloud is gaining traction in terms of usage, a significant share of the market is yet to take the brave step toward a complete cloud migration. Concerns such as **control** and **ownership** of data could be a source of worry to some decision makers and thereby be inhibiting this movement.

The top issue faced in managing data security on the public cloud is as follows:

Granular access control and encryption: Enterprise applications mostly handle critical information about the company's financial data, trade secrets, design files, and leads on a potential client. Due to the nature of the information being used and circulated, there is a need to be extra vigilant regarding the sharing of knowledge. In the wrong hands, leaked information about the company can result in devastating effects on the company's performance.

To-be scenario

Although blockchain technology alone may not be a key enabler for enterprises, it offers companies exposure to a decentralized infrastructure. In this decentralized infrastructure, companies can share, trade, and exchange resources to form a stronger business network. This new method of sharing infrastructure based on blockchains can be less prone to cyber attacks and certainly immune from data corruption intended by malicious users. We will move from a competitive mode to a collaborative mode wherein non-critical resources could be pooled by all the stakeholders in order to achieve a common business goal.

In the future, enterprise applications should be able to leverage blockchain for full accountability and a transparent view of access to corporate information. These applications could also be equipped with **Business Intelligence** (**BI**) tools and AI services, to offer insights based on access patterns in order to neutralize any cyber threat.

Possible solution

You can consider using decentralized databases and data services such as MoiBit to build a document-centric application that can be designed effectively, to ensure that the data integrity of the business documents will stay intact. We can also use a blockchain separately to store the metadata of the files and maintain access logs. In conjunction with using blockchains, you may also build new visualization tools and basic regression models that allow users to draw insights from the data stored in said decentralized database. User authentication can be enhanced dramatically with the advent of several DIDs and name resolvers.

The following diagram summarizes our approach in a compartmentalized reference structure to help you understand the solution better:

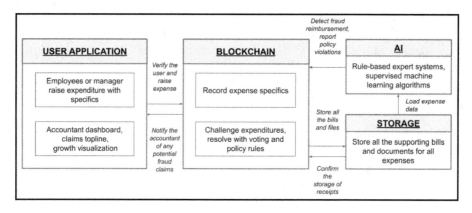

Fig 9.4: Reference solution architecture for identifying security threats in ERP systems with the help of blockchain and AI

As shown in the preceding reference solution architecture diagram, the suggested solution is split across four components, firstly:

- **User application**: As usual, the application component will comprise the client applications used by employees and admins. The employee application could be a simple **Customer Relationship Management (CRM)** application that stores the lead data securely on an IPFS-based permissive network such as MoiBit. In the CRM application, we could have a basic feature that allows employees to create a new lead based on the information gathered by the sales employee. The application could rely on custom name resolvers in order to verify employees. On the other hand, we also need an administrator dashboard in order to closely monitor the health of the network, followed by a list of recent accesses made by employees. Based on the visualization provided by the visualization tools, the admin can take the actions necessary to ensure the stability of the network. An administrator dashboard could also have a multisig-based capability, thereby ensuring that the **power** to make changes is not vested in a single person. The overall security of the system can be enhanced by at least three degrees as follows:

- 1-step verification: Company email ID and password.
- 2-step verification: OTP from the employee's cell phone and/or authenticator.
- 3-step verification: Verify ownership of a wallet belonging to a particular name service. For example, you can ensure that the application allows access only if you have a wallet address that can be resolved to **companyxyz.eth**. Company XYZ's employee, Ms. ABC, will be provided with a wallet address resolved by the name **abc.companyxyz.eth**. If the user is unable to prove that they own a wallet resolved by **abc.companyxyz.eth**, the app should not grant access.

It should be mentioned that the aforementioned enhancements could work as an enhancement alongside enterprise authentication mechanisms including **Fast Identity Online (FIDO)** keys.

- **Blockchain**: The blockchain network will resolve the name service in order to confirm ownership of the wallet. Once the wallet is authorized, the blockchain network is also responsible for facilitating the storage of information in a secondary network. Once the storage operation is complete, the smart contracts in the blockchains will emit transactions for every successful or failed access to a document. This access data is primarily stored on the blockchain and later copied to the secondary storage network for further analysis into failed access to resources. You will understand its purpose in the following section.

- **Storage**: We need a decentralized storage service that can cache all the access logs so that AI systems can get faster access to the data without creating a bottleneck in the primary blockchain network. By using an IPFS-based network, we preserve the immutability features of the blockchain, and also retain the ability to verify the cached content.
- **AI**: Now that the access logs are copied and cached into MoiBit, the administrator can choose a custom trained model of their own or use an unsupervised machine learning technique to detect anomalies in terms of access to a number of critical documents. Once a pattern is generated and analyzed, the anomalies can be recognized in order to act on the attacks.

Let's now explore another domain in the enterprise landscape called finance management and try to address their problems.

Finance management

Most enterprise companies survive based on the stable revenue generated by established product lines. Depending on the products or services, these companies may be generating income ranging from millions to billions of dollars annually. Such huge volumes of income demand proportional costs in the form of expenses that need to be audited regularly and ensure that the books are intact. It is also important to note that most of the large-scale companies who generate such large revenues are public companies, with many public stakeholders watching the growth of the company's sales closely.

As-is scenario

Traditional accounting software used to allow employees such as a clerk or an accountant to manually bill for the sales of goods. However, in today's generation of finance software, accounting modules are already closely knit together with various front-facing modules including **Point of Sale** (**POS**), which is used to bill the items and generate invoices.

Although a majority of accounting operations are now being shifted from manual entries to bar code-driven automation, there could be a high risk of financial fraud and the fudging of numbers in the books.

The top issue faced by enterprises in finance management is as follows:

Accounting scandals: An accounting scandal is defined as an intentionally orchestrated process of manipulating the financial statements of a company in order to achieve the purpose of deceiving someone. Most countries consider this a criminal act, as it allows individual employees and the company to overemphasize an asset or misrepresent current financial liabilities, thereby exposing the stakeholders to risk.

To-be scenario

In the future, accounting software will not only be automated with other modules. Transparency may be embraced by using blockchain in order to enable simpler and cheaper audits for interested parties. Also, accounting applications should be able to leverage deep learning techniques to identify any potential anomalies in the company's cash flow transactions.

Possible solution

You can consider building an accounting application that maintains a virtual ledger recording the ledger as per the norms. The accounting application can also transparently broadcast the virtual ledger if the company wishes to do so. Meanwhile, this blockchain application will also be responsible for managing the states of every wallet, so as to monitor any bad actors within a department. The application can also leverage deep learning models to detect anomalies found in the financial statements and to ensure that no fraudulent acts are being committed.

The following diagram summarizes our approach in a compartmentalized reference structure to help you understand the solution better:

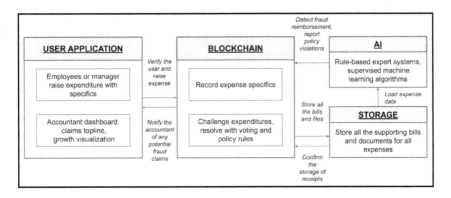

Fig 9.5: Reference solution architecture for managing expenditures and identifying any fraudulent transactions

As shown in the preceding reference solution architecture diagram, the suggested solution is split across four components, namely:

- **User application**: There may be one form that could be used by employees to claim expenses. You can simply build a secure application as explained in the previous *Data security* section and allow users to raise the expenses.
  There may be another form that can be used by the accounts department in order to review and resolve claims. Although you could automate a significant portion of this section today, we can rethink transparency and fraud detection with the help of blockchain and AI, respectively.

- **Blockchain**: The blockchain network will provide wallets for each employee, including the accounts department, to manage the company's capital. The blockchain-based smart contract can also be used to challenge a few suspected transactions in a democratic manner in order to resolve expenses within a department.

- **Storage**: We need a decentralized storage service that can store the bill copies, receipts, purchase orders, and many other supporting documents provided by the employees who raise the expense claims. These supporting documents will be reviewed by the accountant, alongside an AI model that reduces the human effort involved in tracing the origin and verifying the authenticity of the transactions made by employees. We require an IPFS-based network that can persist these documents without giving way to any cyber attack or posting invoices with doctored values. The supporting documents can be encrypted and shared between the accounts department for further review.

- **AI**: Now that the supporting documents are stored in an IPFS-based network such as the MoiBit, we can use the APIs and the accounts department's credentials in order to load the expense data into machine learning algorithms in order to identify potential fraudulent expenses. Rule-based expert systems can also be used to identify any claims that are beyond the scope of a company's policy so that the claim can be rejected without expending too much energy.

Following this detailed walkthrough of problems across several domains in the enterprise landscape, let's now explore the problems faced by governments.

Converging AI and blockchain in government

At the time of writing, the total market size of government software business is estimated to reach around USD 15 billion over the next 3 to 5 years. A lot of progress in society depends on services offered by local government, as well as national-level governments. Some countries, such as the United States, refer to it as the Federal Government. Citizens are dependent on government in one way or another for basic services such as ID enrollment, and obtaining birth and death certificates.

In the following sections, let's try to understand some of the real-world challenges faced by governments across the globe today. We will also observe how to address them with the application of blockchain and AI technologies.

Let's begin by exploring the challenges faced by governments in the taxation domain.

Taxation

To develop a long-lasting economy and to provide public services, governments rely upon levying direct and indirect taxes on its citizens as well as businesses. Direct taxes are levied on the income of an individual citizen or a business. Indirect taxes are levied on goods and services in the form of duties. At the time of writing, the global market size of sales tax software is expected to reach an estimated USD 11.25 billion by 2026.

As-is scenario

Taxation is considered one of the prominent revenue streams for the majority of governments in the world. During the 2018-2019 financial year in India, the **Central Board of Direct Taxes** (**CBDT**) reportedly collected around 11.17 lakh crores in **Indian Rupees** (**INR**). Although this figure seems staggering, it has been reported that the collected amount is still in a shortfall of around 83,000 crores, accounting for nearly 7.4% of the collection target that had been set. Similarly, indirect taxes will also be collected at the point of service. The amount of indirect tax collected may directly depend upon the state of the economy, wherein the buyer has enough purchasing power to afford a product or service. The medium of payment can also directly affect the collection of indirect taxes, as it becomes extremely difficult to trace cash transactions taking place in every nook and cranny of the country.

Let's look at the top issue faced by governments in taxation:

Evasion: Tax collection may decrease severely in situations where the service rendered to a customer is not recognized through a taxable sales invoice. Unfortunately, this may still occur if the customer and service provider mutually agree on exchanging the cash for service, thereby evading the payment of taxes.

To-be scenario

In the future, businesses could be encouraged to use a blockchain-enabled application that keeps track of all inventories in the form of a **Non-Fungible Token** (**NFT**) to distinguish between the raw materials in a distinctive manner. Service providers could be compelled to transfer or account for the said NFT in the blockchain network. This can help identify the input and output of the item in the inventory and track the movement of goods across multiple stakeholders. Based on the transfer or sale of such resources, an invoice can be automatically generated by the smart contract and the customer asked for payment. By onboarding the entire supply chain process and sales life cycle on top of a blockchain, we may be able to curb indirect tax evasion significantly.

Possible solution

You may use any blockchain network to establish a public or a permissioned network, governed by the business owners as well as concerned tax authorities. All the incoming raw materials can be considered as inputs, with an NFT assigned to each unit of the raw material. Later on, once the product is manufactured from the raw materials, the corresponding NFTs could be burned and a new NFT created that is a composite of all the NFTs belonging to the raw materials used in the product. The sale of the product is now an auditable record persisted on the network, with a clear relationship establishing the composition. This will not only make the recording of input and output taxes easier, but it will also enable more tax collection along the way.

The following diagram summarizes our approach in a compartmentalized reference structure to help you understand the solution better:

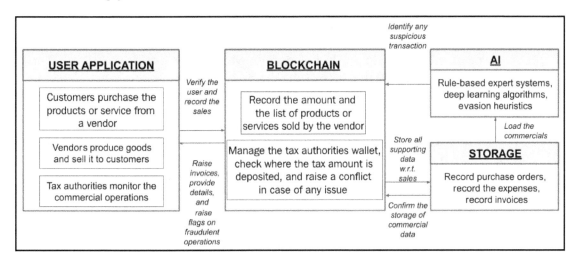

Fig 9.6: Reference solution architecture to reduce tax evasion

As shown in the preceding reference solution architecture diagram, the suggested solution is split across four components, namely:

- **User application**: Unlike the solution architectures proposed previously, we have three main actors in this use case. There could be one application that can be used by end customers that allows the purchasing of finished goods at a retail level. There could be another application that allows vendors to sell raw goods among one another and also sell the finished goods to an end user. All the goods sold by users can be an NFT on a blockchain network such as Ethereum. While the sales are made, there could be a need for a dedicated application used by the tax authorities to monitor the B2B and B2C transactions in a pseudonymous format. Each sale can be drilled down as each can be recorded as a transaction on the blockchain with a rich context of supporting documents made available on a secondary network.

- **Blockchain**: The blockchain network will provide wallets to all three actors. Customers require a wallet in order to pay for the product or service. Vendors need the wallet to perform business and receive the quoted amount. The tax authorities need a wallet in order to transfer the indirect tax amount deducted at the point of sale. Vendor wallets will not only persist rupees or other local currencies, but also persist the balance of raw materials they have in stock. This balance is designated in a unique manner to each unit of the raw material. Once the raw material is converted into a finished product, the NFTs can be burned to mint a new NFT that can represent said finished product. Whenever a sale occurs between a customer and vendor (B2C), or among vendors (B2B), each sale is recorded as a transaction on the blockchain network, triggered by the payment action in the respective application.

- **Storage**: We need a decentralized storage service that can persist the paper trail of this process, ranging from purchase orders to invoices. We need an IPFS-based permissioned network that respects company privacy, and yet remains useful in sharing relevant data with authorities.
  Every time a paper document has been added to a vendor account, a new transaction bearing the relevant priority will be emitted in the network. Only eligible actors in the network should be able to view the transaction. This is an essential part of the design, so as to preserve the competitive spirit among all participatory stakeholders in the market.

- **AI**: Now that we have the paper trail as well as the ledger balance, we can run rule-based expert systems to identify the tax amount to be collected. In order to identify any missing tax goals, we also need to use heuristics to identify potential evasion. Deep learning can also be employed to identify any money laundering activities.

Let's now explore another domain in governance, voting, and try to address the problems associated with this domain.

Voting

Elections are regarded as a celebration of democracy, wherein each citizen is given the opportunity to exercise their rights in choosing the right representative to assume office. Hence, it is crucial that elections are held in an apolitical manner, without favor for any candidate or party. Also, it is beneficial to observe the latest changes in the technology community and apply the relevant technologies for the efficient and fair conduction of elections.

As-is scenario

Currently, the majority of elections take place offline, meaning citizens are expected to enroll themselves and vote at a specified polling booth announced by the respective election authorities. This traditional process is regarded as outdated by a number of people. Based on the growing reach of the internet globally, a customer can place a purchase order on any e-commerce website to avail a product or service. Similarly, it may be convenient to allow citizens to vote from home or the office using their own mobile phones. This not only enables easier access to voting through a digital platform, but also reduces the time taken to announce the election results from days or hours to near-immediate.

The top issue faced by government in voting is as follows:

Speed up results: Many democratic nations offer holidays for citizens, to ensure that people are available to show up at the local constituency office, cast their votes, and then await the results. Although governments can facilitate voting, the process is largely a manual one. Hence, it takes time to handle, transfer, verify, and count all the votes at a designated secure location, a process that involves a lot of resources.

To-be scenario

In the future, governments and citizens should be encouraged to vote for their candidates using secure mobile applications that can be very simple to use. Each vote is cast by applying the citizen's private key, which could be resolved into a biometric signature, thereby proving the presence of the citizen during polling.

Possible solution

You may build a sample voting application on a mobile device or the web that communicates to a smart contract deployed on a blockchain network. The vote can be cast by each user by proving ownership of the private key associated with said account. Also, the application could leverage several pattern recognition techniques and computer vision to identify whether the person in front of the mobile device or the browser is a real person, and not a system-generated graphic. This can be made possible by using **Generative Adversarial Network** (**GAN**)-based classifiers. Once the votes are cast, we can double check the numbers and announce the winners of a hypothetical election.

The following diagram summarizes our approach in a compartmentalized reference structure to help you understand the solution better:

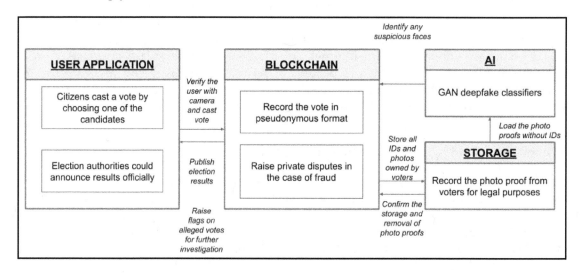

Fig 9.7: Reference solution architecture to reform election technology with a view to saving time and costs

As shown in the preceding reference solution architecture diagram, the suggested solution is split across four components, namely:

- **User application**: There could be one mobile application that could be used by citizens or users. This application must be tightly bound to one SIM in order to prevent Sybil attacks. This client application also needs to be able to capture the photo ID followed by a video of the poller in order to ensure that the vote is being cast by said person only.
Similarly, there could be one web application or dashboard to monitor overall voter turnout and also to handle suspicious votes. The web dashboard can also provide topline information on the votes polled against each participant or candidate.

- **Blockchain**: The blockchain network will provide wallets for every single citizen or user. Votes are cast in a smart contract where mapping exists to count the votes made for each candidate. The blockchain can also be used to provide conflict management in case the AI identifies or warns of a false proof provided by a user.

- **Storage**: We require a decentralized storage service that can store the photo proof that can serve as legal evidence of the participation of users during the vote. It is very important to note that the video is uploaded by the respective citizen, another self-declaration on the part of the participant. Such data must be stored on an IPFS-based network in order to ensure that the data cannot be corrupted.
- **AI**: Now that the photo ID proof and the video of the citizen or user is made available, we can use the APIs of any IPFS-based network in order to vet the proofs shared with the authorities. With the recent release of GAN-based deep fakes, we can consider future-proofing this sample application by using advanced classifiers built on top of GANs only.

Let's now explore another domain in governance, legislative reforms, and try to address their problems.

Legislative reforms

Legislation reforms are one of the key result areas of a government. Although bills are passed into acts, the enforcement of these acts may not be effective on occasion. Many reforms result in changes to financial planning, endorsements, and entitlements. One such example is social security.

There may be one or several acts passed by a governing body that may require immediate and swift adoption. In such cases, we need to be able to ensure that the beneficiaries of these reforms are able to enjoy their benefits without a significant delay.

As-is scenario

Social security reforms, such as an increase in pension levels, may take time to be reflected on the checks. This transition may take time and not necessarily maintain transparency. We can address this issue of social security reforms once suitable legislation has been passed.

The top issues faced by governments in managing legislative reforms are as follows:

- **Enforcement**: Updated rules of law are seldom notified and acknowledged by common citizens. This information gap could create problems. Also, we need to make sure that the updated surplus amount is not pocketed by anybody across the value chain.

- **Documentation**: Once the legislative branch of government makes plans for an amendment, all the relevant documents must be tethered under a single repository. This will aid all members in reaching a common understanding regarding the background, objectives, and goals of the bill.

To-be scenario

In the future, governments could encourage the use of blockchain and AI to tackle numerous problems during legislative reforms. You could build a pilot solution to address the changes made to social security programs. Also, AI could be used to detect any anomalies in the functions of the beneficiary and the benefactors. AI could also be used to identify any misappropriation of funds by employing deep learning techniques.

Possible solution

You could use any suitable blockchain platforms to record the votes on a proposed bill. You could also use blockchain to manage pension funds by locking and unlocking them based on a certain set of conditions. The blockchain platform could also identify each beneficiary by means of a wallet and utilize AI-based face recognition models to ensure that the funds are received safely by the respective beneficiaries.

The following diagram summarizes our approach in a compartmentalized reference structure to help you understand the solution better:

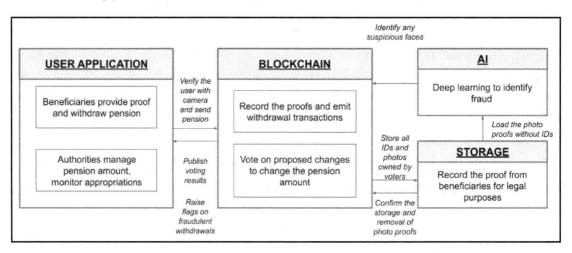

Fig 9.8: Reference solution architecture to rapidly support legislative reforms in social security

As shown in the preceding reference solution architecture diagram, the suggested solution is split across four components, namely:

- **User application**: There could be one form used by citizens, who are the entitled beneficiaries of the social security programs. There could be another form used by government agencies and the legislative house in order to vote on any changes and to also monitor appropriation of the funds in an open environment.

- **Blockchain**: The blockchain network will provide wallets for each beneficiary as well as legislators. It will also host two separate contracts: a **voting contract** can be used to facilitate voting *for* and *against* the bill. A **pension contract** can also be used to facilitate the transfer of funds designated to the respective beneficiaries upon the set conditions. The beneficiaries could simply prove their existence in order to avail themselves of the pension.

- **Storage**: We require a decentralized storage service that can store the aforementioned proofs. These proofs may be required as a legal document for authorities. The proofs will be owned by the users and could be shared with authorities for a predetermined amount of time, in order to check for potential fraud or any other edge cases. Permission may be relinquished by the authorities once the proof is verified.

- **AI**: Now that we have proof of the existence of beneficiaries safely stored on an IPFS-based network, we could feed them to GAN-based classifiers and deep learning algorithms to identify any suspicious activity. Any suspicious or fraudulent transaction could be flagged by the model for dispute resolution with a backend team, where human effort can be involved.

Let's now explore another domain in governance, the census, and try to address the problems encountered here.

Census

A census is a planned and articulated process organized by governments to calculate the latest population count in any given area. A census is also helpful in identifying the cultural and economic diversity of a particular area. As you may already know, a census is carried out every 10 years in India. The latest census was organized by the government of India in the year 2011, and it resulted in observing the latest population of 1,210,193,422 people.

As-is scenario

The government of India is organizing the 16th census during the year 2020-2021 with a key differentiator. The census operations will be digital, all driven through a mobile interface. **Enumerators** are given the option to either use the mobile app, or opt in for traditional paper-based record keeping, which are then submitted for digitization.

The top issues faced by governments in conducting a census are as follows:

- **Time to results**: Although the submissions made by enumerators could be digital, some manual efforts may be required to verify the authenticity of the data recorded by the enumerators. Also, it is imperative to reduce the time associated with verification, which could directly affect the turnaround time required to publish results.
- **Transparency**: The census process is all about knowing changes in terms of the cultural, social, and economic diversity of a region. As a community, it is a healthy and recommended practice to establish certain basic parameters and process checkpoints that could be published in an open network to address everyone's curiosity.

To-be scenario

In the future, census operations should not only go digital, but also emphasize the basic practices that enable communities to understand themselves in a fair manner. This can be made possible by using public blockchain networks to communicate progress transparently. Future census operations could be powered by AI, in order to save costs and gain insights about the communities by drilling down on the large amounts of data collected.

Possible solution

You may consider building a pilot smart census application powered by blockchain and AI. The application can use a suitable blockchain to record and communicate all the checkpoints in the census operations. Blockchain wallets coupled with decentralized data stores can also be used to ensure that the information collected by enumerators at ground level cannot be reproduced in another medium. The application can also leverage visualization tools and deep learning models that allow agencies and interested third parties to drill down on the accumulated data for demographic insights.

The following diagram summarizes our approach in a compartmentalized reference structure to help you understand the solution better:

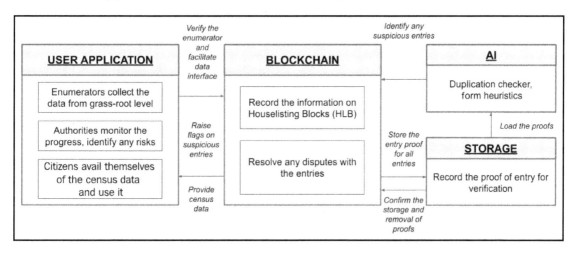

Fig 9.9: Reference solution architecture to introduce a safe and transparent digital census

As shown in the preceding reference solution architecture diagram, the suggested solution is split across four components, namely:

- **User application:** There are three actors in the proposed system: enumerators, the census authorities, and the citizens of the country. To build this sample project, I am recommending three different forms. One form is used by the enumerators, who collect the data from every home at a grassroot level. The second form will be used by authorities to monitor the progress of the census operations and resolve any disputes with any suspicious entries. The third form will be used by common citizens who are interested in understanding about the cultural, economic, and demographic aspects of our society.

- **Blockchain**: The blockchain network will facilitate a wallet for each enumerator. The enumerators will receive a designated wallet address to be used while signing on entries in their app. Since each wallet is unique, it helps maintain accountability in the process. Each entry is a transaction with a signed message representing a hash of data added to the IPFS-based network.

- **Storage**: We require a decentralized storage service that can persist the information of all the citizens in a manner that ensures privacy. Proof of suspicious entries can be retained and access to the remaining entries relinquished.

- **AI**: Now that the proof of entry is made available on an IPFS-based immutable record keeping network, we could use several supervised machine learning algorithms to detect duplicate entries. We could also use form heuristics in order to assess the quality of the data and compare between several **Houselisting Blocks (HLBs)**.

HLB is a term used widely in the census domain to identify a specific geographic habitat area. Each enumerator is allotted one or more HLBs to perform the census and submit all the required information.

Following this detailed walkthrough of problems across several domains in governance, let's now explore the problems faced by financial services.

Converging AI and blockchain in financial services

The financial services industry provides the economic backbone for institutions, organizations, and individuals to operate in a well-defined digital environment today. Although financial services maintain a good reputation as one of the earlier adopters of all technologies, the same may not apply to the blockchain technologies. This may be due to the complications that arise from the transparency achieved in the process. However, we must understand that the application of blockchain with AI is almost inevitable at this point because most tech companies are starting to provide banking and insurance solutions to customers. This is clearly disintermediating people from traditional banks and insurance companies. In the interest of future usage, I suggest that you consider developing applications in the following use cases.

In the following sections, we will cover the issues faced by the insurance sector in the financial services domain and try to address their problems.

Insurance

The market size of insurance software is growing at a rapid rate. There is quite a lot of diversification we may find in the insurance industry. With the latest coronavirus COVID-19 outbreak, there is a multifold increase in demand for health insurance all over the world.

As-is scenario

We are living in a world of **Volatility**, **Uncertainty**, **Complexity**, and **Ambiguity** (**VUCA**) with a dire need to afford protection from various unintended consequences. It may be interesting for you to learn that insurance is not limited to humans, animals, organs, and vehicles. Nowadays, you also find that smart contracts on several blockchain networks are also being insured, to protect against hacking or misuse. Hence, it is important to revisit how insurance management is operated today vis-à-vis a tech-enabled digital process of the future.

One of the top issues faced by insurance industries is as follows:

Claims management: Let's take the case of health insurance, which accounts for a significant portion of the insurance industry. The process for making a claim may become complicated, based on the circumstances of the admission and the nature of the illness or accident.

This calls for drastic measures in managing claims.

To-be scenario

In the future, hospitals and insurance companies could consider working closely in order to reduce costs and cut down on the time to process a claim. Hospitals, diagnostic centers, and insurers could form a consortium, create tokens, and settle using the same tokens for liquidity. Given the dire situation associated with a pandemic outbreak, we need to identify the best mechanisms to sustain. Let's explore a solution approach that could help better in managing claims.

Possible solution

If the patient is being admitted to hospital for treatment, this event could be recorded on the blockchain with the zero-knowledge proof, without giving away the personally identifiable information to anybody. Perhaps a simple biometric signature could be of help here. Once the medical procedure is over, there could be a regular medical check by devices that can directly communicate with the blockchain and establish provenance at several levels. Also, several AI-based advanced techniques can be leveraged to identify any fraud claims. It is a notable effort if insurance companies can expect doctors or any relevant certifiers to stake money on the blockchain before allowing them to approve any claims. This could also significantly reduce the losses arising from fraud claims. In case a claim is known to be fraud, the insurance of the buyer could be barred, and the stake of the doctor or certifier could be liquidated, thereby rendering them non-functional.

The following diagram summarizes our approach in a compartmentalized reference structure to help you understand the solution better:

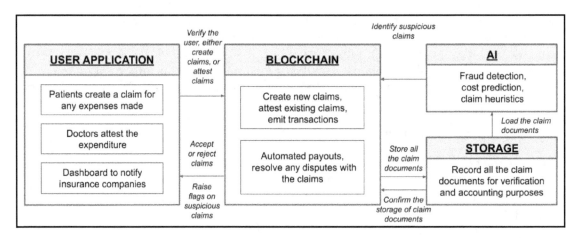

Fig 9.10: Reference solution architecture to optimize the health insurance claim process for transparency and accuracy

As shown in the preceding reference solution architecture diagram, the suggested solution is split across four components, namely:

- **User application**: In this use case, I am suggesting three different apps. One app is to be used by customers or patients who have purchased insurance. They can fill out a form and attach the requisite information in order to successfully create a claim.

  The second app is suggested to be used by the resident doctors who treated the patient. Every time a new claim is created, the doctor is requested to verify and attest the claim. It is important to understand here that the doctor needs to stake a significant portion of their salary in order to perform attestation. In case the system identifies that the doctor had attested a fraud claim, the stake will be liquidated.

  The third app is a dashboard application suggested for insurance companies in order to monitor the topline information, such as the total payouts made in the past 24 hours, along with suspicious claims made in the past 24 hours.

- **Blockchain**: The blockchain network will provide a wallet for insurance companies to manage their funds. Users can pay their premium and expect the payout from such a wallet. The network will also provide a wallet to the doctor, in order to allow them to stake a significant portion of their salary in it. The same wallet could be used to remunerate doctors in case of valid claims. Finally, the network also needs to provide wallets for consumers or patients. They will receive payouts in the wallets.

Notably, the blockchain network also needs to facilitate automatic payouts to eligible claims with the help of a smart contract. The validity of the claim will be decided based upon the supporting documents attached to the claim.

- **Storage**: We require a decentralized storage service that can store all the supporting documents related to the claim. Once the documents are persisted, we could use relevant AI models and techniques to validate claims and also identify potentially fraudulent claims. We need to use any IPFS-based network in order to store these documents in an immutable manner so as to prevent any changes to the bill amount, dates, and other details.

- **AI**: With the critical claim-related documents stored on a secondary storage network, we could use a rule-based expert system to validate the claim structure and formats. We can also use machine learning techniques to identify any duplication in claims and also identify similar patterns to contrast the costs. If the conditions are satisfactory and below a programmed level of risk, an automated payout can be triggered. If the pattern observation looks suspicious, the models can post about the claim on the network in order to vote and resolve the claim issues.

Following this detailed walkthrough of problems across several domains in the financial services landscape, let's now explore the problems faced by human resource management.

Converging AI and blockchain in human resources

Hiring new talent and retaining existing talent has become one of the crucial agendas for organizations of all sizes. At the time of writing, the unemployment rate of the United States of America has been one of the highest since the last decade. This unprecedented rate of unemployment can be attributed to the COVID-19 outbreak. As the economy recovers, hundreds of thousands of new jobs will be created across multiple public and private sector organizations over the next few years. Although the opportunity for employment is growing at an exponential rate, there is also a difficulty in identifying the right talent who can match skills with salary.

Especially in the tech domain, it is becoming extremely difficult to manage talents at two levels:

- **Retaining existing talent**: This means that current employees are jumping companies in favor of a higher salary and better perks. This can be mitigated by a positive company culture accompanied by attractive salaries.
- **Onboarding new talent**: This means that it is becoming difficult to hire new people who have entered the industry very recently. This can be mitigated by refining existing traditional processes to identify potential hires.

While HR experts are making efforts to solve the first challenge mentioned above, I believe that it is important to welcome a new breed of talent into the tech industry. Although other industries may equally deserve a new breed of talent, let's limit the scope to our IT industry.

In the following section, we will see how to address the issue of performing background checks on some critical technical resources in the IT industry. We will discuss the challenges faced by current managers in the industry. We will also address these challenges by using blockchain as well as AI appropriately in the solution architecture. We will also address the issues in onboarding a new wave of talent using technology enablement and gamification of a few checkpoints in the process.

Background checks

Background checking is a process of formally verifying the information furnished by a job applicant. It is a process carried out by human resource managers and may vary in terms of when the process is carried out. Some companies and HR managers perform background checks after the applicant is successfully hired. However, there are a few companies that demand strict compliance of the background checks prior to confirmation of the application.

The following are some of the common documents required during the background checking process:

- **Criminal documents**: Some companies may be required by law to check and verify whether an applicant has committed any criminal act. Such documents are accessed by respective law and enforcement offices of the land. Once it is confirmed that the applicant has not been involved in any criminal proceedings, the company may confirm the hiring of the candidate.

- **Financial documents**: Some companies may require the applicant to confirm the current salary offered by the existing role at the company. This could be verified if financial documents, such as bank statements, are furnished by the applicant.
- **Drug test**: Some companies may have strict policies against the abuse of drugs, and hence may require the applicant to undergo a drugs test. Based on the results of this test, the applicant may be confirmed or rejected on the grounds of company policies or the rule of law, as applicable.
- **Physical fitness**: There are a few jobs in government agencies across the world that may require a strict adherence to a few physical fitness criteria. Hence, the companies may require the candidate to undergo a new physical fitness test. Based on the results of the physical fitness test, the employer may make suitable decisions.
- **Previous work history:** Employers are usually required to maintain a record of the employment history of all of their employees. Employers may require a bona fide certificate from applicants, which may serve as certified proof.

With a basic understanding of the background checking process and the common documents involved in the process, let's now understand the problems faced by the HR managers as well as applicants.

As-is scenario

Currently, most of the documents mentioned above are furnished by a job aspirant via email. The files sent by the applicant are received by the HR managers. It is worth pointing out that documents such as drug test results and physical fitness reports may be shared with HR managers internally by the third-party vendors who conduct the test. Some of the files pertaining to the applicant may contain sensitive and personally identifiable information.

The top issues plaguing the recruitment process and human resources management are as follows:

- **Lack of data ownership by the applicant**: Most of the aforementioned documents are furnished by a job applicant via email. The files sent by the applicant are received by the HR managers. It is worth mentioning that documents such as drug test results and physical fitness reports may be shared with the HR managers internally by the third-party vendors who conduct the test. Some of the files pertaining to the applicant may contain sensitive and personally identifiable information.

- **Inability to perform strong automated background verification**: Once the documents are received by the HR managers, the documents go under scrutiny depending upon the company's policies. It should be noted that most of the verification efforts made by managers involve a manual process, meaning that this is time-consuming and may also be error-prone.

Now that we have identified some of the vulnerabilities in the process, let's go through a simple solution proposal that can address a number of critical challenges in the background checking process.

To-be scenario

In the future, governments and companies should encourage the use of blockchain-based DIDs, to control the data that applicants share with employers. Applicants would be comfortable using a system wherein the data of the applicant could be redacted if they are not offered the job. Also, it is important to streamline the whole process with AI-enabled automation using **Optical Character Recognition** (**OCR**) for reading test results, and critical other documents such as financial statements. The applicant would be more comfortable if there is a specialized OCR program that can read the bank statement just to confirm the current salary of the applicant and immediately redact the document. This transformation in the background verification process will not only save the company time and money, but also provide for a more secure environment that could be applicant-friendly.

Possible solution

We could use a suitable blockchain platform and build a smart contract that allows applicants to safely sign declaration forms with the company or the HR managers. Also, we can separate data from this process by allowing the applicant to store the data on a personal data storage medium such as MoiBit, so as to customize access to all the documents required by the employer in the process. We can also use OCR programs and carefully design a **Zero-Knowledge Proof** (**ZKP**)-based system that can confirm a number of attributes of the document without allowing the HR manager to access the data unnecessarily.

The following diagram summarizes our approach in a compartmentalized reference structure to help you understand the solution better:

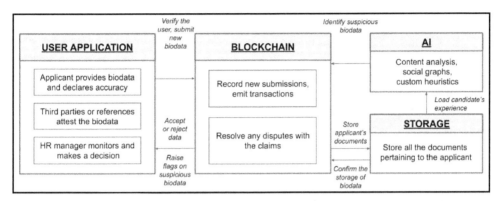

Fig 9.11: Reference solution architecture to optimize the background checking process while interviewing a candidate

As shown in the preceding reference solution architecture diagram, the suggested solution is split across four components, namely:

- **User application**: In this use case, I am suggesting three different applications. The first app can be used by applicants to apply for a company and share their biodata and all supporting documents already stored in their personalized data space. In this case, I suggest using an IPFS-based network such as MoiBit, in order to provide access to users. The second type of app can be used by third parties who perform drug tests and so on. It can also be used by previous employers and references in order to confirm the data declared by the applicant. Once the third parties or references provide information, it can be validated, and their efforts can be incentivized. However, in order to incentivize good actors, staking needs to be implemented. We will discuss this in the following section. Finally, the third type of application is used by HR managers to post job descriptions, shortlist candidates, review the automated verification results, and so on.

- **Blockchain**: The blockchain network will be used to provide wallets for all four actors: applicant, HR manager, references, and the third-party service provider. To prevent permanent access to information, we could use wallets and provide temporary read-only access to HR managers of prospective companies. Similarly, the efforts expended by the references and third-party service providers must be incentivized. Hence, wallets can be used to transfer to them directly tokens of their choice. Apart from the wallets, the blockchain network of choice should also be able to facilitate smart contracts to record updates to biodata. We can also use smart contracts to resolve the disputes in a public manner.

- **Storage**: We require a decentralized storage service that can store the biodata of applicants and share it with respective HR managers on demand. Each document stored by the applicant will be recognized on the network with a transaction.
- **AI**: With the documents made available on a secondary network, we can validate the biodata with custom heuristics. We can also consider identifying the relevant references using social graphs. If anomalies are identified, we can have the system report it on the network for resolution.

Following this detailed walkthrough of problems across several domains in the sphere of human resource management, let's now explore the problems faced by the healthcare industry.

Converging AI and blockchain in healthcare

The healthcare industry has transformed from an institutional system into a service-driven system enabled by many technologies. Many healthcare services, including diagnosis, treatment, and preventive medication, have become digital and engage with patients in a personal manner. Healthcare devices such as fitness bands, trackers, and medication pumps are replacing some of the medical personnel we rely upon. This transformation at the customer level can also be enhanced with the help of new drugs. Let's understand some of the issues faced by the healthcare industry in becoming successful in manufacturing drugs.

In the following sections, we will go through some of the major issues faced by the healthcare industry. We will not only observe the issues, but make some innovative suggestions for pilot projects using blockchain and AI.

Pharmacovigilance

Pharmacovigilance (**PV**) can be defined as a group of activities that includes various processes such as drug formulation, testing the newly formulated drugs, assessing the risks, and finally preventing any side effects from a drug before it can be introduced to the market. The main focus of pharmacovigilance is to ensure drug safety for consumers.

These activities are carried out by many personnel and also require cross-industry stakeholders, under the careful oversight of the local drug administration agency. Hence, there is a need for software that can facilitate these processes in a digital manner, reduce costs, and also identify any potential risks amid the testing based on the data available. Also, it is important that any adverse effect of using a drug is commonly reported to local drug administration authorities, as applicable. Pharmacovigilance software is being used to report such cases. At the time of writing, the global market size of pharmacovigilance software is expected to exceed an estimated USD 250 million by 2027.

As-is scenario

The basic requirements of any pharmacovigilance software could be to collect and assess data pertaining to drug experimentation. Another notable requirement for such software is to automate some of the processes and complement the need for human personnel. Such software is also expected to prepare well-defined and structured reports that are applicable under local regulations and the rule of law. Most of the successful pharmacovigilance software today offers flexible features to facilitate most of these requirements and cut down costs.

There are several phases through which the safety of the drug will be assessed. The software is used to collect the reaction data, analyze it, and report it to applicable drug administration authorities. The software may also provide the insights needed to make the drug safer and reduce associated costs in the process.

The top issues faced by pharmacovigilance software are as follows:

Personal information of subjects: People subjected to a drug trial are usually referred to as **subjects**. While subjects are undergoing such a trial, they are instructed to consume a prescribed amount of a given drug. Drug consumption is monitored over a period of time to observe the reaction, understand more about the side effects, and gather useful information from the test. This information may be passed on to the drug formulation team to improve the product over the next iterations. During the course of testing, the subject may experience a number of adverse effects, including death. Local drug administration agencies may require the drug manufacturers to confirm such scenarios and debrief such adverse instances in a prescribed format detailing the cause. Due to the sensitivity attached to the personal information of the subject, not all the reporting data can be made accessible to the general public or other concerned authorities.

The future of healthcare lies in the adoption of advanced transparency, which allows stakeholders to provide a larger exposure to such adverse data regarding a drug that may already be on the market.

To-be scenario

In the future, the local drug administration authorities may encourage the publication of all the adverse effect data in an anonymized manner, wherein each adverse situation faced by the subject under the drugs trial is briefed, but the personal identity of all those subjects who have experienced side effects is anonymized. Here, blockchain can be used in pharmacovigilance software to establish transparency and provenance of the reports published by the respective stakeholders. AI can also be used to analyze critical data points from the reports and help confirm whether the adverse situations, such as the death of the subject, were caused by the drug alone, or other health conditions.

Possible solution

We can choose any suitable blockchain platform with the ability to handle the reporting of data in a public as well as a permissioned manner. There may be several reports strictly limited to a small number of stakeholders, thereby preventing the exposure of trade secrets. Similarly, we can use AI models to predict any side effects during drug trials, since a third of subjects may suffer from a side effect as a result of drug-to-drug interactions.

The following diagram summarizes our approach in a compartmentalized reference structure to help you understand the solution better:

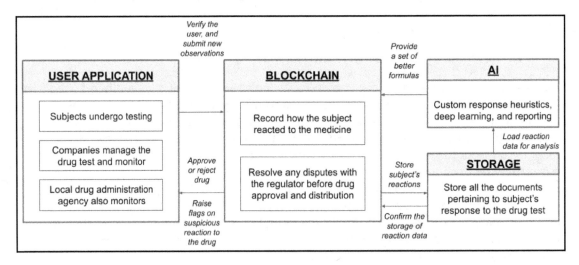

Fig 9.12: Reference solution architecture to enable efficient drug approval and transparency in pharmacovigilance

As shown in the preceding reference solution architecture diagram, the suggested solution is split across four components, namely:

- **User application**: I would like to propose three applications in this use case. One application can be used by the subjects in order to upload the reaction to the drug along with suitable photos or vital information prescribed by authorities. The information will be stored under a pseudonymous wallet, without giving away too much personal information to the public. There could be another application used by drug companies to review the reactions submitted by the subjects. This data can be very helpful to companies in formulating a better drug with lesser, or no, side effects. Finally, we may need a separate dashboard for the local drug agencies to monitor any critical cases, report fatalities during drug tests, and also to approve or reject a drug.

- **Blockchain**: The blockchain network will provide wallets for all three actors: subjects, drug companies, and regulators. The drug reaction data will be safely shared to all three wallets. Also, it is important to maintain an auditable provenance of all the tests undergone by a drug. This may help future investigations and help identify the actors accountable. We will also need a smart contract in the network to facilitate the approval of drugs through a smart contract. This smart contract could simply run under the vigilance of a regulator, or showcase the collective interest of the group by digitally signing on the approval request transactions collectively, using the private keys of more than one wallets in the network. This approach is often referred to as multisig.

- **Storage**: We require a decentralized storage service that can store the exact unchanged version of the drug reaction from subjects. I again recommend using an IPFS-based network in order to customize access to the data.

- **AI**: Now that the drug reaction data is made available on an IPFS-based network such as MoiBit, we need to be able to use deep learning techniques and drug reaction heuristics. If a serious injury or fatality is identified, we can use the models to regenerate the drug formula to address the side effects.

Following this detailed walkthrough of problems across several domains in the healthcare industry, let's now explore the problems faced by the supply chain industry.

Converging AI and blockchain in supply chain management

Supply chain management is defined as a group of activities that streamline the flow of all goods and raw materials that are required for the production of a finished good. It involves the storage and movement of raw materials, monitoring inventory, and the delivery of finished goods to the point of consumption. All these processes need to be digitally monitored and communicate any disruptions in real time. Hence, there is a need for intelligent supply chain management software that is flexible and accurate. The market size of supply chain management software is expected to reach a figure of around USD 25 billion by the year 2025.

There are multiple approaches and solution architectures available for building intelligent **Supply Chain Management** (SCM) software. I have mentioned some of this supply chain management software in Chapter 3, *Domain-Specific Application of AI and Blockchain*. Hence, we will cover one simple problem faced by the supply chain industry and try to address this with a blockchain- and AI-based solution.

In the following sections, we will explore the top issues faced by the supply chain industry and try to address their problems.

Volatility

Volatility can be experienced in the price of a commodity, due to a variation in supply and demand. Geopolitical issues, biohazardous issues, legal and other economic issues may also affect the price of a commodity. Managing the volatility of a commodity's price is a crucial element in supply chain management. Conversely, any risk arising from a supply chain could disrupt the price of commodities.

We need intelligent supply chain software that can address some of the vectors causing price volatility. Let's address this in the following section.

As-is scenario

The price volatility of goods in the supply chain may incur losses. Currently, supply chain stakeholders may incur these losses since the software may not be able to identify rapid changes in prices.

To-be scenario

In the future, supply chain stakeholders should form consortiums, identify liquidity problems in advance, and facilitate trade and logistics using blockchain and AI.

Possible solution

We can use any suitable blockchain platform that can facilitate all the supply chain activities through a scalable smart contract support. I suggest you carefully understand the capabilities of a blockchain and the volumes it can handle, before delving into the development aspects. This simple research could help save time and effort before initiating the project. Also, you can consider using decentralized data storage options such as MoiBit to store all the critical paper trails necessary for maintaining audit purposes and establishing provenance. Finally, AI models could be developed to tap into the transparent ledgers to identify the current volumes of raw materials and make necessary arrangements for the same. However, if the supply is inhibited, the models could resort to hedging current raw materials in order to cover the surplus cost and carry forward with the operations.

The following diagram summarizes our approach in a compartmentalized reference structure to help you understand the solution better:

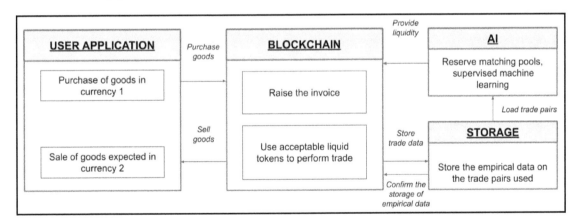

Fig 9.13: Reference solution architecture to reduce volatility risks in supply chains and settle faster

As shown in the preceding reference solution architecture diagram, the suggested solution is split across four components, namely:

- **User application**: I am proposing a simple application that can be used by buyers and sellers. Maybe you can consider enhancing an existing marketplace application with real trade data.
- **Blockchain**: The blockchain network will provide wallets to the buyers and sellers. Instead of converting the local currencies to a global reserve, you can consider trading with custom stablecoins instead, which may be available in abundant numbers at lower conversion fees.
- **Storage**: We require a decentralized storage service that can capture the trade pairs, without giving away the specifics of the trade. This can be made possible by persisting only those trade pairs that can be made available to anybody without harming anybody's privacy.
- **AI**: Now that the trade pairs are available, we can run supervised machine learning algorithms to optimize the search for finding traders who can sell stablecoins at a cheaper price. This could help reduce the volatility issues while converting the currencies, thereby reducing the overall time and cost required to settle.

Following this detailed walkthrough of problems across several domains in the supply chain industry, let's now explore the problems faced by other domains.

Converging AI and blockchain in other domains

In this section, I will be outlining the problems and a *to-be* scenario with benefits. However, you will not see solution approaches. I expect you to carry out further research regarding these challenges, expand on the analysis, and propose a solution architecture by yourself as an exercise.

With the *to-be* scenario and the *as-is* scenario suggested for each domain, you are encouraged to come up with a solution approach of your own. You can follow the format from the possible solutions I have suggested from the sections in this chapter.

Let's now explore the issues faced by law and order authorities and try to address their problems.

Law and order

The police department, local administration, and judiciary system work closely together in order to protect people from scams, violence, and other forms of criminal activities. This group of government agencies could collectively be referred to as **law and order**.

As-is scenario

Monitoring the actions of people, entities, and organizations in developing economies can be tedious with limited resources. We need to consider transforming some of the critical processes in our current system in order to maintain peace and grow businesses in the society.

The top issue faced by law and order authorities is as follows:

Conflict and arbitration management: When an act is passed, it becomes challenging as a citizen to track and understand as to when said regulation will be applicable. You may have also observed that although a rule of law has been passed by an upper house, it takes a significant time to see it materialize. Sometimes, a common rule of law may affect two or more government organizations, thereby leading to more confusion regarding the enforcement of said rule. These issues will result in a delay of service to citizens.

To-be scenario

In the future, law and order needs to strike a balance between the need for human intelligence in contrast to the efficiency offered by machines and networks. This can be made possible by tightly knitting our executive, legislative, and judicial branches. Optimizing the flow of a certain set of decision-making processes already occurring in a repetitive manner could help serve the community better. A consortium of government agencies could not only help the administration achieve the performance expected, but also bring down the costs of enforcement significantly.

Let's now explore the issues faced in achieving national security and try to address their problems.

National security

National security is of the utmost importance for every country. For developing countries, efforts are made in order to ensure that they secure a better position in the global political arena. Similarly, developed countries may make efforts in ensuring that they do not lose their relatively higher position in the global political arena. Between these two aims lies the interest vested in potentially sabotaging the efforts of another country through proxy wars, internal political instability, and espionage. We must find a way to identify such issues plaguing many countries and try to address them with the help of blockchain and AI.

As-is scenario

India's geo-political position is that of a relatively higher status compared to some of its adversaries. This is due to the geographical challenges faced by some of its adversaries and also the economic progress the country is making as a developed country. In the midst of such remarkable progress, we may encounter a few efforts to sabotage initiatives taken by the nation's administration. Hence, we must identify these issues and handle them in a suitable manner.

The top issue challenging the forces in addressing national security matters is as follows:

Unmanned Aerial Vehicles (**UAV**): Many of these domestic drones that fly in the form of a quadcopter are referred to technically as UAVs. UAVs pose a threat to both civilians and the military. Hence, it is important to identify all the drones that are imported, operated, and destroyed in India.

To-be scenario

In the future, governments could encourage the authorities to enroll all the UAVs and any other supporting equipment with the help of a blockchain. Also, the agencies could set up a local UAV response center in each zone of the city in order to mitigate any live risk by the drones. These response centers could use AI-based techniques to analyze the feeds from radio sensors in order to predict any unscheduled flight of a UAV. This intelligence could help assess the risk of an attack before it takes place.

Let's now explore the issues faced in conserving our environment and try to address the problems encountered in this sphere.

Environment conservation

I believe that it is a fundamental duty and a moral obligation to protect the Earth, our only home. One approach to protect the planet is through the conservation of our ecological diversity that contributes to the stability of our planet. As you may already know, climate change is visible across several parts of the world in different ways. Although it may not be at devastating levels, it will soon reach an irreversible point of destruction. To prevent this from happening, we can try our best to conserve our wildlife and our ecological diversity on land as well as water.

As-is scenario

Currently, several greenhouse gases, including carbon monoxide (CO), carbon dioxide (CO2), and methane are prevalent in our atmosphere as a result of burning fossil fuels, cattle rearing, and the manufacture of a number of industrial goods.

The primary issue inhibiting energy conservation efforts is as follows:

Carbon pricing: Carbon pricing is a method of reducing greenhouse gas emissions by charging a surplus on the fuels or setting an allowance on the quantity of gas that can be emitted by an entity. Under the Paris Agreement, many countries have already volunteered for carbon pricing. However, a few countries are yet to support the movement. Although many countries have already volunteered, it may become difficult to communicate the progress of this movement if the changes are not made visible in a transparent manner.

To-be scenario

In the future, all the countries who volunteer to join the Paris Agreement could log all the carbon offset data into the blockchain. This information may transition from the basic consumer to the supplier, all the way to governments and back to the Paris Agreement members who may also join the consortium.

Let's now explore the issues faced by the agriculture industry and try to address their problems.

Agriculture

Agriculture is the backbone of India's economy. At the time of writing, it is one of the foremost contributors to our **Gross Domestic Product** (**GDP**), with a global market size estimated to reach nearly USD 12 trillion over the next 3 years.

As-is scenario

Over the past few years, the agriculture industry in India has been facing some serious issues. Aside from the distress faced by farmers due to irregular monsoons, floods, and famine, we will go through some of the economic problems faced by farmers in the following section.

The top issues plaguing the agriculture industry are as follows:

- **Fair price discovery for farmers**: With the advent of the internet, it was easier to discover prices through some of the co-operative systems that decide the price for the yield. Farmers were also able to discover the price of the yield from the neighboring markets. However, there could be a larger game at play if brokers plan on corroborating on a price that favors their personal motives. This is achieved by brokers sourcing the yield locally for a low price and exporting it to a market that may not be aware of the local yield price.
- **Instant lock-in and payments**: Even if farmers are okay with the price set by the brokers, there is no guarantee of instant payment once the yield is deposited at the warehouse. Once the yield is hoarded in the warehouse, the broker may find a suitable buyer, take the cut, and then make the payment back to the farmer. In India, this may take many days, or weeks. A farmer's obligations may not be met in case payment is delayed. Some farmers have lost their assets, while others have resorted to suicide, a very sad state of affairs.

To-be scenario

In the future, all farmers should consider joining a price discovery app hosted on a blockchain network in order to share the price information of all yields at district as well as state level. Farmers should also consider trading the yields and collateralizing loans among themselves in the short term.

Summary

This chapter has articulated how we can empower blockchain and its decentralized applications using various AI techniques and models. The chapter also introduced you to some of the real-world challenges faced by enterprises, governments, financial services, human resource managers, healthcare, and supply chain management, among other domains. The aim of the chapter is to inspire you to use these ideas in your upcoming projects. You can also reapply the thinking from this chapter to other future problems in your research on blockchain and AI.

Both AI and blockchain are the two major technologies catalyzing the pace of innovation. The combination of these two technologies is expected to revamp innovation in the IT industry. I hope that this book has enabled you to develop a paradigm of thought by combining both technologies to ship productive and robust applications aimed at the next generation of the internet and its users.

I congratulate you on finishing this book and encourage you to keep open tabs on these two revolutionary technologies. I hope the book helped you to improve in a number of areas. Thank you for reading. I wish you the best of health, happiness, and success in all your future endeavors with blockchain and AI. Namaste.

Moving Forward - Resources for you

In this appendix, we are enclosing a list of important links to various blockchain and **Artificial Intelligence** (**AI**)-related resources accessible over the internet. The following resources should help you to further your learning beyond the scope of this book.

The resources will help you further in acquiring skills and experience in blockchain and AI by identifying new resources online, providing you with deeper insights. With this upskilling, you can connect the proposed concepts and techniques in this book with real-world problems and solve them in a collaborative manner with the help of the blockchain and AI communities mentioned in the appendix.

In this appendix we will cover the following topics:

- Blockchain resources
- AI resources

Blockchain resources

We hope this book has provided you with basic knowledge of the fundamental concepts of blockchain, followed by the hands-on knowledge needed to build applications on blockchains such as Ethereum and Hyperledger. To enable you further, we are sharing a few more important resources to delve deeper into other blockchain platforms and protocols.

In the following sections, you will go through an exhaustive list of internet resources required to upskill beyond what you have learned in this book.

Awesome Blockchain

This repository on GitHub is a curated list of resources for the top blockchain platforms. It also enlists the best links on research articles, case studies, books, and so on. You can access the Awesome Blockchain repository on GitHub using the following link: `https://github.com/yjjnls/awesome-blockchain`.

News

Blockchain is one of the most agile industries, transforming almost every day. If you are interested in staying on your toes with the latest information, here are some of the best newsrooms I recommend keeping an open tab on:

- **Week in Ethereum News**: If you are an aspiring Ethereum developer, I urge you to sign up for this awesome newsletter. Evan Van Ness does a fantastic job of sourcing the best links to keep you abreast of the weekly developments in the Ethereum community. You can subscribe to Week in Ethereum News here: `https://www.weekinethereum.com/`.
- **Blockmanity**: Co-founded by Ishan and Shrikar in Bengaluru, India, Blockmanity is one of the go-to websites for catching up on the latest market trends. I recommend keeping an open tab on the Blockmanity website to stay updated. The website link is `https://blockmanity.com/`.
- **Cointelegraph**: Cointelegraph is one of the earliest crypto news outlets that I personally subscribe to for the latest information on all blockchain news across various landscapes in the industry. I suggest keeping an open tab here also. The website link is `https://cointelegraph.com/`.

Communities

Blockchain would be nothing if it weren't for the community presence across the globe. It is very important to be part of your local community to discover job opportunities and learn the latest in tech and business, some of which is not spotlighted by the major newsrooms. Based on my observations, I am recommending some of the best meetups held in Bengaluru, the blockchain capital of India. Apart from Bengaluru-based meetups, I am also sharing some handy links to help you identify blockchain meetups globally:

- **Blockchained India**: This blockchain community has been one of the most active since the dawn of blockchain development in India, during the years 2016 and 2017. You may stay tuned to their telegram community for updates on any upcoming developer meetups or conferences near you. The website of the community is `https://blockchainedindia.com/`.
- **Namma Blockchain**: This is a tightly knit blockchain developer and start-up community in Bengaluru, focused on technology, decentralization, and showcasing the latest products. It is anchored by Aicumen Technologies Inc., one of the earliest **Research and Development (R&D)** establishments in India, working on blockchain and AI since 2017. I recommend you join this meetup group if you are based near Bengaluru. You may see me occasionally attending this meetup if I am around! Join the Namma Blockchain meetup at `https://www.meetup.com/Namma-Blockchain/`.
- **Blockchain meetups for readers outside India**: If you are reading this book outside India, the Meetup.com link, `https://www.meetup.com/topics/blockchain/`, can be extremely helpful in identifying blockchain meetup groups near you. Some of the best international blockchain meetup groups are spread across New York, London, Singapore, Toronto, Zurich, San Francisco, Berlin, and other major IT hubs.

Quintessential blogs

Reading blogs can help us connect to the latest trends in blockchain technology from all corners of the world. In this section, I am recommending a must-read blogging site that you can browse through during your leisure time, to capture new design patterns, **User Experience (UX)** perspectives, and also learn about the development of **decentralized applications (DApps)** on several blockchains.

Hackernoon: Hackernoon is my favorite go-to website to stay up to date on the latest on blockchain. It is not only limited to technical posts, as the website also focuses on economic aspects and various other facets of blockchain technology. Please visit Hackernoon at `https://hackernoon.com/`.

Design

Let's now explore the resources required to keep your DApp design skills on their toes.

ConsenSys Design: If you are an aspiring developer hoping for a job in blockchain, or a product manager looking to lead a blockchain team, it is imperative to understand the challenges in designing a pro-customer UX. ConsenSys Design is on a mission to demystify those barriers for a better UX strategy in blockchain applications. On the ConsenSys Design website, you will find some great articles and a few open source initiatives, including product demos. The website is at `https://consensys.design.`

Development and how-tos

Next, we will explore the resources required to keep your DApp development skills.

Simple as Water: Simple as Water is a community-driven website offering easy-to-understand tutorials for everyone, from beginners to experts. Founded by Vaibhav Saini, one of the top contributors at Hackernoon, this website is a go-to site for developers to understand and build applications on diverse web3 stacks, including Ethereum, Bitcoin, IPFS, Libp2p and so on. You can also find some of my articles here. The website is accessible at `https://simpleaswater.com/`.

Now that we have covered blockchain resources, let's now explore learning materials and communities for AI.

AI resources

AI is a vast ocean and growing into its own industry. We hope this book introduced you to the fundamentals and basic information required to understand the context of building smart applications for the next economy. In the following sections, I provide you with links and information that will help you delve deeper into building innovative complex applications using different AI techniques.

All-in-one list for beginning with AI

Let's now explore resources that will help you gain more practical AI knowledge.

Awesome AI: This repository on GitHub is your one-stop link. It is dedicated to documenting all the AI resources online, in a collaborative manner. You can access the GitHub repository at `https://github.com/owainlewis/awesome-artificial-intelligence`.

Case studies

Let's now explore resources that will help you understand the impact of AI in life-changing scenarios.

Experiments with Google: This dedicated page from Google showcases a curated list of AI case studies that can be very helpful in observing how humans and AI coexist to solve an interesting challenge. The website is at `https://experiments.withgoogle.com/collection/ai`.

Communities

Let's now explore resources that will help you connect with some of the best communities in India. Apart from Bengaluru-based meetups, I am also sharing some handy links to help you identify AI meetups globally:

- **Applied Singularity**: As a closely knit community in India, Applied Singularity is a group of like-minded people using AI, IoT, and biotechnology with the aim of creating a perfect ecosystem for the technological singularity and harnessing its advancements. Their app provides information on the latest journals and best reads, and very actively posts any relevant job opportunities in India. You can access the app here to explore more features and get in touch with an active community: `https://appliedsingularity.com/app/`.
- **AI meetups for readers outside India**: If you are reading this book outside India, the Meetup.com link, `https://www.meetup.com/topics/ai/`, can be extremely helpful in identifying AI meetup groups near you. Some of the best international blockchain meetup groups are spread across New York, São Paulo, London, Paris, Tel Aviv, Istanbul, Toronto, Mountain view (a city in California), Berlin, and other major IT hubs.

Quintessential blogs

Let's now explore resources that will help you upskill your capabilities in data science.

Towards Data Science: As a technical expert, I prefer a blog that can keep me posted on the latest trends in AI technologies, without delving too much into research all the time. Towards Data Science is one of the best medium publications, driven by the global AI community, to share ideas, code, and best practices on AI. The blog is accessible at `https://towardsdatascience.com/`.

Research

Let's now explore resources that will help you stay on top of recent research and development progress made in the AI landscape:

- **arXiv recent AI submissions**: If you are a research scholar and are required to stay on your toes with recent papers in AI, this is your go-to site. It lists all the AI paper submissions classified by date. Here is the specific URL to access the latest AI-related papers on arXiv: `https://arxiv.org/list/cs.AI/recent`.
- **AITopics**: This is my go-to link to fetch the latest information on AI market trends. If you are a decision-maker reading this book, I highly recommend keeping an open tab on this one! The website is accessible here: `https://aitopics.org/`.

Development and how-tos

Let's now explore resources on Kaggle, which will help you upskill your capabilities in the practical implementation skills required as a data scientist. They are as follows:

- **Hands-on Python tutorials on Kaggle**: As someone who wants to enter the AI industry, you need to be well acquainted with either R or Python. Recently, the demand for Python has been growing very rapidly. Hence, I recommend you get a good grip on programming and become versatile with Python. Although there are a lot of Python tutorials that are a search away, I think this tutorial from Kaggle will provide adequate exposure to basic Python, as well as knowledge of using essential features of the Kaggle platform. You can enroll on the course here: `https://www.kaggle.com/learn/python`.

- **Hands-on Introduction to Machine Learning on Kaggle**: This is an introductory course by Dan Becker that outlines the basic concepts of machine learning. The course teaches the basic hands-on machine learning skills required. You will be taught how to build a model using the Kaggle platform's features, validate the model, and optimize it. You will also get exposure to the competitions available on Kaggle, and how to make submissions. You can enroll on the course here: `https://www.kaggle.com/learn/intro-to-machine-learning`.

- **Intermediate Machine Learning on Kaggle**: This micro-course by Alexis Cook exposes you to real-world situations in data science. It will help you to address data leakage, write better testing programs, and optimize your models. Don't miss going through this course before attending an interview, as it can help you prepare for some of the quality problem statements based on optimization. You can enroll on the course here: `https://www.kaggle.com/learn/intermediate-machine-learning`.

- **Micro-course on Pandas**: Pandas is revered as the swiss-army knife for data analysis. This hands-on course by Aleksey Bilogur teaches you how to use the library for data manipulation. You can enroll 0n the course here: `https://www.kaggle.com/learn/pandas`.

- **Deep learning course on Kaggle**: This is one of my go-to recommendations for people who would like to learn about deep learning. This micro-course by Dan Becker will teach you new hands-on skills while using TensorFlow and Keras for image processing and other facets of deep learning techniques. You can enroll 0n the course here: `https://www.kaggle.com/learn/deep-learning`.

Other Books You May Enjoy

If you enjoyed this book, you may be interested in these other books by Packt:

Blockchain Development for Finance Projects

Ishan Roy

ISBN: 978-1-83882-909-4

Learn how to clean your data and ready it for analysis

- Design and implement blockchain solutions in a BFSI organization
- Explore common architectures and implementation models for enterprise blockchain
- Design blockchain wallets for multi-purpose applications using Ethereum
- Build secure and fast decentralized trading ecosystems with Blockchain
- Implement smart contracts to build secure process workflows in Ethereum and Hyperledger Fabric
- Use the Stellar platform to build KYC and AML-compliant remittance workflows
- Map complex business workflows and automate backend processes in a blockchain architecture

Securing Blockchain Networks like Ethereum and Hyperledger Fabric
Alessandro Parisi

ISBN: 978-1-83864-648-6

- Understand blockchain consensus algorithms and security assumptions
- Design secure distributed applications and smart contracts
- Understand how blockchains manage transactions and help to protect wallets and private keys
- Prevent potential security threats that can affect distributed ledger technologies (DLTs) and blockchains
- Use pentesting tools for assessing potential flaws in Dapps and smart contracts
- Assess privacy compliance issues and manage sensitive data with blockchain

Leave a review - let other readers know what you think

Please share your thoughts on this book with others by leaving a review on the site that you bought it from. If you purchased the book from Amazon, please leave us an honest review on this book's Amazon page. This is vital so that other potential readers can see and use your unbiased opinion to make purchasing decisions, we can understand what our customers think about our products, and our authors can see your feedback on the title that they have worked with Packt to create. It will only take a few minutes of your time, but is valuable to other potential customers, our authors, and Packt. Thank you!

Index

www.ingramcontent.com/pod-product-compliance
Lightning Source LLC
LaVergne TN
LVHW081519050326
832903LV00025B/1546